PHOENIX
FROM THE ASHES

PHOENIX FROM THE ASHES

THE LITERATURE OF THE REMADE WORLD

EDITED BY

Carl B. Yoke

CONTRIBUTIONS TO THE STUDY OF SCIENCE FICTION
AND FANTASY, NUMBER 30

Greenwood Press

NEW YORK · WESTPORT, CONNECTICUT · LONDON

Library of Congress Cataloging-in-Publication Data

Phoenix from the ashes.

(Contributions to the study of science fiction and fantasy, ISSN 0193-6875 ; no. 30)
Bibliography: p.
Filmography: p.
Includes index.
1. Science fiction, American—History and
criticism. 2. Regeneration in literature. 3. End of
the world in literature. 4. Myth in literature.
5. Science fiction, English—History and criticism.
6. Apocalyptic literature—History and criticism.
I. Yoke, Carl B. II. Series.
PS374.R39F76 1987   813'.0876'09   87-12035

ISBN 0-313-24328-X (lib. bdg. : alk. paper)

British Library Cataloguing in Publication Data is available.

Library of Congress Catalog Card Number: 87-12035
ISBN: 0-313-24328-X
ISSN: 0193-6875

First published in 1987

Greenwood Press, Inc.
88 Post Road West, Westport, Connecticut 06881

Printed in the United States of America

The paper used in this book complies with the
Permanent Paper Standard issued by the National
Information Standards Organization (Z39.48-1984).

10 9 8 7 6 5 4 3 2 1

For Sherry, Alex, Andrea, and Chris

CONTENTS

ACKNOWLEDGMENTS

Only with the help of several people has it been possible to produce this book. I am grateful to my wife, Sherry, my family, and my associates, who encouraged my progress. I am also grateful to the Research Council of Kent State University, which provided a grant to type the manuscript. I am equally grateful to Barbara Burner for her patience and skill in typing a difficult manuscript, to Janet Lucks for retyping portions of it, to Tom Hrach for all the leg-work he did, and to Professors James R. Carpenter and Radd K. Ehrman of Kent State's Department of Classical Studies for their work in translating the Latin quote from the *Fortuna Imperatrix Mundi*. I am indebted to Greg Shreve for his continued counsel on text grammars, which gave me insights into the literature that I might not otherwise have had, and to Marshall Tymn for conceiving and implementing the series that makes this book possible. But I am especially indebted to my contributors, not only for the excellent articles they produced but for their patience and understanding of some unforeseen circumstances that delayed the completion of this book an unreasonably long time.

PHOENIX
FROM THE ASHES

PHOENIX FROM THE ASHES RISING: AN INTRODUCTION

Carl B. Yoke

I shall die in my nest, and I shall multiply my days as the phoenix.[1]

Job, xxix: 18

The phoenix takes many forms. In the apocryphal *Book of Enoch,* it appears as a great serpent with a crocodile head. In Arabic lore, it is the *Al-Salmandra,* a four-footed animal that changes into a bird and lives in fire. It is the Persian *simurg,* an animal comprised of thirty birds in one (the same as the Arabic *'anka*), and it bears resemblance both to the Hindu *rukh* and the *Garuda,* a half man, half bird with a golden body, white face, and red wings.

It is also the Egyptian *bennu*—the fabulous red and golden bird that came to symbolize the rising, regenerated sun, the bird that appeared at the Heliopolis once every five hundred years bearing a ball of myrrh in which it had embalmed the body of its own dead father and which it later buried in the Temple of the Sun. From this phoenix, dead in its nest of cassia and frankincense, a worm crawls that will grow into the new phoenix.

Beneath each of these variations of the phoenix is a universal concept—rebirth.[2] It lies at the core of the bird's symbolic meaning and is the reason that it eventually came to stand for the Resurrection in later Christian symbolism.[3] But the symbol is not simply limited to rebirth. By logical extension, it must also include an initial birth, and death because rebirth can occur only if preceded by initial birth and death.

All of the countless rebirth symbols found in the world's mythologies encompass, at least by implication, the broader pattern. Some, like Kali, the Black

One, are more obvious about it. She is described, for example, by Joseph Campbell as the "world creatrix, ever mother, ever virgin . . . the life of everything that lives" and "the death of everything that dies . . . the whole round of existence . . . from birth . . . to the grave . . . the womb and the tomb."[4]

She is the archetypic Great Mother, or Cosmic Mother, who is understood more abstractly as the "world-bounding frame: 'space, time, causality'—the shell of the cosmic egg"[5] and from whose womb comes all the possibilities not only of creation but of destruction as well. Like the phoenix, she encompasses not only the archetype of rebirth but the broader pattern of birth, death, and rebirth as well.

Rebirth itself is a principle invoked in literally thousands of stories comprising what is commonly labeled postcatastrophe literature but which would be served better if labeled literature of the "remade world."[6] For though the stories in this subgenre of science fiction begin with the end of the world, they use the end of the world only as an artifice to relate a particular kind of tale and as one phase of a universal, mythical cycle whose pattern is birth, death, and rebirth.

Remade world stories have been written for decades. While they probably officially begin with Mary Shelley's "The Last Man" (1826), the theme of the destruction and rebirth of the world has existed since time immemorial in mythology and religion.[7] The form of the modern remade world story, however, was born, according to Peter Nicholls, in Richard Jeffries' *After London* (1885).[8] It roughly sketches a pattern that becomes synonymous with the form, a pattern with stable and recurrent structural features which has been more specifically identified by critic Gary K. Wolfe as (1) the experience or discovery of a cataclysm, (2) a journey through a wasteland created by the cataclysm, (3) the settlement or reestablishment of a new community, (4) the reemergence of the wilderness as antagonist, and (5) a final or decisive battle to determine which values will prevail in the new world.[9]

In other words, Wolfe has determined that remade world stories have common structural features that are transformed to create particular stories. This means that any remade world story is simply a variation of all remade world stories, generated from a common formula but tailored to a specific text. The processes by which this occurs have been identified and labeled through the structural study of myth and fairy tale, and while not all text linguists agree about how to classify and label them, most systems include addition, deletion, permutation, and substitution as methods to modify the elements of the basic pattern.[10]

Functionally, this means that any feature common to the pattern—the cataclysm itself, for example—may be modified by a predefined process to create a specific variation. In *After London,* while the catastrophe affects the actions of the characters, it occurred in the distant past. In Nevil Shute's *On the Beach* (1957), on the other hand, the catastrophe is immediate, and the actions of the characters are more tightly linked to it. In Jack Vance's "Dying Earth" series, the catastrophe is protracted an inordinately long time, while in Ranald MacDougall's film, *The World, the Flesh and the Devil* (1959), it occurs in an instant. Or, one form of cataclysm may be substituted for another. In John Bowen's *After the Rain* (1959) the catastrophe is a flood, while in Walter Miller's *A Canticle for Leibowitz* (1960) it is nuclear holocaust. Significantly, while the formula is generative, it does not require that each story variation contain all of the elements common to it, nor each element to the same degree.

Moreover, within the parameters set by Wolfe's formula, there may be several distinct models of the story. One easily identifiable model, for example, is that in which virtually the entire story is an extended journey through the wasteland; yet another would be one in which humanity is ultimately and completely destroyed.

Putting aside the controversies involving story grammars and structural analysis,[11] and running the risk of oversimplifying and generalizing in order to provide an overview of this material, I would suggest, further, that deeply buried beneath Wolfe's formula for remade world stories is an ancient and universal pattern,[12] a deep narrative process. It is the birth, death, and rebirth of vegetation as illustrated by the myths of Osiris, Tammuz, Adonis, Orpheus, Mithra, Attis, Persephone, and Dionysus, to mention a few.[13]

These vegetation myths are themselves, of course, part of a more general category of myths called re-creation or "end of the world" myths. All reflect the same basic birth, death, and rebirth pattern. In *Myth and Reality* (1975), Mircea Eliade recognizes, however, that these myths are less about the end of the old world than they are about the beginning of a new one. He writes:

The myths of the End of the World have certainly played an important role in the history of mankind. They have shown that the "origin" is "movable." For after a certain moment, the "origin" is no longer found only in a mythical past but also in a fabulous future.[14]

The reader will remember that . . . we emphasized the extreme importance of the mythico-ritual scenario of annual World regeneration. We saw there that this scenario implies the motif of the "perfection of the beginnings" and that, after a certain historical moment, this motif becomes "movable"; it can now signify not only the perfection of the beginnings in the mythical past but also the perfection that is to come in the future, after this World is destroyed.[15]

I believe that remade world stories are impelled by the same motives that impel re-creation myths, and, while it may be argued that they are not true myths, they are isomorphs of re-creation myths. In other words, they are fictional equivalents of re-creation myths and serve mythic purposes in modern society.[16] As such, they have structural features common to the most common of re-creation myths—the vegetation myths—and they stand in a metaphoric relationship to the deeper narrative pattern that the vegetation myths reflect, that is, the birth-death-rebirth pattern.

The common structural feature of vegetation myths derived from common purpose—the need to assure that fertility would return to the earth in the spring.

Primitive people needed this reassurance because their welfare depended upon the rebirth of vegetation. The structural features of these myths are (1) the violent death of a god (or someone who would eventually be raised to godhood), usually as a sacrifice; (2) a trip through the underworld; (3) a return to the surface after consummating a pact that assured the return of fertility and explained the natural cycle of the year; and (4) a subsequent rebirth of vegetation, or return of fertility. After a period of teeming fruition, the cycle then repeats itself. That remade world stories are megametaphors for this process becomes apparent when the features of both forms are compared structurally.

Each begins with a violent death. In the vegetation myths it is that of a god, or someone who will achieve godhood because of the sacrifice. In the remade world stories, it is the death of a world (world being defined here as the culture, civilization, nation, or community of the hero), as well as the symbolic death of the hero himself, usually marked by some sort of displacement from his community.

There is a trip through the underworld. In the myths, it is a literal trip to the underworld appropriate to the culture. In remade world stories, it is a trip through a metaphoric wasteland, which is often hellish in character. In some stories, like Tanith Lee's *Days of Grass* (1985) and Daniel Galouye's *Dark Universe* (1959), civilization does, in fact, literally survive for long periods underground.

There is a return to the surface. In the myths, the hero physically returns. In the remade world stories, the return is metaphorically expressed when the hero finds a haven, arrives on a new planet, finds an enclave of the former civilization or reaches a new civilization, or even when he reaches the surface as in Lee's and Galouye's novels.

There is a rebirth. In the myths, vegetation returns in the spring. In the remade world stories, the rebirth is usually implicit (though not always). The stories usually end with a double promise: that there will be a new world, in the sense that man has survived and may even thrive, and that whatever civilization or culture finally emerges will somehow, *eventually,* be ''better'' than that which preceded it. This is the promise of redemption implied in the death and resurrection of Christ and which is the central secret of cults like the Eleusinian mysteries.[17] It is also the implicit promise of renewal and regeneration myths.[18] It is important to note the promise because while some stories, like Philip Wylie and Edwin Baumer's *After Worlds Collide* (1934), take us to a world that is actually better, most do not. They end instead in very tough, dystopian worlds which assure man's survival but leave the question of better to the judgment of the reader. Whether or not it is a better world is certainly subjective and is circumscribed not only by the values of the story and its author but by those of the reader as well. Often, though the world is primitive in the sense that knowledge or technology has been lost, it is deemed better because man has returned to a simpler life in closer harmony with nature, a kind of return to *Walden*. This is an antitechnology theme, quite common in remade world stories,[19] though in a number of stories the hero determines to re-create the lost technology because he feels it will make a better world. It is clear in this variation of the remade world story that better is defined in terms of a higher technology and more knowledge.

A few stories take us through a complete cycle of birth-death-rebirth and death again. *A Canticle for Leibowitz* does this, as does the movie *Virus* (1980).[20] Both stories show man surviving not one cataclysm but two, both born of his own stupidity. And both, therefore, are a very black commentary on human nature.

Like re-creation myths, remade world literature is pessimistic only in that it begins with a disaster. Otherwise, it is generally optimistic, naive, romantic, and unrealistic. Even though the ultimate lot of the protagonist may not be that of a happy-ever-after, Hollywood ending, I believe these stories are to be read, as Joseph Campbell believes myths, fairy tales, and divine comedy of the soul stories are to be read, "not as a contradiction, but as a transcendence of the universal tragedy of man."[21] Like the other forms, remade world stories provide a "ritual *Katharsis*" from the taint and pollution of the previous world. The myths and rituals of renewal and regeneration occur as a reenactment of the work of the gods; this happens because the world has moved too far from its "beginnings."[22] In other words, the old world simply becomes decrepit and must disappear because *"for something to genuinely begin anew, the vestiges and ruins of the old cycle must be completely destroyed."*[23] Like ancient festivals and mystery plays, the intention of these myths is to celebrate a triumph over death—of the self and of the world.

And like renewal and regeneration myths, the remade world stories must be viewed as part of a cycle. Campbell says that we cannot take seriously the happy-ever-after endings of myths, fairy tales, and divine comedies of redemption unless we view them as part of a single mythological theme and experience encompassing both tragedy and comedy. Like tragedy they shatter forms and our attachment to forms, but like comedy they express "the wild and careless, inexhaustible joy of life invincible."[24] Only then will we see that they constitute "the totality of the revelation that is life," and which the "individual must know and love if he is to be purged . . . of the contagion of sin . . . and death."[25] While most remade world stories do not end with the hero in a state of wild joy, they do end with an affirmation that man is a survivor and that humanity can survive the most profound catastrophe. What could be more positive? Like myths, fairy tales, and divine comedies of the soul, they should be read in the context of a broader theme—in this case, that of the birth, death, and rebirth cycle.

Affirmation is not simply reflected in physical survival, however. It is also reflected in the transformation of the protagonist. As the world of the story follows the vegetation pattern, so too does the psychology of its hero. As he struggles to survive the dangers of the physical wasteland through which he must pass, he also struggles to survive the mental wasteland through which he must journey. He is party to the double quest. And as the hero dies symbolically by journeying through the wasteland (equivalent of the underworld), he also dies psychologically.

Typically, this is symbolized by the hero's displacement from his community. The catastrophe is more than sufficient to do this (when it is an immediate event) inasmuch as it destroys his comfortable world; usually kills off his friends, relatives, and family; and destroys familiar values, values which have shaped his life and character. But in cases where the catastrophe is nothing more than a distant memory, there is usually a more immediate event that causes displacement. For example, in Andre Norton's *Star Man's Son* (1952), the hero fails his initiation rite and is ostracized from the primitive, postcatastrophe community in which he lives. Sometimes puberty brings sudden and painful recognition of some mental or physical difference which forces the protagonists from the community. Norton's heroines, for example, often suffer this fate. They look different, or they develop some power that makes them different from, and sometimes dangerous to, other members of their community. Or the hero's connection with the community is somehow severed, perhaps by spaceship crash, by enemy capture, or by an injury such as amnesia. The ways by which displacement can occur are literally limited only by the imagination of the author.

Regardless of how this happens, the hero is then forced to journey through a wasteland (metaphorically equivalent to the underworld trip of the dying and reviving god), which is fraught with peril. The journey is a survival test and an inevitable rite of passage, usually from adolescence to adulthood. At this stage of development, the protagonists are often deeply alienated and psychologically distanced from their previous cultures. But the experiences they have in the wasteland usually put them in touch with themselves, makes them appreciate being in tune with nature, and force a transcendence of their own personalities.

The trip complete, they return to their tribes or communities, which may be an actual remnant of the previous community or an equivalent group, with the power to transform them in a significant way (metaphorically equivalent to restoring fertility to the land in the dying and reviving god myths).[26] The capacity to transform the existing tribe, nation, or culture may be in the form of some special knowledge or some special ability or power. It is frequently the product of maturation, as it is with Esther's newly found ability for leadership in *Days of Grass*. In this case, maturation has honed or developed some latent ability or quality of the character. In the course of the process, the protagonist suffers a symbolic death and rebirth, and the process of the journey represents, in toto, an archetype of initiation. Often the major focus of a remade world story is the journey (see, for example, Roger Zelazny's *Damnation Alley* [1969] and therefore a prolonged metaphoric rite of initiation).

According to Carl Jung, initiation archetypes become active when individuals encounter difficult transitions in their lives. Initiation events provide meaningful and spiritually satisfying transitions between stages of maturation. Though such events are lifelong, these rites of passage are most dramatic and obvious in youth and most traumatic when the child passes into adulthood. The most common theme used to express this particular passage is the ordeal, or the trial of strength. (Surviving a wasteland passage through a postcatastrophe world certainly qualifies as an ordeal and trial of strength.)[27] Successful passage requires that the initiate submit to the ordeal, giving up all willful ambition and desire and experiencing the trial without hope of success—even to the point of death.[28]

Symbolically, initiation rites are rites of death and rebirth, and only by submission to a greater power can the child give way to the adult. In interpreting Jung, Joseph L. Henderson wrote:

The ritual takes the novice back to the deepest level of mother-child identity, or ego-Self identity, thus forcing him to experience a symbolic death. In other words, his identity is temporarily dismembered or dissolved in the collective unconscious. From this state, he is then ceremonially rescued by the rite of new birth. This is the first act of true consolidation of the ego with the larger group, expressed as totem, clan, or tribe, or all three combined.[29]

Put yet another way, this is a weaning process in which the relationship of the child to the mother is injured and can be healed only by assimilation into the larger group. The group becomes a second parent to which the young are symbolically sacrificed before reemerging into a new life. Such passages mark the reestablishment of the ego's relationship to the self, a continuing process necessary to maintain psychic health. Successful passages mean that "the individual can live a useful life and can achieve the necessary sense of self-distinction in society."[30]

In this process of breaking away from the mother and reidentifying with society, the child usually suffers a sense of alienation from the powers of the unconscious.[31] That alienation is not fatal, however; it is evolutionary. In his book, *Underground Man* (1973), Edward Abood points out how alienation can be a positive factor when, as in the works of Camus, Sartre, and Malraux, it is used as a foundation to construct new and positive value systems which permit individuals to reach some reconciliation with their cultures.[32] In believing that man can transcend his alienation, they agree with several philosophers and psychologists, who have been termed "utopian existentialists." One of them, psychologist Erich Fromm, states this position as follows:

Human nature drives toward unity with the "all," with nature; but unity on the highest level requires a temporary separation, and consequent loneliness. One goes out in order to return enriched. Separation, though painful, is a progressive step.[33]

This journey, which enables the individual to establish a sense of his own identity by experiencing self as both subject and agent of his own powers, produces a transcended character who displays a productive orientation in which the ability to love and create is predominant.[34] His actions are, of course, heroic, and once he has purged himself of his *hybris,* he becomes the hero of Joseph Campbell's monomyth, *The Hero with a Thousand Faces* (1973).

The formula for the nuclear unit of the hero monomyth is separation, initiation, and return.[35] In other words, *"A hero ventures forth from the world of common day into a region of supernatural wonder: fabulous forces are encountered and a decisive victory is won: the hero returns from his mysterious adventure with the power to bestow boons on his fellow man."*[36] This is clearly analogous to the death, trip through the underworld, and return to the surface pattern displayed in the prototypic vegetation myth. It is equally clear that both the hero and remade world story formulas are metaphors for a deeper narrative process.

A word should be said about stories such as Nevil Shute's *On the Beach* and Mordecai Roshwald's *Level 7* (1959), where the action is confined to a relatively brief period between the catastrophe and a real end of life on earth. In these stories the pattern is fulfilled. The heroes do symbolically die (before they really die), they do undergo initiation rites, and they do transform. However, their "trips through the underworld" fail to produce the necessary return of fertility. These are negative statements of the pattern and a different model of it.[37] They have therefore been included in this book.

Like most of the remade world stories where humanity survives, they focus on the initiation part of the formula—that is, the journey through the wasteland. Virtually the whole story, in those cases, becomes a metaphoric initiation event, usually a complex ordeal requiring the development of skills, intelligence, and talent which in turn produces psychological growth in the form of a new maturity.

While remade world stories become increasingly more probable in terms of their scenarios for world destruction as our technology advances and our understanding of events like nuclear winter increases,[38] they still generally stand in strong contradiction to reality. When and *if* the world does end, it might well be dramatic, but it might also be without drama or fanfare and it might well be unintentional.

For example, we might accidentally pollute ground waters or aquifers; saturate our soils with toxic substances; or dump some altered bacterium, like *E. coli,* which could evolve into some deadly new form that produces a new cancer. Or an epidemic of a disease such as AIDS or Legionnaire's Disease might do the job instead.

Or we might follow an even slower course. We could trigger a "runaway greenhouse effect." We could destroy the ozone layer.[39] We could so completely pollute the air that no plants will grow and therefore no crops could be harvested. Or we could destroy ourselves with drugs, as do the humans and natives of Joan Vinge's "The Crystal Ship" (1976) and as do the wandering bands of addicts in Leigh Brackett's *The Book of Skaith* (1976).

If these ideas, many of which have been treated by science fiction authors already, seem farfetched and fanciful, consider reality. The July 30, 1986, issue of the Cleveland *Plain Dealer,* for example, contained four articles about recent disasters whose potential for world destruction is diminished only by scale. One was about a $9 billion toxic waste bill that would force the Environmental Protection Agency to clean up 375 of the nation's most deadly pits, ponds, lagoons, and landfills. One is immediately reminded of the Love Canal landfill in Niagara, New York, which caused so many problems. Another story reported on chemicals leaking from sixteen tank cars blown off a railroad bridge into the Des Moines River Valley. A third reported on a trial that determined that the W. R. Grace Company was responsible for polluting two drinking wells in Woburn, Massachusetts, and announced that yet another trial would be held to determine if the company was responsible for the high cancer death rate in that community. And a fourth story reported the cost of a train wreck in Miamisburg, Ohio, in which leaking phosphorus ignited to create a cloud that necessitated the evacuation of hundreds of residents. Mercifully, the paper did not include articles on the Chernobyl reactor meltdown, the Union Carbide chemical leak in Charleston, West Virginia, or the deadly methyl isocyanate mist that killed two thousand in Bhopal, India. All of these unnatural disasters occurred since December 1984.

It may be that the world will be destroyed by a more subtle means, one we have not yet anticipated. In his book *The Biological Time Bomb* (1969), Gordon Rattray Taylor speculates about a future in which "gene warfare" is a reality. Discussing research on viruses and in genetic engineering done in the 1960's, he projects a future where designer viruses, encoded with instructions to alter human genetic material, are fired as bullets into a host. The messages, known as episomes, might make targeted populations hypersensitive to some common element like carbon dioxide or oxygen. Made lethal and dumped into a water supply, such viral bullets might kill off entire populations without damaging property. Or, to construct an even subtler scenario, a government might encode and distribute a designer virus that would lay dormant in a population's genetic material for decades, or even generations, before it manifested itself. Or, in a third scenario, a population's genetic material might be encoded to enfeeble its heredity.[40] In yet another scenario, designer viruses might be used to blackmail a population or nation into submission. Such a scheme might be carried out, for example, by spreading the virus and then either withholding an actual antidote, perhaps in the form of a second virus that could reprogram the tainted genetic material, or denying the targeted population the information necessary to save itself. In any of these scenarios, the possibility always exists that the viral bullet could become a viral bomb, which once detonated would end the world as we know it.

Exotic? Perhaps. Yet, as unpalatable as it may be, our own death may be a foregone conclusion. The very grammar of the universe may dictate it. As someone is alleged to have already observed, man simply may be the missing link between ape and human—like the dinosaur, an evolutionary step on the way to somewhere else.

While the remade world stories are not necessarily realistic, they do offer a powerful metaphor for exploring man's relationships to his social structure, his values, and his fellow man.

While the sheer number of novels, short stories, and films using the remade world motif prohibits a complete examination of the form, the contributors to this volume have attempted to cover the general questions raised by many of its principal works. Carl Goldberg, for example, explores the psychological motives of writers who remake the world in their stories. C. W. Sullivan defines the parameters of postcatastrophe literature, Paul Brians discusses the responsibility of the scientist and the role of science in the literature, Joe Sanders examines flood motif stories, and William Lomax discusses character and myth in the genre and takes an intriguing look at the cuckoo motif. Nadine St. Louis, Edgar Chapman, Donna DeBlasio, Thomas P. Dunn, Carolyn Wendell, Gregory Shreve, Judith Kerman, Michael Collings, Joseph Francavilla, Theodore Steinberg, and Harold Prosser, while examining specific works and specific authors, also address such general questions as the nature of the world and of human relationships after the catastrophe. Wyn Wachhorst, David Desser, and Dunn (in a second chapter) examine the postcatastrophe film.

NOTES

1. This line is variously translated. Most authorized versions of the Bible, including the King James and the New Oxford Bible, use the word "sand," but "phoenix" seems to fit better the concept according to the editors of Funk and Wagnalls' *Standard Dictionary of Folklore, Mythology, and Legend*.

2. In this chapter, "rebirth," "renewal" and "regeneration" are used interchangeably.

3. *Standard Dictionary of Folklore, Mythology, and Legend*, ed. Maria Leach (New York: Harper & Row, 1972), pp. 868–69.

4. Joseph Campbell, *The Hero with a Thousand Faces* (Princeton, N.J.: Bollingen Series, 1973), p. 114.

5. Ibid., p. 297.

6. The terms "postcatastrophe literature" and "remade world literature" should be understood as being synonymous throughout this collection.

7. Mircea Eliade, *Myth and Reality*, trans. Willard R. Trask (New York: Harper Torchbooks, 1975), p. 54. For an excellent discussion of why primitive man needed to renew the world, see especially the chapters entitled "Myths and Renewal Rites" and "Eschatology and Cosmogony."

8. Peter Nicholls, "Holocaust and After," in *The Science Fiction Encyclopedia*, ed. Peter Nicholls (Garden City, N.Y.: Doubleday, 1979), pp. 290–91.

9. Gary K. Wolfe, "The Remaking of Zero: Beginning at the End," in *The End of the World*, ed. Eric Rabkin, Martin H. Greenberg, and Joseph D. Oleander (Carbondale and Edwardsville: Southern Illinois University Press, 1983), p. 8.

10. These transformations are those of Teun Van Djik, who provides an excellent discussion of the problems of textual transformations in his book *Some Aspects of Text Grammars: A Study in Theoretical Linguistics and Poetics* (The Hague, the Netherlands:

Mouton, 1972). See pp. 156, 288–89, and especially the section entitled "Narrative Transformations and Literary Operations," pp. 297–309. Initial work on a system of transformations was done by Vladimir Propp, who identified reduction, amplification, deformation, inversion, and substitution of several kinds. See Propp's "Transformation in Fairy Tales," in *Mythology,* ed. Pierre Maranda (Baltimore: Penguin Books, 1972), pp. 139–50. Propp's work has been severely criticized, mainly along the lines that it is simplistic and incomplete, as the field of text grammars has developed. However, his work was pioneering, just as Sigmund Freud's was, and the idea of transformations in story grammars is basically sound even though much work remains to be done.

11. There are many legitimate concerns about story grammars. Some of them result from the fact that the field is so new. Others result from the fact that the study of narrative structures in literature is but one part of a broader and more general field. And yet other concerns result from the fact that this study is dependent in many fundamental respects on other disciplines such as cognitive psychology and brain physiology, which are themselves in a state of accelerated development. I believe that most of these issues will eventually be resolved. For a discussion of some of the critical issues in this emerging field, see Teun Van Dijk, especially the chapter entitled "Semantic Macro-Operations. Narrative Structures," pp. 273–309. In order to avoid confusion, I have tried to avoid the terminology of text linguistics.

12. Wolfe's essay "The Remaking of Zero" is an excellent study of remade world literature. In it he hints at a deeper pattern but does not explore it.

13. James G. Frazer, *The Golden Bough: A Study in Magic and Religion,* abr. ed. (New York: Macmillan, 1950), pp. 371–73.

14. Eliade, p. 52.

15. Ibid., p. 75.

16. Joseph L. Henderson, in interpreting Jung, makes the point that the dream and fantasy sequences of many men and women in modern Western cultures who are questing religiously reveal the fact that they are still very much in the grip of early pagan vegetation beliefs. See Joseph L. Henderson, "Ancient Myth and Modern Man," in *Man and His Symbols,* ed. Carl G. Jung, M.-L. von Franz, Joseph L. Henderson, Jolande Jacobi, and Aniela Jaffe (New York: Dell, 1968), pp. 134–35. Another isomorph of re-creation myths are "Fall from the Garden of Eden" stories.

17. Ibid., p. 145.

18. Eliade, pp. 54–55.

19. Wolfe, p. 8.

20. *Virus* is based upon Sakyo Komatsu's novel *Fukkatsu No Hi,* which was translated into English as *Resurrection Day* (1964).

21. Campbell, p. 28.

22. Eliade, p. 55.

23. Ibid., p. 51.

24. Campbell, p. 28.

25. Ibid.

26. An excellent and more detailed discussion of this process can be found in Bruno Bettelheim's *The Uses of Enchantment: The Meaning and Importance of Fairy Tales* (New York: Viking Press, 1977), pp. 10–11.

27. Henderson, p. 124.

28. Ibid.

29. Ibid., p. 123.

30. Ibid., p. 120.

31. Ibid., p. 121.

32. Edward F. Abood, *Underground Man* (San Francisco: Chandler and Sharp, 1973), pp. 7–9.

33. Guyton B. Hammond, *Man in Estrangement* (Nashville, Tenn.: Vanderbilt University Press, 1965), p. 122.

34. Ibid.

35. Campbell, p. 30.

36. Ibid.

37. Information about "negativity" in story grammars can be found in Van Dijk, pp. 152–53.

38. An article in the Cleveland *Plain Dealer* by Andrew C. Revkin (reprinted from the *Los Angeles Times*) reports on a massive experimental fire to be set in the fall of 1986 in the Angeles National Forest. The purpose of the fire, which is to burn 1,200 acres of chaparral in a rugged canyon in the San Gabriel Mountains, is to test what effect smoke would have if there were a nuclear holocaust. (Attempts to set the fire failed and it was rescheduled for spring, 1987, but objections by environmentalists have caused an indefinite postponement.) Increasingly sophisticated computer simulations run by scientists suggest that nuclear winter may not be as harsh as initially indicated. This mitigation has generated the term "nuclear fall" to describe what might happen. Cleveland *Plain Dealer*, September 9, 1986.

39. An article in the Cleveland *Plain Dealer* by Earl Lane (reprinted from *Newsday*) reports on an attempt by scientists to discover the cause of the depletion of the ozone layer over Antarctica. A cyclical phenomena, beginning in late August every year, the size and severity of the affected area have increased every year since 1979. Cleveland *Plain Dealer*, August 19, 1986.

40. Gordon Rattray Taylor, *The Biological Time Bomb* (New York: Mentor, 1969), pp. 185–87, 224–25.

1

A PSYCHOLOGICAL ANALYSIS OF THE MYTH OF THE REMADE WORLD

Carl Goldberg

Who has driven the light out of my world? What has happened to the warm, protected and rejoicing days promised to me in my youth—the summers of pride—if I chose the virtuous life? They have vanished like lost sands into a starless night! I live in a world in which I am a stranger, a world I do not know. I seek to find an intimacy . . . that from which I have always felt excluded. I seek to return to innocence so that I might taste the fruits that seemed once so much the promise of my world and which are impossible to obtain alone.

—C. Goldberg, *In Defense of Narcissism* (1980)

The purpose of this chapter is to explain the psychological motivation that impels writers of science fiction to create new worlds. I have not been asked in my more familiar role as a clinician to interpret and make psychological inferences about the precursors of behavior of a person referred to me for psychological evaluation, nor have I been asked as a behavioral scientist to decipher the psychological manifestations of a single dramatic or literary work. I have been asked to explain the creative endeavors of all writers of science fiction—perhaps even all creators of fiction.

It would be presumptuous to imply that I expect to explain creative endeavor comprehensively. Even if I had sufficient insight into the matter, it would require more than a single volume, let alone a single chapter.[1] A comprehensive account of creative endeavor requires a multidimensional explanation. Creative endeavor is overdetermined. Consequently, in this chapter I will choose several levels of explanation to account for it. I will examine the invention of fictional worlds both as the author's personal statement and as a representation of universal myths and archetypical imagos regarding the societal dilemmas of the era in which the work was written.

Briefly stated, my theses are as follows: First, the recurring theme of human existence is the self's striving for personal identity, significance, and unification. The saga created by the writer of fiction reflects (mirrors) the author's own personal needs for personal identity. Each work of fiction involves a personal journey into the author's unconscious self. At the same time this endeavor represents the journey of the hero of universal myth and legend. The protagonist in this journey revisits and rediscovers the symbols and myths that countless other adventurers have encountered through the millennia, from the dawn of human consciousness. Second, regardless of the form (time, place, or treatment) of the issues with which the fictional work is struggling, these endeavors reflect societal themes that are current and conflicting in the world in which the author resides. Third, for the author to experience the created work as intellectually and emotionally satisfying, he needs to incorporate into the fictional tale the hidden wisdom of the past. This is to say, through his own personal journey during the incubation of the story, he must first rediscover and then integrate into the work of art the symbols, myths, and universal strivings of the human race. Fourth, the satisfactions of the reader will also reflect the successful, archetypal integration of the sage in such a way that existential options for viewing and dealing with vital societal concerns are tendered by the tale.

THE EXISTENTIAL FOUNDATION OF SCIENCE FICTION

One can, of course, argue that science fiction is nothing more than a revamping of ancient tales, which are devised to divert the reader for a period of time from the banal or even painful moments of his existence by transporting him to a new and exciting fictional world. In *Flying Saucers* (1978), Carl Jung indicates that a major reason for our sensitivity to possible evidence of extraterrestrial beings is that we would like to flee our banal confinement because the earth has grown too small for us.[2] I would be the last to deny the manifest purpose of science fiction as entertainment and diversion. However, I also would be among the first to insist that despite the author's ostensible endeavors, science fiction evinces a struggle with the meaning of human existence. Again, Jung points out that

sensationalism, love of adventure, technological audacity, intellectual curiosity may appear to be sufficient motives for our futuristic fantasies, but the impulse to spin such fantasies, especially when they take such a serious form . . . springs from an underlying cause, namely a situation of distress and the vital need that goes with it.[3]

To understand this better, let us look at the universal issues behind the invention of fictional worlds in our own day. We live in conflictual and distrustful times. The ordered society of yesteryear has dissipated, leaving behind eroded, social structures and clouds of cynicism and discontent. We feel immobilized by complex social problems that appear insoluble. We yearn for the warm regard and assurance of others. We want to touch others deeply and caringly, but instead we draw back in fear of our own malevolence, no less than that of our neighbors. We impute that we are not responsible for the destructive actions we have accorded others. We have tried to act as best we can to survive and to survive with our integrity intact. But we are plagued by a loss of courage and a destructive and irresponsible freedom which has been granted without limitation. In a word, we live in an era in which men find it onerous to accept responsibility for their own actions and for the embittered and hollow course their existence has taken.

The above description, I submit, is a generally held phenomenological view of the world in which the postcatastrophe literature of science fiction and fantasy has germinated. This account touches upon some of the basic archetypal anxieties in mankind since the dawn of consciousness. But what is the nature of this anxiety?

Impeding our attempts at personal identity, significance, and unification is the realization that we are essentially frail, limited, vulnerable, and finite. The recognition of vulnerability may be assuaged somewhat by the busy work of our daily endeavors. There are moments, however, such as serious illness in ourselves or those we care about, which baldly force us to face the impermanence of our existence. Such moments evoke more than just anxiety; they often unleash sheer terror. Not only is this terror concerned with an individual's mortal being, it is also concerned with questions about his achievements, his reputation, and his remembrance by others. In short, the terror his vulnerability bares has to do with the fear of erasure, or distortion of all for which he worked, struggled, and created—in a word, the meaning of his life.

Some mortals experience this terror more acutely than others. Those who have worked with profoundly psychotic people will recognize the psychotic reaction, in its ultimate sense, as an inability to defend against terror—the prospect of total loss of meaning of oneself as a person. In *The Denial of Death* (1975), Ernest Becker indicates that the person who suffers from a psychotic condition feels the overwhelmingness of life, his finitude, and dread of death more acutely than other people

because he has not been able to build the confident defenses that a person normally uses to deny them. [His] misfortune is that he has been burdened with extra anxiety, extra guilt, extra helplessness, an even more unpredictable and unsupportive environment. [As a result, he cannot] *confidentially deny* man's real situation on this planet.[4]

It is this underbelly of terror, which all of us experience at least in some subliminal way, that provides a major impetus for the creation of fictional worlds. In science fiction the fatal course of mankind's destiny may be creatively reversed and, through fantasy, recast.

THE ROMANTIC QUEST

Let us pause a moment before we reduce science fiction to nothing more than a desperate flight from our tragic, ontological condition. Heretofore, I have described man's condition in gloomy and pessimistic terms. The reader might ask why, if the human condition is so bleak, any of us persevere in trying to improve ourselves and the world in which we live. First, we must realize that our survival in itself has little or no significance. As Avery Weisman points out in *The Coping Capacity* (1984), human significance requires that our survival be lived competently and purposively.[5] An examination of the human condition suggests that our awareness of human possibility is as much invigorated by romantic passion as it is foreclosed by desperate terror. There is actually no acceptable reason for continuing to live except because we want to exist.[6] The meaning man craves for his existence is derived from his passions. These passions induce us to become involved in our existence. Why else would we continue to struggle with "the slings and arrows of outrageous fortune" other than in the fervent desire to participate in their full enrichment![7]

Thus, human consciousness is double-edged. While revealing the tragic substratum of life, it simultaneously provides us with romantic imagination and fantasy to transcend the given state of affairs of our present world. Anatole Broyard has reassuringly posed the rhetorical question "Why should not the analysis of the human soul be a romantic affair?" Our romantic nature, he argues, is our most redeeming attribute. It enables us to love and care for others and to strive for what we believe in.[8] It is our romantic passions that enable us to express these sentiments not only through interpersonal interaction but also in poetry, music, art, and all other forms of creative and intellectual endeavor.

It is the romantic aspect of our consciousness that recognizes that for our lives to be purposive a personal quest and journey in search of self is required.[9] The process of life involves each of us in an endless series of developmental challenges and frequent crises. Our human condition requires a personal exploration in order to meet these challenges. It is this journey that provides the foundation for all imaginative adventure.

THE PERSONAL JOURNEY IN SEARCH OF SELF

We may begin to unravel the conditions that have fueled the age-old journey of the seeker of self-knowledge by asking why no other species of being appears in need of such a journey. When we study nonhuman creatures closely, we observe that all animals of a species are highly similar in nature and that their natures are fixed at birth. That is not true for humans. To the contrary, human nature, as such, is a potential for living wisely and purposively and is to be discovered and personally shaped by the individual himself.

In an epigenetic sense, then, the limits of development and maturation are set at birth for all species except humans. Joseph Campbell tells us that myths from earliest times plainly show that unlike other creatures humans are born too soon—they are unfinished and unprepared to deal alone with the world.[10] The infant, still to be shaped and directed, is cast into the world in concert with a nurturing other. The infant encounters the external world as part of a dual physical and psychological unit with the mother. This union continues many months after birth in face of countless catastrophic dangers, any of which could instantaneously annihilate the neophyte if the infant were not protected. The susceptibility to danger without the protection of a caring other is the human creature's initial source of vulnerability. It is, at the same time, the source of human creative potential. Early inability to be separate and autonomous mandates protection against external danger by caretakers. This custody, when caringly provided, gives us the freedom to explore our own psyches unhampered and to develop and shape our own destinies.

The potential for creative development, of course, is neither unlimited nor undemanding. There are inherent strictures that must be attended to in order for creative growth to ensue. Chief among these is the requirement of finding a direction to pursue along the journey. Myth and legend reveal that although each person's journey is somewhat unique, each journey, if dutifully pursued, is also a rediscovery of what countless other seekers have found before.[11] These redis-covered signs provide a pathway for the seeker of self-knowledge to venture forth and to study how others before him have interpreted those universal con-ditions of the human psyche that must be addressed if wisdom is to emerge.

We see, then, that intimate bonding with the mother provides the individual with an initial sanctuary so that he may develop curiosity about his psyche. However, although each of us begins our personal journey, few of us relentlessly continue the trek of self-discovery. Something more than a capacity for growth and development, which is inherent in our human condition, is required. Alfred Lord Tennyson revealed this necessity to us poetically when he wrote of Odysseus telling his son, Telemachus, after twenty years of separation, that he is the father that his boyhood lacked. Tennyson spoke here of father as a mentor and guide.

In our earliest myths and folk legends the seeker is accompanied during his journey by a wise man who leads him through perilous ordeals so that he may become purified and transformed and may integrate his human nobility and spirituality. According to Campbell, mythology evolved in part to serve the psychological function of providing a marked pathway to carry the individual through the stages of his life.[12] The role of mentorship is crucial and well-articulated, although often metaphorical, in these mythical accounts.

Regardless of the methods they employ, mentors play a vital role in normal development. Adolescence and young adulthood, particularly, are marked by the search for a person wiser and more inspiring than one's self, who can help the individual through difficult life situations and what psychologists call "identity crisis" in such a way as to avoid what the young person experiences as the uncertainties and tribulations of dealing with these situations in ordinary ways. In this role the mentor serves as a psychological teacher by examining and searching the human psyche for ways to live one's life with purpose. Generally, the mentor influences a new perspective in his disciple by offering him a socially useful and creative solution for his teeming energies and ambitions— by providing not only a role model but active tutoring and encouragement as well. Without this relationship, the young person might turn with unconstructive rebellion against those elders whose power controls those areas of life to which he aspires.[13]

Finding a suitable mentor is not a matter of happenstance. The tragic manifold of destructive, charismatic leaders makes it clear that it is easy to fall prey to false messiahs.[14] To find a suitable mentor, the seeker of self-knowledge must himself acquire several essential characteristics. One of the most important of these is the willingness to postpone immediate gratification in order to acquire more durable satisfactions in the future. This endurance makes possible a serious commitment to undergo ordeal. The implicit message in myths and, as Bettelheim indicates, most particularly in fairy tales, is that a struggle against severe obstacles in life is inevitable.[15] However, if the seeker faces up to these difficulties forthrightly and courageously undergoes hardship, he will master all dilemmas and emerge victorious.

A personal journey is, among other things, a creative venture. In this endeavor, the seeker's whole identity may be forged upon the task at hand. The seeker must secure for himself a means of guidance when the mentor is absent in order to remain on an enlightened path to self-discovery.

It has always been the prime function of myth and rite to supply the direction and purpose that carry the human spirit forward in a constructive way.[16] Since empirically we cannot acquire absolute truth, we attempt to create reliable guides for living through myth and metaphor. They serve to explain to us how things became as they are. The revered poet Stanley Kunitz has said,

Old myths, old gods, old heroes have never died. They are only sleeping at the bottom of our mind, waiting for our call. We need them. They represent the wisdom of our race.[17]

The myth-symbolizing process is at the heart of endeavors that make us human. Susanne Langer has indicated that there is a human tendency to envision stories with the images we seek.[18] This tendency to create narrative from minimal sense data forms the basis of all creative, artistic, and inventive accomplishments. The seeker who searches for wisdom must rediscover and assimilate precisely those basic "archetypical imagos," as Jung called them, contained in universal myths. These symbols have inspired people throughout the millennia to face the longings and the suffering of the human psyche with courage, compassion, and vision. These symbols are the wisdom that the seeker of self-knowledge rediscovers. According to S. Kopp (1976) a considerable part of the quest for wisdom throughout the ages comes from the seeker's ability to speak "the forgotten language of prophecy, the poetic language of the myth and of the dream."[19] According to Erich Fromm (1951), the symbolic language of myth "brings us in touch with one of the most significant sources of wisdom. . . . [I]t brings us in touch with the deeper layer of our own personality."[20]

Examining the obstacles in the seeker's path through the symbolic meaning of enduring myths provides viable options for understanding human experiences, while, at the same time, sharing the spiritual tradition with those kindred who have preceded the seeker. Once he or she begins a personal journey, the seeker commences a trek as venerable as human existence itself.

All mentors share their symbols and their prophecy with their disciples. The wiser mentor, however, encourages the seeker to find or reshape his own knowledge, and the requirement of finding one's own symbols necessitates a separation from the mentor.

The message conveyed by the millennia of these knowledge seekers is that wisdom is best found beyond the abodes of mankind, out in the great solitude. Moreover, they have emphatically insisted that only privation and suffering can open the mind of the seeker to mysteries of human existence which are hidden from the more intrepid.[21]

It may be of interest to note that in shamanic tradition only a person who has healed himself is regarded as a wise man, because only such a person truly knows the dark secrets of the psyche. Thus in a psychological sense the seeker of knowledge is ill. His illness is usually due to a combination of physical and conflictual psychological tensions. During the course of his illness the seeker struggles, dramatically and valiantly, against powerful forces that have persistently afflicted his life. Acquaintance with the dark secrets of the psyche, which comes from bouts with illness and the possession of venerable symbols from myth and rite, provides the seeker with a visionary wisdom. The vision not only represents the struggles of the present society but also articulates ancient truths by means of which society is perpetually reborn and reformed.[22] Rediscovering the wisdom of the past in mythology reveals to the seeker the universal theme of death and rebirth. Jung has said that the major problems of our lives are never fully overcome.[23] However, by having struggled with them and having subdued them for the moment, we are enabled to continue our development of self-knowledge. In a word, the seeker who has deeply suffered and recovered can boldly face other sufferers' deepest feelings about man's tragic being.

The crisis of acute suffering offers a crucible for the mysteries of life. It involves an encounter with forces that decay and destroy, together with those that resuscitate and inspire. Suffering can thus become a vehicle to a higher level of consciousness[24] if the seeker has kept his inner fires and utilized them as a means to direct his life. These inner fires, ignited from fierce passion of combat with illness and suffering, may be employed to inspire others as well. In reality, what the wise man offers is guidance toward accepting the imperfections of a temporary existence in an ultimately unmanageable world through the utilization of romantic imagination. In imagining a better world, we are provided a vision with which to create a better world.

How valid is my explanation of the universal themes that foster the motivation for writing science fiction? One way of assessing this question is to extrapolate the various motifs I have emphasized in my discussion of the personal journey into the self—rediscovering the wisdom of the past from symbol and myth, the importance of privation and struggles with illness and suffering, the ubiquitous appearance of rebirth cycles, and the indispensable role of a mentor—and then to compare them with the cardinal motifs in the works of science fiction. Even a casual comparision reveals a congruent fit.

After detecting the connection between the universal themes in the epigenetic requirement and the theme of science fiction, however, our explanation remains incomplete because there are countless people, other than writers, who use archetypal imagos in attempting to transform man's tragic condition. Therefore, the unique ways different people represent their struggles with man's tragic condition must be accounted for. In short, why do some people become writers of science fiction rather than physicians, psychologists, engineers, philosophers, and so forth?

This question can be best answered by examining the psychological development of the creative person. All creative endeavor has an interpersonal aim. This aim is an attempt to fulfill the requirements of the personal journey heretofore discussed. In order to comprehend creative endeavor meaningfully, therefore, we first must examine the conditions that have fostered its etiology. Not only are we born too soon, but we also inevitably fail to attain the magically desired relationship with others that our romantic imagination desires. Creative endeavor is at least an attempt to reverse the disappointments and failings of our early, intimate bonding relationships. Since we have already tied the themes of mythology with science fiction tales, we can now confidently apply Otto Rank's thesis about mythology to them. Rank tells us that myths are the daydreams of children and adolescents that have continued long after puberty. They serve to wish-fulfill and to rectify the "injustices" of early life.[25] The most ubiquitous of these is the fantasy of replacing the real father with a more distinguished surrogate and mentor figure. Fantasies, such as these, attempt to recover the vanished happiness of childhood, when the father still appeared to be the wisest, strongest, and most noble of men and the mother the most beautiful, caring, and dearest of women.

The unfinished crucible of the mother-child bonding sets the stage for the personal journey. How courageously the seeker is able to face creatively the ordeals encountered in this quest depends upon early bonding. Stated succinctly, aspects of the personal journey are necessarily struggled with and experienced in solitude. The ability to withstand aloneness, however, is dependent upon prior, satisfying experiences in intimate relatedness to others.

The creative person shares the epigenetic, unfinished quality of selfhood with all other humans. What differentiates him from them, however, is his active curiosity and passion for self-discovery which has been thwarted in the less creative person's early bonding relations. This differential development needs delineation. Consequently, a theory about how intimacy develops in the mother-child bonding and its relationship to the personal journey is required in order to explain creative endeavor more fully.

HOW INTIMACY DEVELOPS

The earliest and most basic aim of social behavior is the striving for intimate relations with a caring other. Important socioemotional needs are served in this way. Intimate connectedness is a mechanism of survival. The infant who is able to respond appropriately to what the mother wants and requires of the child is more adaptive in pleasing the mother and more likely to be rewarded by her. The quality of the early bonding relationship between mother and child mirrors and models how the child will subsequently relate to others. It is the bonding relationship that gives the child a sense of self. Developmental studies suggest that a rather important phase of the child's development of a sense of self, referred to as the mirror phase of personality development, occurs between the child's sixth and eighteenth months.

In this phase the mother serves both as a mirror and as a representation of how the larger world will respond to the child. Courage and nonintrusive caring are essential attributes in the development of meaningful intimacy. When the mother is not straightforward, that is, when she tries to hide her fears and limitations, she is more likely to relate to her child by controlling his responsiveness to her. The child who is denied the open, inner being of the mother for identification of his own psychic experience will search for external mirrors—other people and objective mirrors. The child uses these mirrors to reveal his own psyche and at the same time, paradoxically, tries to control the information these mirrors render, so that he conforms to the ''acceptable'' self demanded of him in his early bonding relationships.

The unacceptable parts of the self of a child whose mother controls him are disavowed. This results in a division of the self from itself. Collectively, over time, these parts are sensed as a magical or second-self. I will refer to this sense of self as the ''magical self.''

In the mirror phase, the child needs to be looked at, smiled at, and approved of by an active, loving, and supportive person. Without this emotional nurturance, the child experiences the world as persecutory and regards part of himself or herself as unacceptable. In a word, a person subjected to an unresponsive or distorted mirroring relationship will be handicapped to a greater or lesser degree in his or her capacity to mirror another person accurately and, as a consequence, to respond empathically to the other and to experience what the other person may be feeling.

Intimacy is a uniquely personal experience, operationally defined here as the experience of being recognized and emotionally touched in the way the self wishes, that is, in a way that self experiences the other as accurately and satisfactorily mirroring its desires for caring and closeness. The other in the intimate encounter is the medium for how the self wishes to be related to and regarded. Therefore, unlike its often associated state of privacy, intimacy always involves the real or imagined presence of the other. Moreover, unlike privacy, which is a reaction of the other's encroachment upon the self's experience of space and time, the experience of intimacy has no sense of time. It is experienced as a flow of tactile sensation. Intimacy is grounded in the immediacy of the present moment, and the present moment is experienced as located in space, not time. Only the past and future have a sense of time. Intimacy leads to an accentuation of how each partner uses the space between them. Anxieties in intimate relating are experienced as going out of space and are projected to moments in the future. Intimacy, then, is a moment that the self experiences as if time stopped and stood on end. The self's intention in the throes of intimacy is that this moment go on forever. Nietzsche wrote that every pleasure wants eternity—deep, deep enternity.[26] This intent has a definitive body locus—even when there is no actual physical contact occurring between self and other.

Developmental and clinical evidence suggests that intimate strivings have to do with an attempt to re-create the events of the tender, caring touch experienced in the mother-child bonding. Consequently, the hunger and potency for this striving have to do with frustrations that occurred in this early relationship, whereas fears about intimate coupling involve the import of painful rejection and exclusion from these intimate relations. According to the psychoanalyst Heinz Kohut, the capacity for intimacy develops in the infant by means of the mother's mirroring function. The mother's role in the child's development of intimacy is to serve as a supportive self-object for the child's curiosity about self and other.[27]

The event of intimacy requires a bond between persons in which each "feels into" the other, as well as an openness with oneself which permits the other to connect with typically hidden aspects of oneself.[28] What does this mean in terms of the bonding relationship between mother and child? The child learns to recognize himself in the eyes and facial expression of the mother. Basically, the mother gives the child one of two very different and crucial options in his response to her. The child may be given tacit permission by the mother to look into her depths and, metaphorically, into her mystery, or he may be constrained to merely looking at her and his own reflection in her eyes. Intimacy between mother and child in the early bonding relationship involves the mother's willingness to be intimate with her own self. It requires courage on the part of the mother in order to struggle with, or at least be comfortable with, her own uncertainties.

Significant in intimate bonding with the mother is the child's witnessing of her willingness to bear pain and suffering in her creative functions. For example, in the act of bearing children, the mother demonstrates her unwillingness to abort her pain and suffering in order to produce hope and possibility. The experimental work of Stanford University psychologist David Rosenman has demonstrated that the individual's pattern of altruism is deeply influenced by parental models in regard to handling issues requiring persistence and fortitude.[29]

Thus, the child witnessing the mother's relationship with her own depths allows him to have a relationship with the mystery of another self. On the other hand, a narcissistic or repressive mother will not allow her child to probe her fears and uncertainties. She will restrict him to the image reflected upon her face and will not allow him to search her own depths or to have his own mystery.

The two basic options the mother may offer her child in the bonding relationship then are (a) sharing her mystery and uncertainties or (b) restricting him so that he sees himself as she wishes him to. The child of narcissistic and repressive mothers, therefore, will be restricted to superficial reflection—that is, literal image (such as in the mirror) for self-evaluation and esteem.

The child whose mother shares with him is allowed to find beauty and contentment within himself. He is allowed to take in and hold onto the inchoate, unfinished aspects of himself, cogitate with them, play with them in fantasy and action, and, if he wishes, share them with others. Without restriction on his inner being, he feels no compulsion or haste to share immediately his inner being or the products of his imagination. He experiences permission to do so in his own time. Exploring his thoughts and feelings becomes a regular process in his ongoing development as a person. It does not require abrupt separation and withdrawal from other people.

The child who is denied the mystery of his mother's inner being becomes uncomfortable with his own psyche and its mysteries. He feels unsettled and perturbed inside. He is continually searching for something or someone in the external environment to relieve the urgent promptings within his psyche which he has not been allowed to explore. Most particularly, he searches for the opportunity to find other people who will mirror acceptable parts of himself, thereby validating his existence.

In a word, it is essential that a child feel tenderly loved in his bonded relationship with his mother. Her inability to share her depths with him makes meaningful intimacy impossible. Those attributes that she feels threatened by and denies in her self she will deny in her child. The mother teaches the child not only how to love and how to be intimate with another person but, as important, how to be intimate with one's own self. If the feelings of the child that threaten the mother are denied, these rejected feelings are then disassociated from the child's experience of himself. However, because they relate to once deeply felt experiences of the inchoate self, they are dynamically retained, but as shrouded images resembling that primal self now obliviscent; when ascendant, the images are sensed as external, hostile, and elusive. These images are similar to the fearful symbols collectively referred to as the "shadow," which are found in the myth and ritual of many cultures. In Jung's psychological theories, the shadow is conceived as externalized self-hatred and plays a significant role in his therapeutics. As the missing, hidden, and secret part of the self, it must be owned for harmonious existence. In Karen Horney's theory, the shadow is described as "alienation from Self"—it is a coterie of despised selves which must be integrated with the idealized selves to create a unified, holistic, real self. In

Heinz Kohut's theory, the missing aspects of the self are those which have gone unmirrored by the narcissistic mother, who possesses her own agenda and is not sufficiently empathic with her child.[30]

I have spoken about the mother's role in the child's development of intimacy but not yet of the father's. What part does the father play in the child's striving for intimacy? In general, we know very little about his role in the child's development of a capacity for intimacy. We do know that in the consanguine family of Western society he cuts the cord.[31] This is to say that the father forces the child out of the timeless space of intense, intimate bonding with the mother. Of course, other siblings and external situations may do so as well, However, in the early, triangular family relationship, this appears to be one of the father's major functions.

According to psychoanalytic theory, the mother, as an object for relating, is experienced by the infant as coming from within the self of the infant. The father, by contrast, exists only as an external figure, as part of a gradual process in which the figure of the mother becomes experienced as outside of the child. In fact, it is the relationship between the parents that helps the child differentiate what is inside and what is outside of himself.[32] By keeping the mother-child relationship from becoming too exclusive, the father serves as a representative of space and time and of the larger society. The father's presence between child and mother enables the child to experience sufficient frustration from the absence of unlimited intimacy with the mother to induce him to seek intimate relations with peers and parental surrogates. Without the structure of time and space created by the father, the child would remain magically and symbolically fused with the mother.

To summarize, the parallel themes in the intimacy paradigm and in the universal myths of personal journey suggest that inevitable disappointment and limitation in early childhood is part of the human condition in greater or lesser degree. As such, they continue as inherent themes of human longing in universal myths.

Moreover, we cannot understand the nature of intimacy if we view the self as a solitary and complete entity. In the act of intimacy the self tries to transcend itself; it tries to reach out and rescue its disavowed and denied aspects. It is the pursuit of these disavowed aspects that, at the personal level of explaining creativity, impels writers to create new worlds.[33]

THE INTERPERSONAL AIM OF CREATIVITY

Why then do some creative people become writers, while others fashion other forms of expression? Writers are people who early in life found, or at least believed, themselves to be inarticulate in verbal and behavioral ways. They also found that they needed a period of quiet incubation of ideas in order to inhibit primary process thinking and convert it into secondary and more abstract expression. This need for the transliteration of feeling to cognition by copiously working out sentiments before sharing them with others may continue into adulthood or may even be modified. However, by adulthood, the written form of expression has become a primary source of personal satisfaction. The evidence for these contentions should be obvious. The feedback and reward of the writer's audience are not immediate. Indeed, most frequently, the writer has no direct contact with his audience and their reactions. The rewards of writing are, at best, delayed. Those who at a young age are verbally articulate are immediately reinforced. Why would such a person seek writing as a primary source of satisfaction if it involved postponing gratification, when immediate satisfaction was easily obtainable?

The problem with explaining the writer's motivation in this way is that satisfaction is narrowly defined here in terms of an individualistic pursuit. It is easy to accept this definition uncritically because creative writing is, for the most part, a highly solitary activity. However, remember that we have argued that science fiction is the prolonged daydreams of childhood and adolescence in which the writer seeks a more perfect, magical world, a new age after the fall, to replace his vanished happiness of long ago. He wants a more perfect order and a new breed of beings. Surprisingly, these attempts to replace vanished worlds are often fostered in the context of other kindred souls. For example, Isaac Asimov tells of being "huddled close to other teen-agers" like himself, feeling "trapped in an alien and unsympathetic world," and collectively reading science fiction stories and inventing their own.[34] Moreover, we can trace back this interpersonal context to, at least, Thomas More, who in creating a utopian world based upon humanistic beliefs of his trusted friends and associates, hoped through satire and symbolism to protect his friends and himself from the retribution of the authoritarian order of his day and, at the same time, to foster responsive sentiments in other humanistic intellectuals.

My comments should suggest that creativity, certainly the works of science fiction, not only is inspired products to amuse others but also is an interpersonal striving for guiding others. At this point it is important to define "creativity" because the term has been subjected to a plethora of meanings and usages. In this chapter it is used with two specific meanings:

1. as a process that leads to a specific artistic product and
2. as a kind of dialogue and attitude toward one's self and others that provides the possibility for intimate relationships through integrating passion, will, and vision.

I contend that these two processes are related but that the former is a partial or compromised expression of the latter. This is not intended to denigrate artistic work itself but to suggest that the impetus for creative expression is not entirely satisfied by the work of art.

Despite persistent efforts by social scientists and literary scholars to understand and explain creative endeavor, few of these efforts have been illuminating. Considerable ignorance remains about the source of the creative urge. I believe this is due to attempts to explain creativity by reductionistic causality. Even modern psychoanalytic theory still accounts for artistic achievement as the manifestation of defense mechanisms against unacceptable, libidinous urges. Briefly stated, the psychoanalytic thesis is that limitation and frustration of the sexual and procreative urges lead to a need to express these biological strivings in the form of art or scholarly achievement. Creativity is, therefore, a sublimated or compromised form of the original biological urge. This is exemplified by the frequent and arrant description by psychoanalysts of the autobiography of the artist or writer as "pathography."

Various explanations of creative endeavor have been suggested. While many of these explanations undoubtedly have a necessary basis in the creative process, they do not actually tell us any more than that all humans have some innate urge for creative endeavor, which may be accentuated from frustration and fostered by the interest and the encouragement of creative expression in the environment in which the individual finds himself. These notions also suggest, however, that creative endeavor, as in the quest for novel stimulation, is a rather aimless search for the opportunity to find something in the external world to relieve boredom within the psyche. The curiosity notion posits that in the creative act the artist projects his or her dimly conscious, or even unconscious, representation of an inner-need satisfier onto the external world. Then, through artistic efforts, the creative person seeks to find, come to terms with, and finally identify with his object-representation in the external world. The result is a feeling of integration and completeness. The problem with this explanation is that it fails to recognize sufficiently the interpersonal dimension in the search for personal identity of the artist which, I believe, is implicit in all creative endeavor. To appreciate this point of view, we need only to take into account the notion of human intentionality, which recognizes that personality consists of the composite of specific acts a person takes toward other people and events and the value and meaning with which the person imbues these acts. How can a person find meaning other than in significant encounters with others?

It is through an interaction that permits a person to articulate and negotiate his intentions that a sense of personal identity is created. Personal identity is meaningful only in terms of other people. There is no need to have an identity or sense of self simply in terms of relations with one's own self.

What are the interpersonal forces which come together in the individual fostering of an artistic bent? H. J. Kleinschmidt believes that "the childhood of creative people seems to be burdened by their awareness of their being 'different' with all the implications of guilt and ambivalence over being 'special.' "[35] This is exemplified, as mentioned earlier, in the writer being a child who did not receive immediate gratification as a speaker or doer. The intensity of response and the greater vulnerability to frustration of such children "puts an added burden on the relationship with the mother, accounting for the dominance of narcissism as a primary defense among artists."[36] Their narcissistic defenses "protect them in the face of their vulnerability and provide them with the rationale for their feeling of being special."[37] What are the specific factors of specialness that the artist experiences?

First, constitutional factors are sine qua non for the development of the artist. In "The Childhood of the Artist," the psychoanalyst Phyllis Greenacre has described the passion for life that the artist manifests.[38] This is exemplified by Sylvia Plath, the poet who died at her own hands and is considered to have written much rage-filled verse. While she was a person in whom one might have expected to find morbidity, she revealed, paradoxically, in her diary an almost pantheistic relish for life. In her words, "I want to be able to sleep in an open field, to travel west, to walk freely at night."[39]

Another common denominator in the lives of artists is loss. Freud put great emphasis, for example, on Leonardo da Vinci's loss of his father. Da Vinci spent the first years of his life alone with his mother, and this had a decisive influence on the formation of his inner life. The absence of an adult male confronted him with the riddle of where babies come from. At an early age, he became a researcher and later claimed that he was destined to investigate the problem of the flight of birds because he had been visited by a vulture as he lay in his cradle (which we may speculate was Leonardo's creative explanation of the riddle about birth). Da Vinci soon lost the protective haven he found in his mother alone, but refound that lost world in his painting and specifically in the woman with the mysterious smile—"the smile he had lost and that fascinated him so much when he found it again in the Florentine lady."[40]

Another special factor is that the great artist is often the firstborn child in a family where the father and, perhaps, other relatives have attained some distinction in the field of creativity. Like Da Vinci, he is doted upon by a loving, empathetic mother who sees him as the most wonderful, beautiful child in the world. A variation of this theme is the narcissistic mother who sees him as an extension of her beautiful self and the future fulfillment of all her exhibitionist claims. Early in life he displays the family gift, a development that is eagerly anticipated and encouraged by both parents.[41]

The early losses or disappointments of the great artist are probably not catastrophically traumatic, as they are to those persons who do not seem able to achieve creative mastery. Generally, they involve some physical separation or an emotional estrangement due to empathic failures. The loneliness leads to the development of fantasy as a mode of consolation and perhaps a form of play related to later artistic activity. Here the denied aspects of self, impeding the sense of self-integration, are reworked in fantasy and daydream and recast in the imagination in the form of a remade world.

Often the decisive disappointments occur with the birth of new siblings when the doting mother is no longer available with her enormously stimulating input. In a study of the relationship between artistic endeavor and traumatic loss, George Pollack (1982) found that a surprising number of writers of all kinds had suffered a premature loss in the family.[42]

Mourning plays a significant role in the writers Pollack studied as well as in the lives of most creative people. Clinically, we know that when a person mourns, powerful or loved aspects of the lost object are taken in and internalized. This leads to a greater sense of integration of self than during the period when the mourner denied the loss because he felt that he could not endure without the lost person. He experiences a feeling of incompleteness, which, if unresolved through mourning, prevents his present world from having a bright tomorrow.

The final special factor that should be mentioned is the physical self. The physical self may have great importance if much attention is focused on the sheer physical beauty of the child who becomes creative. Such attention feeds his fantasies of omnipotence and grandiosity. The artist is, thus, more vulnerable to disappointments and more likely to lack the ability of empathic mirroring. In the process of creativity, he attempts to regain the paradise once tasted and subsequently lost. As George Bernard Shaw indicated, you use a glass mirror to see your face; you use a work of art to see your soul.

Accordingly, creative works may serve both as mirrors for autobiographical reflection and as sources of approval from other people. I. B. Singer has indicated that all novels are autobiographic. Everything is taken from the author's life, because writers can only actually describe their own experiences.[43] This may explain why some writers write only one great novel and others write several. The one important book is probably most painfully autobiographic. Once having produced the work and gained an approving mirror, passion for further risk and exploration may be stifled. The tenuousness of this continuing struggle in the artist between the quest for greater creative satisfaction and the need to feel secure with habitual modes of behavior is probably the source of the popular notion that there is a very fine line between madness and creative genius. Because of this, the artist is often regarded as a deviant from the mainstream of society in any given period of history. My own clinical experience tends to verify that the creative aim emanates from a longing for once-experienced emotional states that have become disavowed and denied because of their threat to the individual's early relations with nurturing others. A number of people about whom I have read and with whom I have worked in a clinical setting were able courageously and successfully to come to terms with denied and unacceptable parts of self through creative endeavors. They have transcended, at least for periods of their lives, rather disturbed personality structures. Their experiences illustrate that the creative act is for some artists a striving to integrate the denied aspects of self into personality. In it the self attempts to transcend itself, to reach out and rescue its disavowed and denied aspects. The source of creativity for these artists is the desire to quell the inner suffering that has resulted from incomplete or lack of self-integration. I assume a Platonic stance in this matter.

While the artist seeks to reach and articulate an ideal form, the form is not conceived by the gods. Rather, it emerges from the quest for an intimate bonding with disavowed aspects of self that were created, experienced, and denied in childhood. The longed-for goal in creative endeavor is to experience completeness and integration, thus, temporarily ending suffering and frustration. The creative person finds a viable means to do this through skill and/or erudition. The artistic endeavor bridges the self and its denied aspects in a temporary, or more enduring, synthesis. This is possible, in no small way, because of the creative person's accentuated awareness of certain aspects of the environment.[44] The artist's powers in these endeavors are distinguished not only by an unusual sensitivity and intellect but also by an outstanding capacity for integration of emotional and intellectual forces.[45] This explanation also accounts for the inevitable suffering of the artist who believes that he can no longer create. The case of Ernest Hemingway is a tragic example of this.

However, if completion and integration is the ultimate aim of creative endeavor, then how can we account for the common observation that some individuals disrupt cognitive balance in the interest of seeking greater stimulus input, such as the creative individuals studied by F. Barron?[46] One clue to answering this question may have been found in a study by the Psychiatric Department of the Cincinnati General Hospital in 1961.[47] The Cincinnati study tends to support theoretical notions about the developmental causes for the ideal types of creative personalities. Investigators found that the creative child is likely to come from a home and family characterized as not tightly organized, not overly intimate, and not particularly well-adjusted. Each parent perceives the marriage and family life in somewhat different terms. The family is one in which there is open and often turbulent expression of strong feelings, but that expression is not used to bind the child to the values of either parent. Nor does either parent use the child against the other to prove himself a better parent or person. In this kind of environment a child learns an adaptive, reconstructive strategy early in childhood, so that he can regress to a more primitive stage of development without fear of disapproval from his parents.

Such children show precious skills at internalization. According to Ernest Kris, a psychoanalyst who has extensively studied the creative personality,

The observation of children who show this early tendency to internalization, in some cases during the earlier phase of the second year . . . supply not only well-known examples of early intellectual achievements, but also evidence of a flourishing fantasy life, or at least of richness of imagination, which makes some of [them] self-contained without forcing them necessarily into actual withdrawal. They are in command of an inner world populated by creatures of their own, but at the same time they are prone to solve complex problems.[48]

In short, each creative act is an attempt to create a bond with another psyche. Once we accept this notion, we can clearly see that creative activities that are limited to products—for example, works of art, music, literature and so forth—are only partial achievement of the creative effort. Creativity in those who have had untoward experiences with intimacy in the bonding relationship derives from the impulse to compensate for dissatisfaction with contemporary existence by inventing a more harmonious existence. For example, many writers experience themselves as not verbally articulate, and others frequently describe themselves as feeling inadequate in facing life's problems. Each may subvert the anxieties generated by these demands and, at the same time, form a gratifying sense of identity through the structured roles and functions provided by creative work.

But we should not lose sight of the fact that the subversion is a compromise. In all of these efforts there is an attempt to relate with vision, passion, and innovation to one's creative endeavors in ways the artist subliminally desires would be possible with other people. To the extent that the artist channels his existence into creating products rather than relating creatively to both his work and other people, inhibitions and compromises may be inferred in the artist's psychological functioning. The artist whose life is emotionally impoverished because he lives for his creative endeavors is living a subverted life—"subverted" in the sense that the psychopathology of the artist comes from the extreme channeling of creative effort into making products rather than into meaningful interpersonal relations. Thus, regardless of how abstract the product of an artist's creative efforts is, these activities have at their source an interpersonal aim. In short, creativity, at least in its ideal state, is not simply those activities that lead to artistic products; more important, it involves a process of creative living.

Correspondingly, my theory of creative development posits that there are two kinds of creative artists. I am not saying that there are only "A" artists and "B" artists. I am referring to ideal types rather than real people, and creative people fall along a continuum between these ideals.

According to my theory, the need for creative endeavor derives from the need to master a segment of the environment in innovative ways which enable the artist to symbolically integrate dissonant and unfinished aspects of himself. But if that were the only impetus, he would have a far greater need for immediate completion than we observe in creative genius. Therefore, he may also derive considerable pleasure and satisfaction from reaching others and sharing his innovative and creative way of experiencing the world in a kind of ongoing dialogue with them.

The need to complete his work quickly comes from the experience of the artist who has suffered deeply from disturbing intimate relationships. It is not that his work is less creative or less insightful than more tranquil artists but that he keeps repeating the same themes and struggles in his work.

All writers seek external worlds to match those with which they are internally preoccupied. However, they frequently need to expel toxic and painful introjects that cannot be internally tolerated or manipulated and that maintain creative monotony in order to create new varieties in the nature of things. The work of these writers is generally pessimistic and violent. The usefulness of this paradigm is that it enables us to see that helping the artist work out his psychological conflicts need not lead to inferior creative work. It can, in fact, lead to greater complexity and quality in the work. Kleinschmidt points out that the artist's narcissistic vulnerability tends to mitigate this realization.

Since creative artists are capable of high levels of integretion, it would seem likely that the same levels could be reached in object relationships; however, such people feel that to allow sustained object relationships would mean to lose everything, namely, the special ability and unique identity, when, in reality, they have nothing to lose but their isolation.[49]

Incompleteness and the need for creative endeavor in order to experience brief periods of integration make the artist's sense of well-being, his relationship to self and the world, depend upon his continued creative production. In a sense, he is addicted to this need. To quit would produce a painful withdrawal, so, in the context of his art, he eagerly awaits the next "fix." In a word, he may experience the underbelly of terror discussed earlier in this chapter. As a consequence, he cannot exist either for himself alone or immersed in the interpersonal realm without the intermediary of his art. He is destined to feel incomplete and to search for completeness in a variety of ways and in a variety of mirrors.

The artist is hero in his ability to take risks, to disregard convention, to create new order, although to what extent this remains choice is questionable. In reality, he probably has no choice but to walk the tightrope between reality and illusion. To hesitate means to fall into an abyss of nothingness, with no identity. Artists must have courage because their sentiments, and how they express them, will often be provocative and unusual, but when their ideas are accepted, or tolerated, they stretch the limits of human understanding.

THE FUNCTION OF ART FOR THE SPECTATOR

Our world does not simply require more creative artists, rather it requires creative people to teach others to live more courageous, passionate, and creative lives. It has been aptly said that creativity represents a temporary triumph over human conflict[50] and that every child is an artist, but the problem is how to remain an artist once the child grows up.[51] We find ourselves in need of new and creative means to redress the suffering we find in a world that is filled with eroded social structures and clouds of cynicism and discontent.

Science fiction writers destroy worlds and create new ones when they sense that the myths that support their societies are no longer viable or have become destructive to human growth and development. Jung indicated that only an idea or an experience that is "overwhelming, no matter the form of expression it takes, can challenge the whole man and force him to react as a whole."[52] In this sense, writers of science fiction try, perhaps without consciously realizing it, both to shock the reader into reacting as a whole person in a world of peril and, ironically and simultaneously, to create a fantasy to distract the reader from his ostensible personal concerns. There is no contradiction in this dual function if we realize that we may need to subdue the daily preoccupations of the individual in order to reach his archetypical self.

Art has many functions but, perhaps, one of its most important is frequently ignored. Art can and often does have a moral function. It serves this aim to the extent that the protagonist, say in science fiction, asks eternal questions about the human condition. Many artists, especially Oscar Wilde,[53] have denied this contention. They have referred to novels as ''art without value.'' On the other hand, the novel may serve to represent and mirror, by creative expression, the highest ideals of human thought and ambition. As such, creative work may with inspired examples lead us to noble action. Wilde and other proponents of valueless aesthetics point to the function of art, as Aristotle described it, as a purgation of untoward emotion. They have indicated that to interpret and derive values from the work other than the simple pleasure of aesthetics is unreasonable.[54] It seems evident, however, that purgation leads psychologically to encourage action. Indeed, art is inspirational in the emotional sense. The moral aim of art is to move the observer to participate more fully in an artistic work that proved to be vague, unarticulated, or unconsciously experienced within his own psyche in previous encounters. Art has the effect of kaleidoscoping a series of emotional options by associating the externalized object (the work of art, music, drama, and so forth) with states of emotion heretofore suppressed. The art object is a condensation of the longed-for expression of ''unfinished'' experience, ''unfinished'' in that no emotional solution or harmony had been achieved, and in this sense it is related to the need for personal journey. This is clearest in the dramatic arts, but it follows in principle for all forms of art. The harmony created by the work provides solutions, emotional expressions through identification in the viscera of the observer.

Furthermore, as inspiration, the work of art may provide the impetus for purposive action. Musical bands have preceded armies from the earliest tribal battles. One could argue that this may follow for a work of art of a Michelangelo or a Leonardo da Vinci but not in the tormented struggles in the work of Edvard Munch or van Gogh's later work or in grotesque science fiction tales. I would contend that this argument still consistently follows. The tortured beauty of these works creates a unique symmetry in its revelation of truth, which we all experience but fear to express. The artist may become our Pied Piper by enabling us to participate more fully in our emotions in ways we could not identify until we encountered the artistic work.

In summary, the occurrence of a close similarity between the age-old journey of the seeker of self-knowledge and science fiction tales is no mere happenstance. We all dream and long for imagined new worlds. This is, as I have tried to demonstrate, because we are born incomplete. We require a personal quest to fulfill our human destiny. The creators of fictional new worlds, by casting important archetypal and social images in their stories, not only provide the vision of a better world which we hope to build but also help alert us to the concerns of the human race which flow subliminally from one generation to the next and which we must face if the new world is to flourish.

NOTES

1. The reader who is aware of the literature on creativity may note with some dismay the lack of conviction these theories and explanations offer, even when written by the most outstandingly creative people.

2. Carl Jung, *Flying Saucers* (Princeton, N.J.: Bollingen Series, 1978), p. 17.

3. Ibid.

4. Ernest Becker, *The Denial of Death* (New York: Free Press, 1975), p. 63.

5. Avery D. Weisman, *The Coping Capacity* (New York: Human Sciences Press, 1984), p. xii.

6. Ibid., p. 14.

7. Carl Goldberg, *In Defense of Narcissism: The Creative Self in Search of Meaning* (New York: Gardner Press, 1980), pp. 68–80. See especially the section entitled "The Passionate Self," pp. 77–79.

8. Anatole Broyard, "Life before Death," *New York Times,* June 9, 1982.

9. Carl Goldberg, *To Be a Psychotherapist—The Journey of the Healer* (New York: Gardner Press, 1985). The entire volume is devoted to the issue of personal journey.

10. Joseph Campbell, *The Hero with a Thousand Faces* (Princeton, N.J.: Bollingen Series, 1968), p. 6.

11. Ibid., p. 39.

12. Ibid., p. 10.

13. Daniel J. Levinson, *The Seasons of a Man's Life* (New York: Ballantine Books, 1978), pp. 251–56.

14. Carl Goldberg, "Courage and Fanaticism: The Charismatic Leader and Modern Religious Cults," in *Psychodynamic Perspectives on Religion, Sect and Cult,* ed. David A. Halperin (Boston: John Wright, 1983). See especially pp. 164–167, 176–79.

15. Bruno Bettelheim, *The Uses of Enchantment* (New York: Vintage, 1977), pp. 3–19.

16. Campbell, p. 11.

17. Stanley Kunitz, "The Presence of Myth in Contemporary Life," Conference Presentation at the New School for Social Research, New York, October 1984.

18. Susanne K. Langer, *Mind: An Essay on Human Feelings,* vol. 1 (Baltimore: Johns Hopkins University Press, 1967), pp. 59–61, 63–64, 67–69.

19. S. Kopp, *If You Meet the Buddha on the Road, Kill Him!* (New York: Bantam Books, 1976), p. 12.

20. Erich Fromm, *The Forgotten Language* (New York: Grove Press, 1951), p. 10.

21. Joan Halifax, *Shamanic Voices: A Survey of Visionary Narratives* (New York: Dutton, 1979), p. 6.

22. Campbell, p. 4.

23. Carl G. Jung, "Approaching the Unconscious," in *Man and His Symbols*, Jung, M.-L. von Franz, Joseph L. Henderson, Jolande Jacobe, and Aniela Jaffe (New York: Dell, 1975), p. 75.

24. Halifax, pp. 10–11.

25. Otto Rank, "The Myth of the Birth of the Hero." In *The Myth of the Birth of the Hero and Other Writings,* ed. Philip Freund (New York: Vintage, 1964). See especially the section entitled "The Interpretation of Myths," pp. 65–96, where this concept is discussed in detail.

26. A. M. Meerloo, "Father Time," *Psychiatric Quarterly* 22 (1948), p. 597, quoting Nietzsche.

27. Heinz Kohut, *The Restoration of the Self* (New York: International Universities Press, 1977), pp. 6–11.

28. A. B. Szalita, "The Use and Misuse of Empathy in Psychoanalysis and Psychotherapy," *Psychoanalytic Review* 68 (1981), pp. 11–12.

29. For further information, see David Rosenman, J. Karylowski, P. Salovey, and K. Hargis, "Emotion and Altruism," in *Altruism and Helping Behavior,* ed. J. P. Rushton and R. M. Sorrentino (Hillsdale, N.J.: Erlbaum Press, 1981), pp. 233–48.

30. For further information, see J. Simon and Carl Goldberg, "The Role of the Double in the Creative Process and Psychoanalysis," *Journal of the American Academy of Psychoanalysis* 12 (1984), pp. 341–61.

31. Meerloo, p. 602.

32. E. Gaddini, "Discussion of the Role of Family Life in Child Development," *International Journal of Psycho-Analysis* 57 (1976). Printed response to a paper entitled "On Father Formation in Early Child Development," presented at the 29th International Psycho-Analytic Congress in London, July 1975, pp. 397–401.

33. Considerably more explanation of how intimacy develops can be found in Goldberg, *To Be a Psychotherapist.*

34. Isaac Asimov, *Today and Tomorrow and . . .* (New York: Dell, 1983), p. 295.

35. H. J. Kleinschmidt, "The Angry Act: The Role of Aggression in Creativity," *American Imago* 24 (1967), p. 100.

36. Ibid.

37. Ibid.

38. For further information, see Phyllis Greenacre, "The Childhood of the Artist," *The Psychoanalytic Study of the Child* 12 (1957), pp. 47–72.

39. L. Schreiber, "Books of the Times," *New York Times,* April 21, 1982.

40. Sigmund Freud, *Leonardo da Vinci and a Memory of His Childhood* (New York: Norton, 1964), p. 61.

41. For further information, see Charles Kligerman, "Art and the Self of the Artist," in *Advances in Self Psychology,* ed. A. Goldberg (New York: International Universities Press, 1980), p. 385.

42. A discussion of Pollack's study appeared in the *New York Times Book Review,* July 11, 1982.

43. I. B. Singer, "Fiction," in *The Creative Experience,* ed. S. Rosner and L. E. Abt (New York, Delta Books, 1970), p. 228.

44. Kleinschmidt, pp. 99–100.

45. Ibid., p. 100.

46. F. Barron, *Creativity and Personal Freedom* (Indianapolis, Ind.: Van Nostrand Reinhold, 1968), pp. 1–6.

47. P. S. Weisberg and Kayla J. Springer, *Environmental Factors Influencing Creative Functions in Gifted Children* (mimeo.), (Cincinnati, Ohio: Dept. of Psychiatry, Cincinnati General Hospital, 1961). Subsequent studies have verified and refined these findings.

48. Ernest Kris, "The Personal Myth: A Problem in Psychoanalytic Technique," in *The Selected Papers of Ernest Kris* (New Haven, Conn.: Yale University Press, 1975), pp. 296–97.

49. Kleinschmidt, p. 120.

50. Ibid., p. 127.

51. Pablo Picasso is reported to have said, "Once I drew like Raphael but it has taken me a lifetime to draw like a child." L. Lecaze, "Young Brains Are Delved for Roots of Creativity," *Washington Post*, April 27, 1980.

52. Carl Jung, *Analytical Psychology* (New York: Random House, 1970), p. 39.

53. Oscar Wilde, *The Portable Oscar Wilde*, ed. R. Aldington and S. Weintraub (New York: Penguin, 1982).

54. Oscar Wilde said, for example, in the preface to *The Picture of Dorian Gray*, "There is no such thing as a moral or an immoral book. Books are well-written or badly-written. That is all. . . . The moral life of man forms part of the subject matter of the artist, but the morality of art consists in the perfect use of an imperfect medium. . . . All art is at once surface and symbol. Those who go beneath the surface do so at their own peril. It is the spectator, and not life, that are really mirrors. . . . All art is quite useless." *The Portable Oscar Wilde*, pp. 138–39.

2

ALAS, BABYLON AND ON THE BEACH: ANTIPHONS OF THE APOCALYPSE

C. W. Sullivan III

1.

Research for this chapter disclosed that very little in-depth critical attention has been paid to Pat Frank's *Alas, Babylon* (1959) and Nevil Shute's *On the Beach* (1957). Each was reviewed positively in numerous publications, both mainstream and science fiction, but neither has been dealt with to any great extent.[1] Mainstream critics have generally avoided anything approaching science fiction whenever possible (exceptions like *2001: A Space Odyssey, Dune,* and *A Clockwork Orange* notwithstanding), but the science fiction community should have paid Frank and Shute more attention. These two mainstream writers have quite clearly defined the boundaries of post–World War III fiction as have few purely science fiction authors. Perhaps it is precisely because they are not primarily science fiction writers that they have been able to do this (after all, anthropologists and sociologists have known for some time that outsiders can often look in and see more clearly than insiders). For whatever reason, it is possible to see all post–World War III fiction as bounded on the optimistic side by *Alas, Babylon* and on the pessimistic by *On the Beach.*

2.

Because they deal with atomic war (as it was called in the 1950s) or, more specifically, the aftermath of such a war, both books have quite a few basic concepts in common. First, both authors spend very little time on the actual war. There is no mobilizing for war, no parading, and no ''shipping out'' in these books; the war is over in a matter of days or, at most, weeks, and the fighting is done largely by missiles—from ground, sea, and air bases—and by bombs. Afterward, there may be a certain amount of "mopping up," but the reader is only dimly aware of that since most national and international communications have broken down, and the reader's attention is focused on survivors who are far from the areas where such lingering fighting might continue.

Alas, Babylon and *On the Beach* are also similar in that they portray this ultimate war arising not out of a direct confrontation between or among super-powers but as the result of activities in areas by secondary or minor powers—Syria in Frank's novel and Albania in Shute's. Of course, the larger countries, especially the United States and the U.S.S.R., quickly enter the action—perhaps willingly—so that the hostilities escalate into an all-out war. But both Frank and Shute seem to adhere to the popular belief that no sane person could give the order to start such a war, that it could certainly begin only through a series of mistakes, misunderstandings, or misinterpreted data.

Both authors place the larger share of the blame for the war not on the specific individuals or the incidents that touched it off but on the leaders and others who allowed their countries to build up a level of armament that permitted such a war. In *Alas, Babylon,* Mark Bragg, an officer in SAC Intelligence, comments, "Nations are like people. When they grow old and rich and fat they get conservative."[2] The United States, he argues, just has not kept up, militarily, with the Russians, and the Russians now believe that they have a significant advantage. And when a young American pilot over the Mediterranean fires a missile at a plane that has been shadowing his aircraft carrier, the missile goes awry, hits a train in the Syrian port city of Latakia (a suspected Russian submarine base), and provides the Russians with an excuse to fire everything they have at the United States. But Frank extends the blame. The references to Babylon in the text imply that as the people of biblical Babylon were responsible for the condition and subsequent destruction of their city so too were the people of Russia and America—all the people, not just the leaders—responsible for allowing the conditions for such a war to develop.

In Shute's *On the Beach,* the war begins when Albania obtains atomic weapons and bombs Naples. Activities then escalate in the Arab-Israeli conflict, and the United States, the British, the Russians, and the Chinese are drawn in. Over four thousand atomic and hydrogen devices are detonated, and lethal fallout begins its worldwide spread. But that only tells how it happened; some of the characters speculate about why. Naval officer Peter Holmes, for example, calls it a kind of silliness in which some people "decide that their national honor requires them to drop cobalt bombs on their neighbor."[3] He suggests that, if the process had begun early enough, people might have been educated out of such silliness:

We liked our newspapers with pictures of beach girls and headlines about cases of indecent assault, and no government was wise enough to stop us having them that way. But something might have been done with newspapers, if we'd been wise enough.[4]

Like Frank, Shute sees the longer process by which the world acquired the ability to wage such a war as the responsibility of everyone—the leaders and the people.

The immediate and much more important long-range causes of the atomic war are more completely described than the war itself. In fact, neither Frank nor Shute provides more than a sketchy picture of what a blast site or the surrounding area might look like. In *Alas, Babylon*, there are eighty pages of action prior to the war and almost two hundred that deal with the survivors and their lot. All of the action in *On the Beach* takes place after the war, and while there are brief sections dealing with the events leading up to it interspersed throughout the novel, Shute's focus, like Frank's, is basically on the survivors. There is, however, a significant difference between the two books in this regard: *Alas, Babylon* provides an optimistically romantic view in which the survivors struggle and succeed; *On the Beach* provides a pessimistically realistic view of survivors trying to cope as lethal fallout spreads over the entire world.

3.

Randy Bragg and the small group of people who surround him in the Florida town of Fort Repose in *Alas, Babylon* are fortunate survivors. They are in the right place with, essentially, the right skills to survive. They are not in or too near a main target area and so are not destroyed by either the initial blast or the subsequent fallout. Their Florida location means that they will not be exposed to extreme cold in the winter and that they will be able to harvest food from their gardens and from the waterways; their community is small and away from most of the refugees from the larger cities. They possess survival skills—there are two mechanics, a sailor (wind power, now, not motor), a doctor, and a librarian (who finds information on edible plants and the like). And Randy Bragg is a natural leader.

They are also fortunate in that Randy's brother, Mark, is an officer with SAC Intelligence. Mark sends his wife and their children to Fort Repose because, as he tells Randy, they stand a better chance of surviving there than they would with him in Omaha. As a result, Randy receives some advance warning that the war is likely to occur and is at least partially prepared when it actually comes. Although some of his purchases prove virtually useless (a large order of milk and meat, and ice cream which becomes a sloppy mess in the freezer when the electricity ceases to flow), he does have a psychological advantage. Warned that the war might occur soon, he is prepared for the psychological shock and then begins to cope with the new situation more effectively than other people.

Ultimately, it is the postwar world and the way or ways in which various characters cope with it that is the focus of *Alas, Babylon*. Some of them do not handle the situation very well at all. Various merchants sell out their stock in the first few days, so happy for the business that they fail to realize until too late that the money they have taken in will be of no use to them, whereas the goods they sold should have been kept for personal use or for barter. The collapse of the economic system hits banker Edgar Quisenberry the hardest; when his financial world crumbles and he is no longer important as the town's banker, he can only commit suicide. And there are several people with weak hearts who have fatal attacks from the strain of trying to cope with the new situation.

Other characters react badly because they do not understand the dangers inherent in a post-atomic-war world. Various tourists, looking for shelter or help, are set upon, robbed, and killed by roving bands of men who have decided that they can do as they please now that no one seems to be enforcing the laws. Hospitals, doctors, and druggists are attacked for the drugs that they carry or store. And men who see untended jewelry stores in blast-area cities as easy picking die because they do not understand that the watches and rings they wear, like everything else that close to ground zero, have absorbed lethal doses of radiation. The most pathetic, perhaps, are the people who continue to live on in the local hotel, refusing to believe that things have permanently changed, assuming that the maids will return and the toilets will begin to work again, and who eventually die in a fire caused by someone trying to cook hoarded food in his room.

Amid this breakdown of much that contemporary Americans take for granted, Randy Bragg and his friends manage quite well—almost too well, in fact.[5] They have the skills and most of the equipment necessary, from hunting and fishing gear to a working artesian well. To be sure, they cannot replace things like coffee, but they can use honey for sugar and, guided by a diary written by one of the first Braggs to settle in Fort Repose, they find a natural salt source when their store-bought supply runs out. But most important is their attitude. Each member of the group is generally intelligent and capable of adapting to the new situation, and none of them is afraid of a challenge. In fact, Bill McGovern, Randy's girlfriend's father and retired president of Central Tool, is transformed from a slowly dying retiree into a man with a reason to live; he has useful things to do in this new situation. By the end of the novel, the Fort Repose group is living well enough to shock the military personnel who contact them, and no one in the group is even interested in the military's offer of transportation to a larger "safe zone." Like a modern Swiss Family Robinson, the main characters in *Alas, Babylon* have made their home in a strange, new world.

4.

Initially, it might appear that the main characters in Shute's *On the Beach*—primarily Australians with a few Americans mixed in—are also fortunate survivors of the atomic war. Although they gave at least their moral support to England, the Australians were not actively involved in the war. In fact, the actual fighting was confined primarily to the Northern Hemisphere where, over a period of approximately thirty-seven days, seismographic records show that at least four thousand, seven hundred bombs were dropped, most containing a cobalt element that produces lethal fallout. As a result, human life in the entire Northern

Hemisphere has been wiped out, either in the initial blast or by the fallout that followed. And radio transmissions indicate, outside of Australia, that there are survivors only in parts of Africa and South America.

As the novel opens, Australia's only problem seems to be a gasoline shortage that has forced people to use bicycles and horse-drawn vehicles for transportation and for hauling goods. Much of the nation's public transportation is still operating, however, as various characters in the novel are able to take the train to and from Melbourne. Although it might appear, initially, that survival for Shute's Australians will be easier than it was for Frank's Floridians, the people in *On the Beach* have no hope at all. The fallout released by the cobalt bomb explosions is working its way down through the Southern Hemisphere and will eventually cover the entire planet. Shute's characters, like Frank's, have to cope with the war's aftermath, but for them it is not a matter of survival against the odds, it is a matter of waiting for the end.

Essentially, *On the Beach* deals with the last year or so in the lives of five people, three men and two women, who represent among them the various ways such a situation might be met. Shute gives very little indication that anyone "went off the deep end" when confronted with his or her fate. American submarine commander Dwight Towers turns to alcohol for a while in an attempt to forget the war and his family (now dead in Connecticut), and Moira Davidson, too, tries to lose herself in alcohol, parties, and men. But Towers soon finds that the alcohol does not really help, and when he and Moira meet later, he helps her to pull herself together. From time to time, one of the main characters sees a drunk in the gutter, and by this Shute may be implying that some people do find alcohol a successful escape.

The characters who cope best are those with something to do. Dwight Towers and Peter Holmes are naval officers, and the Australian Admiralty creates two missions for them on American submarine patrols, first along the Australian coast and then up the western coast of the United States. These patrols not only give the characters a purpose for five or six of the remaining months, they also show that the Northern Hemisphere is completely devoid of human life and that the fallout is moving southward at its predicted rate. Also along on these patrols is physicist John Osborne, whose scientific knowledge and activities explain and confirm the situation for the novel's other characters as well as for the reader. Mary Holmes, Peter's wife, has their new baby, Jennifer, to keep her busy. And Moira Davidson, after pulling herself together, enrolls in college-level business courses toward a secretarial degree. Even some of the minor characters cope by finding purpose: Moira's parents keep working their farm, some of the crew of the American submarine marry Australian girls and settle down, most businessmen keep their businesses open (although many do not bother to collect for the merchandise they "sell"), and the members of John Osborne's club set themselves to finish the choice port and sherry before the end comes.

But the pragmatism of work is not the only way these people cope; they also exercise a healthy ability to fantasize. Peter and Mary Holmes actively plan for a future they will never see, planting next year's garden, buying a garden swing, and generally thinking about their baby growing up. Dwight Towers fantasizes that his family is alive, well, and awaiting his return; when he takes the submarine out to sink it (killing himself and the remaining crew members in the process), he packs presents for the wife and children he is going to rejoin. Moira Davidson, at first puzzled and hurt by Towers' loyalty to his wife and family, not only comes to understand him but, by the end of the novel, hopes to accompany him when he returns to his family. And John Osborne, who seemed to share Moira's despair in the beginning of the book, is rejuvenated by living out one of his fantasies. He buys a Ferrari and becomes a successful automobile racer, winning the last Australian Grand Prix.

Even though Shute's characters handle themselves and their situation every bit as well as do the characters in Frank's novel, there is no happy ending in *On the Beach*. As the fallout begins to affect the population, government-supplied kits are handed out so that people can take their own lives rather than die in agony from radiation poisoning. Peter and Mary inject Jennifer and then get into bed and take their own pills. Osborne prepares his Ferrari for storage, climbs into the driver's seat, and takes his pill. As Dwight Towers takes the *Scorpion* out for her last run, Moira Davidson drives down to the beach and takes her pills so she can be as near to him as possible when they both die. The Northern Hemisphere may have died with a bang, but Shute's epigrammatic use of T. S. Eliot's famous lines from "The Hollow Men" is incomplete; the main characters (and, by implication, much of the rest of the population of Australia) die not with a whimper but with great dignity.[6]

5.

Although Frank and Shute may have defined the boundaries of post–World War III fiction, they did not, by any means, exhaust all the fictional possibilities of the postwar paradigm. Most science fiction writers, both before and after the publication of *Alas, Babylon,* have described, as did Pat Frank, people surviving as best they can in a substantially changed world. The closing section of Ray Bradbury's *The Martian Chronicles* (1950), for example, depicts a few farsighted people escaping to Mars as the nations of earth destroy each other and the planet. Bradbury implies that these escapees will begin a new and better society on Mars. In Leigh Brackett's *The Long Tomorrow* (1955), order in the postwar United States is maintained initially by Amish and Old Mennonites, people still possessing the skills necessary to survive the technological breakdown that will follow such a war. The early sections of Robert Heinlein's *Farnham's Freehold* (1964), on the other hand, show how one man might prepare as thoroughly as possible for the war he knows is on the way. And the science fiction classic of this group, André Norton's *Daybreak—2250* A.D. (first published in 1952 as *Star Man's Son, 2250* A.D.), presents an almost primitive North America containing warring tribes, technological ruins, and mutant humans and animals.

Commenting on *On the Beach,* Donald Wollheim, in *The Universe Makers* (1971), says that Shute's novel presents

the supreme pessimistic view—not surprising since the author is not among the ranks of deep-dyed s-f writers. We s-f writers rarely let the world die. We have the farther vision. It sustains us.[7]

Wollheim is correct—if a bit extreme. Certainly fewer science fiction writers share Shute's vision, but that vision of a closed future contains far fewer fictional possibilities than the open-ended one explored by Pat Frank and the writers who see at least some people surviving the atomic war. Still, a number of science fiction writers have found some interesting fictional possibilities in the war-doomed world extrapolation. For example, although some of the monks and their charges escape the doomed earth in Walter Miller's *A Canticle for Leibowitz* (1960), the cycle of events that produces World War IV undercuts the hope that those who escape this war will never start another. In Harlan Ellison's "A Boy and His Dog" (1969), Vic and Blood seem to be surviving reasonably well, but neither the above-grounders nor the down-unders are fertile societies, growing and developing anything upon which to build a future. And Norman Spinrad's "The Big Flash" (1969) combines the attraction of a rock group, the influence of the broadcast media, and the power of the bomb in an ultimate hard rock concert which causes the listeners/watchers in strategic installations to unlock their weapons, push the red buttons, and cause the big flash.

Surviving the atomic war, if only temporarily, is a crossover topic that, for more than thirty years, has been explored again and again by both mainstream and science fiction writers; it is fair to say that the only science fiction some people have read (or seen in the movies or on television) has come from mainstream authors writing about an atomic war's aftermath. Certainly the popularity of this post–World War III fiction—from stories published since the end of World War II to recent made-for-television specials like *The Day After* and recent novels like Whitley Strieber and James Kunetka's *Warday*—suggests that critics and scholars, at least, need to be aware not only of the history and development of this subgenre but also of the dimensions of this kind of fiction. The success of the survivors in *Alas, Babylon* places Pat Frank's novel at the optimistic end of the scale, while the lethal fallout that destroys all those who survived the initial war in *On the Beach* places Nevil Shute's novel at the pessimistic end. Thus, whatever else they are (and these two books can be discussed as lessons about the uses of power, as warnings of a terrible and possible future, and much more), *Alas, Babylon* and *On the Beach* do provide the standard perspectives of the atomic war's aftermath against which all other postwar visions—in literature, on television, and in movie theaters—can be measured.

NOTES

1. Especially cogent articles and reviews of *Alas, Babylon* appeared in the *New York Times Book Review*, March 22, 1959, p. 43; *Library Journal*, April 1, 1959, p. 115; *Saturday Review*, June 13, 1959, p. 20; *Analog*, September 1959, pp. 145–47; and *Galaxy*, December 1959, p. 150. Articles and reviews of *On the Beach* appeared in the *Magazine of Fantasy and Science Fiction*, October 1957, pp. 102–3; *New Worlds*, November 1957, p. 124; *Analog*, February 1958, pp. 144–45; *Galaxy*, March 1958, pp. 119–20; and the *Journal of British Studies*, Spring 1977, pp. 121–42. In addition, both novels are discussed in Frank N. Magill, ed., *Survey of Science Fiction Literature* (Englewood Cliffs, N.J.: Salem Press, 1979).

2. Pat Frank, *Alas, Babylon* (New York: Bantam Books, 1959), p. 16.

3. Nevil Shute, *On the Beach* (1957; reprint, New York: Ballantine Books, 1974), p. 268.

4. Ibid.

5. In his review of *Alas, Babylon* for *Galaxy* (December 1959, p. 150), Floyd Gale remarks, "Survival in that region, though hard, looks easy." This situation, surviving well in adverse circumstances, is one of the trademarks of romantic fiction, especially the historical/wilderness romance after which *Alas, Babylon* is patterned.

6. In his review of *On the Beach* for *Analog* (February 1958, pp. 144–45), P. Schuyler Miller asserts, "The major air of unreality about the book is the quiet, genteel manner in which everyone, the world over, lies quietly down to die—without panic, without rioting, without private or public hysteria, down to the last dog and cat." It is this calm acceptance of the inevitable that gives the ending of *On the Beach* its dignity. The people in the novel do not, in Dylan Thomas' words, "rage against the dying of the light," but neither do they see Eliot's two alternatives as the only ones.

7. Donald Wollheim, *The Universe Makers* (New York: Harper & Row, 1971), p. 66.

3

THE REVIVAL OF LEARNING: SCIENCE AFTER THE NUCLEAR HOLOCAUST IN SCIENCE FICTION

Paul Brians

One of the basic stereotypes of science fiction beginning with the days of the Drs. Frankenstein and Jekyll is the mad scientist. Both H. G. Wells' invisible man and Dr. Moreau are other notable examples. But by the 1940s, the mad scientist had been relegated, by and large, to radio and movie serials and to the comic strips. Even in the latter medium *Buck Rogers'* Dr. Huer (the original upon which the perhaps better known Dr. Zarkov of *Flash Gordon* was modeled) was more representative of the image of the scientist in the science fiction of the 1940s: one able to invent precisely the needed miracle weapon or device for any contingency. As Albert I. Berger has noted, the dropping of the bombs on Hiroshima and Nagasaki resulted in a certain amount of self-congratulation in the science fiction community which reinforced proscience attitudes already flourishing in the field.[1] The success of the Manhattan Project was felt to mark the beginning of a bright new day for the sciences.

There were few within the confines of science fiction publishing who recognized fully the threat posed by the bomb; even among those who did, there was a tendency to depict the use of various technical devices to avoid an atomic Armageddon. In this attitude authors were reflecting the mood of the time, which not only absolved science and scientists from responsibility for their creation but tended to congratulate them. This chapter will consider how science fiction has attributed responsibility for a future holocaust to science.

One must search diligently in the years immediately following Hiroshima to discover a fictional attack on nuclear scientists; what one finds is eccentric, unrepresentative, and almost unread—F. Horace Rose's *The Maniac's Dream: A Novel of the Atomic Bomb* (1946).[2] Rose depicts a group of atheistic scientists bent on disproving the existence of God by destroying most of humanity with nuclear weapons. They are foiled by the protagonist and the pious daughter of one of the scientists, aided by God himself, who strikes down the maniac of the title with a lightning bolt. Rose makes clear both in his introduction and "An Editorial P.S." that the story is intended to be read as an allegory of the self-destructive nature of modern science unrestrained by traditional religious values. His "maniac" is a classic mad scientist.

Aside from Rose's unusual religious concerns, the attitudes toward science expressed in this novel are such that one would expect them to have been widespread. But he is almost unique. Writers of fiction did not seem to feel even as much concern with the responsibility of nuclear scientists as the scientists did themselves. There is nothing in the science fiction of the period that approaches Leo Szilard's meditation on scientific responsibility in "My Trial as a War Criminal" (1949), for instance.[3]

In Robert Conquest's *A World of Difference* (1955),[4] a scientist loosely resembling Szilard joins a group of antinuclear activists, including one resembling Claude Eatherly, pilot of the Hiroshima weather plane, to seize a Polaris submarine in an attempt to blackmail the world into disarming. Although he is fairly sympathetically presented, he is a madman who must be stopped. Similarly, Professor Bollenden, who asserts his responsibility for building a nuclear-armed space station and tries to destroy it in Edmund Cooper's *Seed of Light* (1959),[5] is a religious madman whose plot is doomed. It would seem that only crazy physicists get involved in disarmament.

Certainly many science fiction writers were aware of the efforts of Szilard and others to restrain the enthusiasm of government officials for the bomb. Chandler Davis, who wrote several early A-bomb satires for *Astounding,* described in one of them a nuclear physicist who uncovers a mad military plot to launch an atomic war.[6] In this story, it is the politicians whose naiveté about science endangers the human race. Probably the most famous postwar mad scientist—Dr. Strangelove, of Stanley Kubrick's film and Peter George's novelization—is not so mad as the general who unleashes the missiles in the first place. And it should be noted that Strangelove was not present in the original novel on which the film was based *(Two Hours to Doom,* 1958).[7]

Philip K. Dick's mad scientist—Dr. Bruno Bluthgeld—was created as a direct response to the film version of *Dr. Strangelove,* as his novel's title makes clear: *Dr. Bloodmoney, or How We Got Along after the Bomb* (1965).[8] Although Bluthgeld is responsible only for a portion of the nuclear holocaust, he is definitely held responsible and punished. In his "Afterword" to the 1977 Gregg Press edition of the novel, Dick made his attitude toward his villain clear: "I hate him and I hate everything he stands for. . . . It is not the Russians I fear; it is the Doctor Bluthgelds, the Doctor Bloodmoneys, in our own society, that terrify me."[9]

One of the few other science fiction novels depicting a guilty scientist is also by Dick, in collaboration with Roger Zelazny *(Deus Irae,* 1976).[10] Conscious of his own responsibility, he longs for martyrdom while most of society worships him as a god, a type of ironic situation which will be discussed further below.

Clearly there was great reluctance on the part of science fiction writers to blame the hazards of the nuclear age on science itself, even among those who warned of a possible holocaust. A good illustration of this attitude is the story by A. M. Phillips entitled "An Enemy of Knowledge" (1947) in which a boy who loves reading pillages the remains of a library in the ruins and is horrified to discover—along with technical books which he finds baffling—bound volumes of popular picture magazines depicting scenes from the atomic war that produced the world in which he lives.[11] He tries to destroy the past by destroying the books, but Phillips does not endorse his attitude, for the boy's wise old grandmother cannily saves several volumes from the flames. Even if the boy cannot, she is able to discriminate between useful scientific and technical knowledge and some of its harmful side effects. And when the father in Ray Bradbury's "The Million-Year Picnic" (1946) burns documents from the preholocaust past, they are such as deal with business and politics, not monographs on nuclear physics.[12]

One theme that occurs from time to time in science fiction and that was first explored in Walter M. Miller's "Dumb Waiter" (1952), is the technology of atomic war run amok, relentlessly continuing a senseless war which the human race has long since wearied of.[13] One also encounters the supercomputer which imposes a dictatorship in order to ban nuclear war (D. F. Jones' *Colossus* [1966] and its sequels). Yet rarely is the scientist blamed directly for the misdeeds of his creation in such stories, or he at least redeems himself by combating the malfunctioning machines. The cure for ills caused by science is more science.

Despite the fact that there was so little criticism initially of scientists for their role in developing the bomb, many science fiction writers were anxious explicitly to defend them from such criticism in their fiction. This anxiety is reflected in a large category of stories that depicts the repression of science in a postholocaust dark age. It is this subgenre depicting the suppression and the rebirth of science which will be the main topic of this chapter.[14]

A typical example is Poul Anderson's juvenile *Vault of the Ages* (1952).[15] In it young boys defy taboos imposed by their elders to explore an ancient time capsule and discover technology (black powder bombs) which helps the tribe to defeat invading barbarians. This success causes the tribe to reevaluate its ban on ancient learning. Anderson does not explain how such an ancient and deeply held prejudice could be so lightly overcome, but clearly he feels that even the violent effects of science, if kept to the appropriate scale and handled in the appropriate manner, should not be shunned. Says the newly enlightened leader: "There is no evil in the vault. There is only evil in the hearts of men. Knowledge, all knowledge, is good."[16]

The bigotry of the commoners is not always so easy to overcome. In Leigh Brackett's *The Long Tomorrow* (1955), three rebellious teenagers must run away from the village in which they have been raised and where antiscientific, antiurban attitudes prevail.[17] They go in quest of the fabled Bartorstown underground research center, complete with a working nuclear reactor, so they can freely explore the exciting world of science. Yet another science fiction novel aimed at a teen audience, A. M. Lightner's *The Day of the Drones* (1969), depicts an African society in which all science except medicine is prohibited until curiosity about the possibility of the survival of another pocket of humanity leads them to use a solar-powered helicopter to explore Europe. In England they discover a culture more primitive than their own, but equally antiscientific. The English have a myth they call "The story about the Rights," who tried to fly: "You see, they weren't right . . . they were wrong. Only the bees can fly. And of course the birds. For men to fly is against the gods, and when these two brothers flew, it brought death and destruction from the gods until they were all dead."[18]

Scientific knowledge is endorsed in a more soberly realistic story like James Blish's "The Oath" (1961).[19] The protagonist is a physician who practices selective medicine to weed out the defective in the postholocaust world. After some reluctance, he joins a profit-oriented government program which uses atomic energy and practices atomic medicine. He is aware of the moral ambiguities involved in his actions but finally concedes that to accomplish any lasting good he must collaborate with the forces he holds responsible for the war. Prejudice against science finds expression in this story in a popular attack by physicians because they cannot successfully treat radiation disease.

In James Tiptree, Jr.'s "The Man Who Walked Home" (1972), a scientific experiment gone wrong is responsible for triggering a catastrophic war, but the antiscientific, primitive culture that ensues is depicted as regrettable.[20] Tiptree is sophisticated enough to avoid a simple solution to the end of civilization of the sort so popular with other authors, but the story—although altogether admirable as a piece of fiction—still does not focus primarily on the responsibility of scientists.

Edmund Cooper's *The Cloud Walker* (1973) reverts to the classic formula; a young man in an antiscientific, neofeudal society defies bans on machinery and experimentation to develop various flying machines.[21] His hot air balloon successfully overcomes an invasion by savage pirates, causing the villagers to cast off the tyranny maintained by the inquisition of the Luddite church. Twenty-one years later, we are back in the world of *Vault of the Ages,* although admittedly on a much more sophisticated level in terms of literary technique.

In these stories, it is frequently a religious priesthood that enforces the ban on learning. Walter M. Miller's *A Canticle for Leibowitz* (1959) is unique in suggesting that the Catholic monks of the new dark age will repeat the task carried out by the monks of the Middle Ages: the preservation of knowledge.[22] The monks are not the instruments of the antiscientific "simplification" but the agency by which its effects are overcome. However, their ignorance is the butt of much gentle humor in the novel. All the efforts that Father Zerchi goes through in trying to prevent his congregation from resorting to euthanasia to relieve themselves from the agonies caused by nuclear war are doomed. In the end, religion will endure only with the aid of science, as the missionaries head for the stars aboard spacecraft. Although he is more thoughtful than most in exploring the relationship between religion and science, Miller is not ready to denounce science as such even in the face of the destruction of life on earth.

Another way in which science plays a role in the postholocaust age is as the exclusive property of a privileged group, as in Vonda McIntyre's *Dreamsnake* (1978).[23] McIntyre's heroine learns that she must not depend on the static culture of Center but can make innovative discoveries on her own. In Piers Anthony's *Sos the Rope* (1968), the technocrats regulate a barbarian culture based on a dueling code in order to keep humanity's violent instincts channeled into small-scale aggression which does not risk leading to a repetition of the holocaust, but this benevolent dictatorship must be overthrown in the name of liberty, even if the result is a revival of warfare.[24] Scientists are criticized here not for practicing their profession but for failing to advance it or for placing limits on it.

Many of the earlier versions of the postholocaust revival of learning do more than endorse the continued importance of science; they advance the proposition—either explicitly or metaphorically—that the technology of the atomic bomb is itself a positive force for good. An early example is A. E. van Vogt's series of stories collected in *Empire of the Atom* (1957) and *The Wizard of Linn* (1962).[25] Although the world has been devastated centuries earlier by a cataclysmic atomic war, contemporary civilization ignorantly worships the fissionable elements which it associates with unlimited power. It is this "holy" radiation that is responsible for the talents of the mutant Clane, who battles alien invaders in the second volume by the use of an advanced technology which outweighs even the enemy's monopoly on nuclear weapons.[26] What might have been an opportunity for satire on the worship of the very force that destroyed their ancestors and threatens to annihilate them (as, for instance, in Russell Hoban's *Riddley Walker* [1982][27]) is negated because the priests who maintain the worship of atomic energy are portrayed as lacking in sufficient scientific knowledge to understand the real potential of the materials they handle, and therefore they direct their devotion toward an inappropriate technology. Since its product—radiation—gives birth to that savior of the human race, Clane, the ancient atomic war proves to be a sort of *felix culpa*. The moral of these stories is that of the serpent in Eden: the human race is advised to eat of the fruit of knowledge so that it will become like gods, knowing good and evil.

Similarly, the world is saved through the use of technology derived from the nuclear science that destroyed the ancient world in van Vogt's "Resurrection" (1948)[28] and in Edmond Hamilton's *City at World's End* (1951).[29] In the latter tale an earth spokesman tells a tribunal of our distant descendants, come from other stars to decide the fate of the last outpost of humanity on the dying earth:

Yes, we fought our wars! We fought because we had to, so that thought and progress and freedom could live in our world. You owe us for that! You owe us for the men that died so there could one day be a Federation of Stars. You owe us for atomic power, too.

We may have misused it—but it's the force that built your civilization, and we gave it to you![30]

Poul Anderson's "No Truce with Kings" (1963) displays a similar hostility toward the idea of outsiders protecting the human race from itself.[31] In a post-holocaust age aliens manipulate history to direct the evolution of a communitarian, nonmaterialistic culture, fearing that if human beings should once more acquire atomic weapons they will invade the rest of the galaxy. The story could easily be read as an allegory of the author's preference for capitalism over a planned socialist economy, but a surprise ending confuses the parallel: the hero's daughter decides to ally herself with the aliens' cause. Perhaps an independence that dooms humanity to racial suicide is not preferable to a planned existence after all.

Anderson's ambivalence on the subject of nuclear was is apparent in his Maurai stories as well, in which he sometimes seems to embrace the concept of placing limits on research and at others to reject it. Anderson is strongly committed to libertarian and proscientific ideals, but he is more aware than most of the very real dangers of nuclear conflict, having written a book on the subject, entitled *Thermonuclear Warfare* (1963).[32] The latest work in the series—*Orion Shall Rise* (1983)—contains a vivid and horrifying description of the detonation of an atomic bomb, but in the end its use is justified by the necessity to remove the stifling Maurai overlordship so that the innovative spirit of ancient America can undergo a rebirth of freedom.[33] Despite his hesitations and doubts, Anderson seems to have been fairly consistent over the years in insisting that the very real danger of nuclear holocaust—which he does not minimize—does not justify the suppression of either the knowledge or the use of the bomb.

Since the 1950s the theme of a highly technical culture interacting with a neoprimitive one has sometimes been treated in a considerably more thoughtful manner. In Suzanne Martel's *The City Underground* (1963), the process of mutual discovery between the highly technical but repressive and sterile society of the people living under the ruins of ancient Montreal and the natural but primitive society of the surface-dwellers is clearly an allegory of the need for improved communication and understanding between the English-speaking and Francophone communities in Quebec (the subterraneans speak English, the sur-face-dwellers French).[34]

Science itself becomes the object of unthinking superstition which prevents its own advance in Paul O. Williams' *The Dome in the Forest* (1981).[35] In a plot resembling that of Robert A. Heinlein's "Universe" and other "generation ship" stories, generations of technicians tend machinery whose complexity is far beyond their understanding. Their empty rationalism must be combined with the ignorant but healthy emotionalism of the tribal culture outside. Williams interestingly depicts the complex relationship between the two groups, avoiding the usual cliches of neobarbarian fiction and minimizing the violence endemic to it. In both Williams' and Martel's work, reason and emotion, nature and knowledge, are seen as complements, not antagonists.

Keith Roberts seems to endorse the idea of the suppression of nuclear science in *Pavane* (1966), a series of stories set on a parallel earth where the defeat of the British by the Spanish Armada has allowed science to be controlled by the Catholic church much longer than in our world.[36] As a deliberate matter of policy, knowing that the premature discovery of fission will be catastrophic, scientific progress is retarded so that civilization can mature more fully before confronting the bomb. The novel seems to illustrate the dilemma of our time—that we have matured scientifically without having matured ethically. Even in Roberts' novel, however, the advance of science is welcomed. Only in the 1960s, then, is a science fiction writer willing to acknowledge in a novel dealing with nuclear war that it might be wise to retard science, even temporarily.

Finally in 1978 appears Joan D. Vinge's "Phoenix in the Ashes," in which a Brazilian mining engineer learns to value the antitechnological but ecologically sound peasant culture of the natives and rejects the exploitative industrial civilization of his homeland.[37]

There remains something of a mystery about the stimulus for the long tradition of strenuous defense of science in the postholocaust world before the late 1960s. As Michael J. Yavenditti makes clear in "The American People and the Use of Atomic Bombs on Japan: The 1940s," hardly anyone in the U.S. press was publicly blaming the scientists for the bomb or even expressing the notion that its invention was a mistake in the years following Hiroshima.[38]

It is probable that science fiction writers, predisposed to be hypersensitive to criticism of science, overreacted to the few expressions of antipathy toward science generated by the bomb's use. The fact that some of them grasped the implications of the bomb more clearly than the general public may even have prompted them to extrapolate a backlash without any other stimulus. Once the first few stories had been written, the image of the new dark age had been formulated; from that point on it probably fed on itself. Science fiction remained ghettoized during the 1940s and 1950s, and it is not difficult to imagine that such a view of public attitudes toward science could be maintained for a considerable length of time with very little confirmation from the world outside.

NOTES

1. Albert I. Berger, "Nuclear Energy, Science Fiction's Metaphor of Power," *Science Fiction Studies* 6 (1979), pp. 125–26. Other useful sources on the subject of nuclear war in science fiction are Albert I. Berger, "Love, Death and the Atomic Bomb: Sexuality and Community in Science Fiction, 1935–55," *Science Fiction Studies* 8 (1981), pp. 280–95; Harold L. Berger, *Science Fiction and the New Dark Age* (Bowling Green, Ohio: Bowling Green University Press, 1976); Gary K. Wolfe's *The Known and the Unknown: The Iconography of Science Fiction* (Kent, Ohio: Kent State University Press, 1979); Warren W. Wagar: *Terminal Visions: The Literature of Last Things* (Bloomington: Indiana University Press, 1982); and Eric S. Rabkin, Martin H. Greenberg, and Joseph D.

Olander, eds., *The End of the World* (Carbondale: Southern Illinois University Press, 1983).

2. F. Horace Rose, *The Maniac's Dream: A Novel of the Atomic Bomb* (London: Duckworth, 1946).

3. *University of Chicago Law Review* 17 (Fall 1949), pp. 79–86. Novels dealing with the scruples of the Manhattan Project scientists, such as Pearl S. Buck's *Command the Morning* (New York: John Day, 1959) and Haakon Chevalier's *The Man Who Would Be God* (New York: Putnam, 1959), are here omitted as non-science fiction.

4. Robert Conquest, *A World of Difference* (London: Ward Lock, 1955).

5. Edmund Cooper, *Seed of Light* (New York: Ballantine Books, 1959).

6. Chandler Davis, "To Still the Drums," *Astounding,* October 1946.

7. Peter George [pseudo. Peter Bryant], *Two Hours to Doom* (London: Boardman, 1958).

8. Philip K. Dick, *Dr. Bloodmoney, or How We Got Along after the Bomb* (New York: Ace, 1965).

9. Ibid., p. 302.

10. Philip K. Dick and Roger Zelazny, *Deus Irae* (Garden City, N.Y.: Doubleday, 1976).

11. A. M. Phillips, "An Enemy of Knowledge," *Astounding,* April 1947.

12. Ray Bradbury, "The Million-Year Picnic," *Planet Stories* (Summer 1946), in *The Martian Chronicles* (Garden City, N.Y.: Doubleday, 1950).

13. Walter M. Miller, Jr., "Dumb Waiter," *Astounding,* April 1952.

14. This theme is explored by Warren Wagar on pp. 161–68 of *Terminal Visions,* although with a different emphasis since Wagar includes nonnuclear holocausts in his discussion.

15. Poul Anderson, *Vault of the Ages* (Philadelphia: Winston, 1952).

16. Ibid., p. 207.

17. Leigh Brackett, *The Long Tomorrow* (Garden City, N.Y.: Doubleday, 1955).

18. A. M. Lightner, *The Day of the Drones* (New York: Norton, 1969). Lightner's novel is very closely patterned after Margot Bennett's *The Long Way Back* (London: Bodley Head, 1954) in which an African expedition also explores savage Britain, but in Bennett's work the nuclear war has been forgotten except as a catastrophe caused by a mysterious god named Thai.

19. James Blish, "The Oath," *Fantasy and Science Fiction,* October 1961.

20. James Tiptree, Jr., "The Man Who Walked Home," *Amazing,* May 1972.

21. Edmund Cooper, *The Cloud Walker* (London: Hodder & Stoughton, 1973).

22. Walter M. Miller, Jr., *A Canticle for Leibowitz* (New York: Lippincott, 1959).

23. Vonda McIntyre, *Dreamsnake* (Boston: Houghton Mifflin, 1978).

24. Piers Anthony, *Sos the Rope* (New York: Pyramid, 1968). Reprinted as part of *Battle Circle* (New York: Avon, 1978).

25. A. E. van Vogt, *Empire of the Atom* (Chicago: Shasta, 1957), stories originally published in *Astounding:* "A Son Is Born," May 1946; "Children of the Gods," August 1946; "Hand of the Gods," December 1946; "Homes of the Gods," April 1947; and "The Barbarian," December 1947. *The Wizard of Linn* (New York: Ace, 1962), originally serialized in *Astounding,* April-June 1950.

26. Poul Anderson has one character criticize the notion of radiation creating positive mutations at the beginning of his story "Logic" (*Astounding,* July 1947), but he goes on to create a radiation-induced superhuman of his own.

27. Russell Hoban, *Riddley Walker* (New York: Simon & Schuster, 1980). See also *Deus Irae* by Dick and Zelazny.

28. A. E. van Vogt, "Resurrection," first published as "The Monster," *Astounding,* August 1948.

29. Edmond Hamilton, *City at World's End* (New York: Frederick Fell, 1951).

30. Ibid., p. 194.

31. Poul Anderson, "No Truce with Kings," *Fantasy and Science Fiction,* June 1963.

32. Poul Anderson, *Thermonuclear Warfare* (Derby, Conn.: Monarch, 1963).

33. Poul Anderson, *Orion Shall Rise* (New York: Timescape, 1983).

34. Suzanne Martel, *The City Underground,* trans. Norah Smaridge (New York: Viking Press, 1964). Originally published as *Quatre Montréalais en l'an 3000* (Montreal: Editions du jour, 1963). Reprinted as *Surreal 3,000* (Toronto: Macmillan, 1966).

35. Paul O. Williams, *The Dome in the Forest* (New York: Ballantine Books, 1981).

36. Keith Roberts, *Pavane* (Garden City, N.Y.: Doubleday, 1966).

37. See Carl Yoke, "From Alienation to Personal Triumph: The Science Fiction of Joan D. Vinge," in *The Feminine Eye: Science Fiction and the Women Who Write It,* ed. Tom Staicar (New York: Ungar, 1982), pp. 103–30.

38. Michael J. Yavenditti, "The American People and the Use of Atomic Bombs on Japan: The 1940s," *The Historian: A Journal of History* 36 (1974), pp. 224–47.

4

DEATHS BY DROWNING

Joe Sanders

A worldwide flood is one of the most fascinating disasters imaginable. First of all, the flood is terrifying, for it shows normal routine being shattered by a familiar, life-giving element turned destructive; moreover, it plays on a fundamental human fear of being swept away from consciously beloved possessions into a formless, fluid existence. Yet it also is awe-inspiring, literally wonderful, as it reveals the power hidden in familiar objects. Finally, and most basic of all, the flood is an appealing disaster. It lifts the burden of past mistakes from the best of humanity and lets them find a new, more appropriate way to live.

In our culture, the archetype of the flood is the biblical story of Noah, which especially gratifies its audience. By its terror it reveals, and by its revelation it comforts. The biblical flood kills only people whom God has judged unworthy. The few people permitted and inspired to survive are given a clean world and shown a definite, healthy role in that world. The biblical flood is the basis of a covenant between God and Noah: God will not flood the earth again, and man will accept the role for which he was created. All other stories of floods must be measured against the appropriateness and satisfying resolution of this model.

Despite the fear, awe, and relief that make the flood such a fascinating disaster, however, it has not been utilized in science fiction until recently. Instead, it remained confined to the subgenre of the Atlantean romance because of the difficulty of imagining a sufficient cause for a worldwide flood after God's clear statement that he would never again drown the world. Moreover, much early science fiction was essentially tentative in its exploration of new ideas, reverting to the status quo at each story's climax;[1] such an attitude obviously was unsuited for considering the profound changes entailed by a flood, in particular the individual's need to find a satisfying, new way to live. Several of the twentieth-century science fiction novels that have considered various kinds of floods thus show a mixture of biblical references and differing postreligious estimates of human potential.

Garrett P. Serviss' 1912 novel *The Second Deluge* describes the earth passing through a watery nebula that raises the level of the oceans above the summit of Mt. Everest. Fortunately, the scientist Cosmo Versal spots the nebula coming and builds an ark to save one thousand superior humans to be parents of an improved humanity. As the story develops, however, the selected group is diluted by Versal's own servants, whom he saves because of their loyalty to him, and later by various other survivors who demonstrate nothing more than extreme tenacity. Thus the idea of a purified humanity is nullified even while Versal's ark makes a tour of the drowning world so that readers can experience the fear and wonder mentioned above. Finally, when the ark returns to America, Versal discovers that his calculations have been in error and that a section of the American West has been thrust above high water; several million survivors already are settled there, commanded by the president of the United States and a conservative scientist who had led those who scoffed at Versal's original predictions. The ark, with neat symbolism, runs aground and sinks so that Versal and his companions must join the existing society—the New America.

Serviss' novel is a clear example of status quo science fiction. The conclusion manages to reduce the apocalyptic force of the flood by stressing how much Versal overlooked and how impractical were his plans for a postdeluge society.[2] In addition, by returning to a system that is a copy of the old, the story validates our present society. If a genius like Cosmo Versal can make mistakes, humanity ultimately is better off with a pluralistic decision-making process controlled by a cross section of humanity representing the present mix, rather than a "scientific" dictatorship of a selected elite. Thus the flood serves merely to confirm the rightness of existing personal and social arrangements.

S. Fowler Wright's *Deluge* (1928) and *Dawn* (1929) approach the flood and its consequences much more seriously. In these novels, the surface of the globe has shifted slightly upward or downward, submerging most of the land. Apparently no major land mass has remained unaltered, and there is no surviving government to reproduce itself. The novels focus on a random assortment of British survivors who must take stock of their resources and organize themselves. The most immediately striking thing about the novels is the joy with which people respond to the disaster. Wright believes that the old civilization was physically unhealthy, as shown in the pollution that mining and industry inflicted on the country and in the ill health that an impersonal social system inflicted on people. More than that, the characters delight in their sudden spiritual liberation. As Claire Arlington, formerly trapped in a loveless marriage to a sick man, muses, "that life had left her, with all its obligations, all its occupations, its loves and friendships . . . they were gone, and here she stood—free."[3]

All their lives, people had been restrained. Sometimes the restraints were comfortable, and sometimes they were accepted knowingly; now, however, survivors recognize that they are "free for the adventure of life untrammeled— or at least trammeled only by forces that are at once beneficial, and blind, and impartial."[4]

After that first rush of freedom, the survivors settle into an ordered system, partly out of habit, partly out of an instinctive companionship, and partly out of recognition that they need some kind of guaranteed cooperation because they are in danger from the elements and from a few survivors who choose to use their freedom to satisfy personal fantasies of power and destruction. But the new system will not be like the old. The survivors choose Martin Webster, a tough-minded former lawyer, as their leader, but they make clear that they do not want him to re-create the mass of laws that had confined them before. Martin appreciates the uniqueness of each individual, but he accepts command with the understanding that there will be no questioning of his orders, ever.

Clearly, "freedom" has limits. Freedom, in Wright's novels, means a chance "to look at things straight, and to see clearly,"[5] not to do whatever one wishes. This accounts for the element of *Deluge* that helped make it a *succès de scandale*,[6] Martin's decision not to choose between Helen, his wife, and Claire, the woman with whom he has fought through difficulties since the flood. It is not simply that Martin desires both women. He has pledged loyalty to both; both deserve his faith and both properly expect him to make a fair decision. Consequently, recognizing that no one is bound by the old form of marriage, Martin decides that the three of them can and should form a new unit. In the same manner— by trying to see conditions as they truly, fundamentally are—Martin is forced to find how other humans survive. Muriel Temple, a former missionary who serves as a commentator in *Dawn*, attempts to see the new world according to part of the old viewpoint, her religious faith. In fact, she accomplishes much good by her sympathy for others and her disinterested actions. Wright makes clear, though, that it is her actions rather than her faith that justify her. Despite resembling the biblical flood, Wright's deluge is a mere phenomenon, a part of uncaring nature. The passage of time (and human life) is described in the novel's last paragraphs:

The night moved round the earth. It followed daylight, as men are followed by the overtaking feet of Death, but there was no finality in its triumph.
For behind it followed forever the indifferent dawn.[7]

Considering "indifferent" and the fact that dawn earlier was described as "regardless,"[8] we see that it would be a mistake to imagine that anything beyond man's will gives meaning to the struggle of life. Wright depicts an almost existential situation, in which the characters must create their identities by acting in a setting that is otherwise a meaningless blank. The fact remains that Martin, Claire, Helen, and Muriel *do* create themselves. Difficult as it is to find a new role without divine aid, it is possible.

In more recent years, science fiction has become more pessimistic about the possibility of viewing things objectively or taking any significant action about them. In fact, one of the most interesting things about John Wyndham's 1953 novel *Out of the Deeps* (also known as *The Kraken Wakes*) is that it is told from the perspective of a husband-and-wife team of broadcast journalists, people whose job is not merely to observe and interpret events but to communicate them to the public. What they observe is a large number of mysterious, glowing objects dropping into the ocean; what they come to believe is an eccentric scientist's theory that aliens are colonizing the water-covered portions of the globe. But what they and the rest of the news media communicate to the public is only what they think will be acceptable, a mixture of government obfuscation and ill-informed belligerence. The scientist (and the newspeople themselves, as individuals) may speculate about whether the aliens are hostile or not and whether it would be possible to communicate with them peacefully, but the actual human response is a combination of groping investigation and inept attack. The aliens answer with increasingly effective hostility that culminates in the melting of earth's polar ice caps and the flooding of low-lying country. All through this the central characters try to process information objectively, but they do it rather badly. The problem is more basic than management control over what they may broadcast; they have trouble approaching the subject in the first place. The woman is more sensitive to this than her husband. It is to her that the scientist remarks, " 'It is mental suicide to funk the data one has.' "[9] A few pages later, her husband reassures her that he is actually as worried as she by saying, " 'My protective coloration isn't intended to deceive you, my sweet. It is intended to deceive me.' " She is not especially reassured: " 'I must remember that,' she said with an air of extensive implication that I am not sure I have fully understood yet."[10]

Wyndham's novel actually raises the question of how much people are willing to know. It appears that we may be unable to respond effectively to a new situation because we insist on interpreting it according to familiar guidelines. We will attack anyone who crowds us, but we will lash out with special viciousness at a stranger. We will choose comfortable nonsense rather than unsettling facts. And this, as Wyndham notes, is mental suicide. At the book's conclusion, it does appear that humanity will survive, because the Japanese apparently have found a weapon that can reach the aliens in their undersea bases. However, readers may not be as encouraged as the characters. Until the scientist reappears in the book's last pages as a *deus ex helicopter*, the story has shown the steady crumbling of human society. In particular, the British government's plan to resettle people in central camps has been a ghastly failure. Yet, while this is going on, the central characters broadcast propaganda for the government, as usual knowing more than they tell:

News reached us mainly by two channels: the private link with E.B.C., which was usually moderately honest though discreet; and broadcasts, which, no matter where they came from, were puffed with patently dishonest optimism. We became very tired and cynical about them, as, I imagine, did everyone else, but they still kept on. Every country, it seemed, was meeting and rising above the disaster with a resolution that did honor to the traditions of its people.[11]

The juxtaposition of these last two sentences may be read as a serious tribute to the people who stick by their duty—or as a bitter comment on the futile self-delusion to which they cling. I believe Wyndham intended the latter, but I cannot shake the suspicion that the newsman would try to argue the former. Even at the end, the journalists undertake a new propaganda campaign encouraging the isolated bands of survivors to cooperate. Though the old government consistently misled them, they must be convinced to trust a central authority again. Necessary as this may be at the moment, and tempting as it would be to suppose that humanity has learned a lesson from its blunders, the story gives readers little sense that the characters have changed enough to avoid exactly the same kind of willful errors in the future. Happy ending and all, Wyndham's novel shows humans still vulnerable to their desire to sink into the unexamined life.

That desire is the subject of John Bowen's *After the Rain* (1959). The flood in Bowen's novel looks much like the biblical version, an unending rain. It is not caused by an angry God, however, but by a crackpot inventor's scheme to get rich by ending a drought. As the narrator, a young writer, discusses the carnival that surrounds the inventor's performance, he comments with wry admiration on the man's shrewd commercial sense, and during the early stages of flooding he himself works as a copywriter with a timely slant:

"STOCKING A RAFT?" I wrote, "Remember OYSTERS! succulent and easily digested, Buxtable OYSTERS give you those RESERVES OF ENERGY you are going to NEED. OYSTERS in your provision box are worth their weight in PEARLS. Ask your grocer for BUXTABLE'S BOTTLED OYSTERS now before it's too late."[12]

Later, after society has broken down completely and the narrator has escaped from a soggy government camp with Sonya, his lover, he is picked up by a kind of ark. However, it is not one of the boats begun during the rain by various eccentric "Noahs"; it is a giant balsa raft launched years before as a promotional stunt for a breakfast cereal, Glub. It was intended to sail around the world and thus prove "that man could live by Glub alone."[13]

From a religious perspective, it might appear that God would be justified in drowning a people so contemptuous of anything except business as usual. But there is no one in the novel to offer such a religious perspective. The one survivor aboard the raft who actually worries about God is a guilt-ridden lunatic. The clergyman present explains that he took up the ministry because every other profession was too difficult, and in any event " 'nobody wanted me to believe in God as a person, or in Christ as anything else.' "[14] No one else on the raft has a belief from the old culture to set in the place of religion. An actress, for example, describes her struggle to hold onto faith in art as a center for life but concludes that she " 'could come away from a performance of *Lear* feeling noble and uplifted. . . . [B]ut [she] also found [she] could get the same feeling from benzedine.' "[15]

This lack of faith makes the survivors vulnerable to Arthur Renshaw. He is described initially as "absurd and frightening."[16] Though physically insignificant, he is intelligent—and burning with belief. Not knowing how the rain really started, Arthur believes that the flood was caused by natural selection to save humanity from smothering in its excess. He believes that the people on the raft have been selected to be the basis of the new humanity and that he has been destined to command them. And the survivors, with differing degrees of speed and gladness, fall in line with Arthur's certainty. They obey him, follow him, and eventually worship him when he proclaims himself God.

Grotesque as this is, it never is quite laughable. Rather, the action is like Arthur himself, simultaneously foolish and frightening. The narrator is convincing in his pliability, as he briefly resists accepting the God Arthur but eventually is willing to promise to sacrifice his baby, which Sonya is about to bear:

The relief [that Arthur does not demand Sonya herself as a sacrifice]! I was filled with relief until it almost ran out of my ears. Not Sonya. Nobody would hurt Sonya. I was not to be tested, not to be required to fight for her. Only the child. Nobody could ask me, nobody could expect me to fight, to risk both our lives—risk them? to lose them certainly—to lose both our lives for a child a few hours old, something without even a personality; nobody could do that. It would not be pleasant, certainly, to sacrifice the child, not easy to explain to Sonya herself . . . , but it was not so bad, not so fearful; it could be borne. "She'd better not be told," I said. "We'll have to say it died or something."[17]

Such rationalization is revoltingly credible. What is incredible is that Arthur is killed immediately afterward by Tony, a young bodybuilder whom Arthur had considered a mindless manual laborer; Tony is too unsophisticated to drift like the others, and he knows that murdering babies is simply wrong. At the same moment, the survivors sight land. Now that Arthur is gone and they cannot act like dependent children anymore, they must take responsibility for building the new society themselves. In the novel's last lines, the narrator assures us that they are up to the task.

Bowen's 1957 dramatization of the story, which preceded the novel, suggests the kind of society the survivors could create and explores the human desire necessary to escape freedom by believing in something at any cost. To solve the problem of showing the massive raft on stage, as well as presenting the novel's vast weather changes and an attack by a giant squid, Bowen presents action as a pantomimed performance at a university history lecture. The lecturer interjects frequent comments on the action, explaining how the people on stage laid the foundations for the way of life enjoyed by the university audience of "two hundred years after the Rain."[18]

Although the new society is never described directly, the lecturer does note that the performers in the skit have been hypnotized, so that they genuinely believe they are the characters they represent, because their performance is a combination of punishment and therapy. They must purge themselves of the criminal traits their roles exhibit; the "Arthur," for instance, "has been guilty of persistently individualistic behavior," and the crimes of the others include "lack of group effort . . . public sarcasm . . . private pleasure and irrational enjoyment . . . [and] doubt."[19] The new society watches for such behaviors, and it obliterates them dispassionately. Thus the action—even the same dialogue—is seen from a different angle than it is in the novel. Arthur becomes almost a tragic hero in his attempt to be extraordinary, superior to the group. At the play's end, during Arthur's fight with Tony, the lecturer suddenly halts the action: "the community does not and will not allow waste of any kind. We cure criminals; we do not kill them. This man will be returned to medical care."[20] A moment earlier, "Arthur" had broken hypnosis to object that "I am myself. I will overcome."[21] In fact, he cannot overcome, and the only way he can remain himself is to trick "Tony" into actually killing him. Though the play ends with the wistfully hopeful words of the characters as they look toward the new land, "I wonder how we shall go on there, then," the play's audience has seen very clearly what they will create—a society in which the lecturer's final commands are "There will be no questions. . . . You will not discuss what has happened."[22]

Probably the most disturbing of these postdeluge science fiction novels, however, is J. G. Ballard's *The Drowned World* (1962), for Ballard questions whether even the notions of social order or social roles would persist if people once were free to examine their own nature. A society does exist in *The Drowned World,* retreating farther and farther north after a solar flare has melted earth's polar caps and after heat and flood have made the lower latitudes uninhabitable; it appears to be a military regime, and it makes periodic attempts to map or reclaim the flooded cities of the south. But its efforts are only inconsistently and arbitrarily energetic. In the final analysis, the general society is irrelevant to much of the earth or the lives of human beings.

What is relevant to several members of a scientific-exploring party in partly submerged London is the posthuman jungle, the heat of the sun that saps their will and turns them away from any conscious purpose. Bodkin, a scientist, offers a more or less lucid explanation to Kerans, the central character:

Every step we've taken in our evolution is a milestone inscribed with organic memories—from the enzymes controlling the carbon dioxide cycle to the organization of the prachial plexus and the nerve pathway of the Pyramid cells in the midbrain, each is a record of a thousand decisions taken in the face of a sudden psysico-chemical crisis. Just as psychoanalysis reconstructs the original traumatic situation in order to release the repressed material, so we are now being plunged back into the archaeopsychic past, uncovering the ancient taboos and drives that have been dormant for epochs. The brief span of an individual life is misleading. Each one of us is as old as the entire biological kingdom, and our bloodstreams are tributaries of the great sea of its total memory.[23]

It is futile to ask whether this is the true explanation of the characters' sinking into a languid, instinctive state. No "explanation" is possible.[24] Whether the drowned world has triggered the organic memory as Bodkin suggests, whether humanity is trying to cure its trauma of leaving the sea,[25] or whether the characters are just attempting to rectify their mistake in leaving the womb[26] does not matter. Nothing "matters." In *The Drowned World,* words lose their ability to refer to abstract concepts and become mere hints of physical sensation and immediate emotion, then lose meaning altogether. All readers can be sure of is that somehow characters arrive at the same condition, in which they make vague plans for what they somehow must do—leave the company of other humans and journey south toward the greatest possible heat and certain death. At the end of the novel, Kerans has destroyed an attempt to reclaim part of the city and is traveling south through the jungle. He is aware of what he is doing, but he ceases to reflect on it. He is unthinkingly, uncommunicably satisfied. Although he is "sure that no one would ever read the message," Kerans scratches a note on the wall of a ruin, ending with the reassurance that "*All is well.*" In the novel's last sentence, Ballard shows Kerans entering a place and a state of consciousness where no reader can follow him:

So he left the lagoon and entered the jungle again, within a few days was completely lost, following the lagoons southward through the increasing rain and heat, attacked by alligators and giant bats, a second Adam searching for the forgotten paradises of the reborn sun.[27]

This is not so much a choice of death as an escape from conscious choice. Kerans has ceased to exist in human terms, just as society or the personal relationships that underlie it have ceased to exist for him. No Eve is waiting for Kerans in a new Eden where they can begin humanity again. The only "paradise" waiting for him is personal oblivion. But that is his desire.

This group of postflood science fiction novels shows the variety of floods imaginable and the imaginable variety of human responses.[28] Since the biblical flood is the archetypal image of a worldwide flood in our culture, these novels compare their action to that story in comments by authors and characters. Without God's presence, the novels' floods are caused by uncaring nature or by man himself. Man must cope with floods without supernatural aid. Early science fiction suggested that man could overcome his terror, that the flood and the struggle to survive it might even aid the future health of humanity. More recent novels have questioned our ability to understand or control life. Defects in the human consciousness make thinking unreliable or actually perverse, leading to deliberate destruction of the self. It may even be that the attempt to know and do is a recent, superficial layer over our non-reflective, death-seeking nature. Doubtless, this reflects our society's general loss of certainty. It still is striking, looking at these novels and considering how many centuries it took writers to lose confidence in God and how few decades it has taken them to lose faith in mankind.[29]

NOTES

1. For a fuller discussion of this label, see Frank Cioffi, *Formula Fiction? An Anatomy of American Science Fiction, 1930–1940* (Westport, Conn.: Greenwood Press, 1982).

2. Serviss suggests that Versal's party provides "a leaven" for humanity, but in the time covered by the novel everyone goes on behaving exactly as before. Garrett P. Serviss, *The Second Deluge* (1912; reprint, Westport, Conn.: Hyperion Press, 1974), p. 397.

3. S. Fowler Wright, *Deluge* (New York: Cosmopolitan, 1928), p. 51.

4. Ibid., p. 109.

5. Ibid., p. 212.

6. For a survey of Wright's career, see Brian Stableford, "Against the New Gods: The Speculative Fiction of S. Fowler Wright," *Foundation* 29, pp. 10–52; the discussion of *Deluge* occupies pp. 19–23.

7. S. Fowler Wright, *Dawn* (New York: Cosmopolitan, 1929), p. 349.

8. Ibid., p. 25.

9. John Wyndham, *Out of the Deeps* (New York: Ballantine Books, 1953), p. 50.

10. Ibid., p. 58.

11. Ibid., pp. 156–57.

12. John Bowen, *After the Rain* (New York: Ballantine Books, 1959), p. 22.

13. Ibid., p. 46.

14. Ibid., p. 83.

15. Ibid., p. 102.

16. Ibid., p. 46.

17. Ibid., pp. 151–52.

18. John Bowen, *After the Rain* [dramatization] (New York: Random House, 1957), n.p.

19. Ibid., pp. 39–40.

20. Ibid., p. 117.

21. Ibid., p. 116.

22. Ibid., p. 118.

23. J. G. Ballard, *The Drowned World* (New York: Berkley, 1962), p. 40.

24. For that matter, the novel provides no convincing explanation of the mountains of silt that choke the drowned cities; they certainly cannot have been created by the floods that followed from the change in climate, and I suspect that those undulating mounds have more to do with the wavy surface of the human brain than any truly possible rearrangement of dirt.

25. Ballard, p. 87.

26. Ibid., pp. 99–100.

27. Ibid., p. 158.

28. This is, to be sure, a selective list of works dealing with the subject, excluding some short stories—such as H. G. Wells, "The Star," which does hint of a new utopia

after the disasters (including immense floods) that accompany a wandering planet's passing close to the earth—and some novels—such as Charles L. Fontenay, *The Day the Oceans Overflowed* (Derby, Conn.: Monarch, 1964), which describes efforts to recover from the chaos when an attempt to gradually melt the polar caps goes awry.

29. When God himself loses faith in man and sends another deluge, the result is described in Bernard Malamud's mordant fantasy *God's Grace* (1982), discussed elsewhere in this volume.

5

FROM THE ASHES COMES THE CUCKOO: CHARACTER AND MYTH IN POSTHOLOCAUST NARRATIVES

William Lomax

Insofar as science fiction is about today rather than tomorrow, postholocaust narratives normally respond to sociopolitical developments stemming from the advent of the atomic age during World War II. Thus, the drive during the 1950s to establish a viable civil defense system and the subsequent scramble to build, stock, and even live in underground shelters inspired a series of stories, including Mordecai Roshwald's *Level 7* (1959), Daniel Galouye's *Dark Universe* (1961), and Philip Dick's "The Defenders" (1952), which questioned, with typical science fiction skepticism, the practicality of such a defense strategy. Less obvious, but equally significant, postholocaust narratives reflect cultural needs and fears which reach far beyond the limited, temporary effects (as devastating as they may be) of the existence or use of the bomb, which, in effect, is only one specific expression of a larger cultural pattern. Furthermore, such narratives achieve this by manipulating traditional literary symbols and conventions within an apocalyptic context of radical change. This melding of the radical and the conventional is particularly apparent in the relationship of character, traditionally one of science fiction's biggest liabilities, to the unique landscapes of postholocaust worlds.

At first glance, it may appear that holocaust fiction renders character superfluous. The vast power of the bomb, multiplied beyond conceivability in the Armageddons which smash civilization, dwarfs merely human scale, and the fates of individuals seem insignificant compared with the fate of the race. This is the case, for example, with Whittley Strieber and James Kunetka's *Warday* (1984), a fictionalized documentary with a cast of well-coached but generally faceless sideline witnesses to the magnificent destruction of America. Here indeed our attention is riveted by (in William Golding's ludicrous phrase) that "big, big, oh enormously, indescribably, big, big bang,"[1] and we do not read on, as James Gunn says, "to become better acquainted with real people."[2] Similarly, the only truly memorable scenes in Philip Wylie's *Tomorrow!* (1954) are those indelible portraits of the vivid, jagged horror of the explosion and its human aftermath. The final pages are a powerful testament to nuclear horror, but individuals are swallowed up in the vast panorama. Other types of holocaust stories—doomsday stories, tales of survival, even preholocaust dramas—utilize character more effectively, but the focus typically remains on the bomb and its real or potential effects.

True *postholocaust* tales, by contrast, narrate the *recovery* of civilization— the rise of the phoenix from the ashes. The Big Bang has long been over, life has stabilized, and survival is no longer in (too much) doubt. With the special effects out of the way, the actors again take center stage. Even though post-holocaust characters may be, in terms of conventional character development, no more noble or flawed, complex or ambiguous than characters in any other story, the peculiarities of their situation and their environment give them a functional role which transcends conventional development.

They walk on stage, first of all, to a dramatic change of scenery. Topography has shifted, and time has been dopplered by an interruption in the linear flow of history. Knowledge has succumbed to ignorance, and distorted memories turn the past into golden myth or dark nightmare. Life has reverted either to medieval or paleolithic levels. Technology is alternately feared, envied, or worshiped, the object of ignorant awe or hopeful recovery. Obsolete machinery furnishes icons or salvage. The dead shells of great buildings shelter livestock, and the stumps of ruined monuments, like Ozymandias' pedestal, give bleak testimony to shattered glory. The social and political megaunits of twentieth-century life have been fragmented into city-states, villages, or clans. Social organization, isolated from outside contact, is regressive and monolithic. Industrial civilization has retrogressed into an agrarian, barter economy. Hunting and foraging provide sustenance. Law and power are centered in authoritarian, peremptory, and often repressively theocratic political systems. Petty tyrannies, primitive democracies, and pocket monarchies litter the map. Security is tenuous at best. Ethics shift violently as people feed off each other to survive. Religion has reverted to superstition, morality to taboo. Man is once again subject to the elements, and radiation has turned nature virulent, alien, antagonistic. The gene pool has been roiled, and man is plagued by induced mutations or he retreats before emerging *homo superior*. Children are nonexistent or bestialized.

At the same time, however, this wild, radically changed environment also seems paradoxically familiar. The landscape is altered, but not beyond recognition. Who is not aware that Edgar Pangborn's Davy is wandering through the northeastern United States, that Brian Aldiss's Greybeard is navigating down the Thames Basin, that David Strorm (in John Wyndham's *The Chrysalids*) lives in a warmer Labrador and is rescued by a woman from New Zealand, or that

Riddley Walker slogs through a wet and muddy Kent? The mutated place names beloved by postholocaust authors are designed for familiarity, not for strangeness; puzzles disguise what is known, not what is unknown. And, just in case someone is not paying attention, we nearly always are told, sooner or later, exactly where we are:

The world . . . was generally thought to be a pretty big place. . . . The civilized part of it . . . was called Labrador. This was thought to be the Old People's name for it, though that was not very certain.[3]

[W]hen I am chief we shall go beyond the great river. We shall go to the Place of the Gods—the place newyork.[4]

It happened in 323, in Nuin, whose eastern boundary is a coastline on the great sea that in Old Time was called the Atlantic.[5]

No 1 uses the old place names now they been unspoak this long time but mos of them are stil there in the places. You know Cambry ben Canterbury in moufs long gone.[6]

In addition, familiar images from contemporary civilization continually pop up to remind us of ourselves: the vine-choked Capitol in the film *Logan's Run;* the crumbling towers of Oxford in *Greybeard,* still majestic but now converted to an inn and marketplace; the rotted shell of an automobile hanging on a tree branch in the film *Glen and Randa;* the letter-filled jeep in David Brin's "The Postman"; the statue of "ASHING" in Stephen Vincent Benet's "By the Waters of Babylon"; the Disney cartoon in Arthur C. Clarke's "History Lesson"; the Mona Lisa in Ray Bradbury's "The Smile"; the books and phonograph records in Walter van Tilburg Clark's "The Portable Phonograph"; and, of course, the buried Statue of Liberty in the final scene of the film version of *Planet of the Apes.*

Besides the stage dressing, those popular social institutions—war, superstition, tyranny, repression, suffering, irrationality—remain recognizable although reduced in magnitude. David Strorm runs from a rural tyranny as superstitiously fearful of mutants as Europe was of witches in the seventeenth century. Len Colter (in Leigh Brackett's *The Long Tomorrow)* flees a Mennonite homeland which blindly and violently represses scientific knowledge and has banned large cities with an amendment to the Constitution. John, in "By the Waters of Babylon," lives a life of noble savagery but must break rigid tribal taboos in order to go east[7] to the Dead Places and rekindle civilization. Brushfire wars plague the pioneer-level statelets in *Davy.* Kieron's reinvention of balloon flight in Edmund Cooper's *The Cloud Walker* is immediately applied to aerial bombardment. The rediscovery of gunpowder in *Riddley Walker* quickly separates a couple of characters from their heads. And in Walter Miller's *A Canticle for Leibowitz,* the whole pitiful cycle revolves, and nuclear war *again* devastates the earth.

Postholocaust landscapes, then, are simultaneously radically alien and con-

ventionally familiar. In its wild, fragmented radicalization, this environment
forces the individual to be independent. He can no longer hide, like his preholocaust ancestors, behind social anonymity or depend on the inertia of civilized
systems to sustain him. He is no longer a mote in the megalithic sociopolitical
institutions of twentieth-century life nor just a single cell in the body of the race.
He cannot escape himself now, and his survival depends almost entirely on his
own inner character. Scott Sanders' argument that science fiction characters are
one dimensional because of the loss of identity in modern society[8] is, in effect,
reversed in a postholocaust setting, which, although chronologically postmodern,
is a reversion to a premodern world in which the problems of anonymity and
identity still lie far in the future.

At the same time, in its conventional familiarity, the postholocaust landscape
is linked inextricably with our contemporary world and clearly serves as an
analogue for it. This suggests that postholocaust narratives are setting up experimental alternatives, almost in the manner of naturalistic fiction. By wiping
the board clean with the bomb and setting it all up again, but with the Brob-
dingnagian institutions of modern life reduced in a sort of Gulliverian reversal
to a size where an individual can once again make a difference, the human race
can try again, not literally but analogically. The institutions still exist, as we
have seen, but in microcosm, as the symbols of their former power lie fragmented
and crumbling across the surrounding landscape.

In other words, the radicality of the postholocaust setting gives character the
independence to function, free of the restrictions of modern life as reflected in
the rigidity of dystopian scenarios; the familiarity of that setting, as an analogue
for today, dictates the nature of that function which the character has been given
the freedom to perform. In short, postholocaust heroes are designed to perform
that which we—preholocaust moderns—are incapable or unwilling to perform
for ourselves. The cosmic irony in this is that, if we could do it for ourselves,
we could probably prevent the holocaust.

Before we can determine what it is that postholocaust heroes actually do, we
must examine more closely the nature of their character, for, despite their theoretical independence, it turns out there is a remarkable consistency of character
in nearly all postholocaust narratives. They are, in fact, a variation on a stock
figure into which Western man has for over five hundred years projected some
of his most fundamental fears and desires—the *wild man*.

The fictional wild man[9] spans human history from Enkidu in the *Gilgamesh*
to Hercules and bacchants to the fantastic forms of travelers tales and antimasques
to Caliban and Bremo to the Houyhnhnms and Mr. Hyde. By the twelfth century,
he (and she, for there were wild women too) had become a symbol of man's
bestial nature—a gigantic, hairy, naked, libidinous, cave-dwelling beast-human,
without speech, rationality, or spiritual knowledge, despising order and restraint,
rebelling against social and religious norms—the antithesis of knighthood. He
was, above all, insane and, as such, a potential prophet. By externalizing and

objectifying his own violent nature in such a repulsive figure, man could laugh or throw stones and thus exorcise his own fears and guilt; by metaphorically exiling the forces of disorder to the wilds, away from human communion, he could assure the stability of his social contracts.

With the breakdown of medieval unity and the growth of nations and societies into modern megaunits, society itself became the evil. As discontent with civilization mushroomed, the wild man was transformed into a symbol of man's rejection of his own civilization and thus became a model for human conduct and a reminder of what man had lost by becoming civilized.[10] Now civilization was insane, and the wild man was a type of virtue, love, and nobility possible only in the wild, away from society. This was the noble savage, personified in Cervantes' Cardenio and Spenser's "salvage man," whom Vico saw as a natural poet, and who in a sixteenth-century poem by Hans Sachs laments for the "unfaithful world."

In this transition from wild man to noble savage was born a third figure, a complex literary image that expressed the ambivalence of men who recognized the benefits of civilized life but abhorred the inhumanity and savagery that inevitably accompany mass organization. Neither a collective objectification nor an ethical model, he was an individual, an outsider, a solitary, self-sufficient, resourceful, peripatetic figure, with neither parents nor home (either having lost or never known them), the only sane figure in an insane world. Alternately pariah, picaro, robber, fool, innocent, orphan, or combinations thereof, he lived *in* society but was not *of* it and so was an apt and ironic observer of the inhumanity and irrationality of society.[11] Sometimes wild, sometimes noble, sometimes both at the same moment, he wandered through a strange land, coming and going mysteriously, equally adept at survival and satire. He was, in other words, a sort of "cuckoo," and, like the young of a cuckoo, he grew in an alien environment which rejected him but to which he had to adapt in order to survive.

He appears in the seventeenth century as the wandering innocent fool turned soldier of fortune in H. J. C. von Grimmelshausen's *Der Abenteuerliche Simplicissimus* (1669), a grim, bizarre, episodic tour through the Thirty Years' War, a preatomic holocaust which, Eric Bentley implies, was, in its devastation and suffering, not unlike the conflagrations envisioned by futurists.[12]

He reappears as Frankenstein's monster, who has neither home, parents, nor companions. "Like the savage," writes Milton Millhauser, with some understatement, "the monster approaches our society as an outsider, tests it by natural impulse and unsophisticated reason, and responds to it with a mixture of bewilderment and dismay."[13] In fact, the horrified reaction of the De Laceys to his deformity and Frankenstein's obsessive rejection of him transform the monster from an innocent to a literal wild man, the violent product of society's failure to assimilate the individual.

A half century later, Nemo, another homeless, parentless, nameless outsider valiantly struggles, alone, against governments which destroy or enslave the individual. Like Frankenstein's monster, he too responds to his anger and frustration by becoming a wild man, using the tools of his science rather than his own sheer physical strength to destroy that which he perceives as evil.

Finally, in modern postholocaust narratives, beginning with H. G. Wells' *The Time Machine,*[14] cuckoos appear with remarkable consistency. Characters are homeless, or they choose to leave home; they are sharply aware of their identity and name and are frequently nameless or adopt new names; they are rational and self-sufficient with unique skills, often mental or creative skills; they repeatedly have visions of cities and technological wonders, or they simply dream of *someplace else;* they wander aimlessly or journey purposefully, but always in quest of their vision; above all, they are outsiders, different, out of step with the traditions and conventions of their society and are therefore treated with suspicion, persecuted, exiled, or attacked. They see what others cannot and so are strangers in the land. But rather than simply adapt and survive like Simplicissimus, or merely accuse and destroy like the monster and Nemo, they seek to reshape the world or, like the time traveler, to find another in which they can live.

In the characters of Simplicissimus, Frankenstein's monster, and Nemo, and in their individual responses to collective insanity, we can see a very distinctive progression from innocence to sensibility to rationality. To put it another way, Simplicissimus is the conscience of his age, the monster is the indicter of his age, and Nemo is the reformer of his. Each is a cuckoo—a homeless, nameless (Simplicissimus has a name, but he prefers his adopted name), wandering outsider with perspectives on humanity hidden to nearly everyone around him. But in the progression from commentary to indictment to dynamic, if futile, action, there is a sense of change and evolving purpose. As a seeker—one who searches for a foundation on which to build a new world—the cuckoo in the postholocaust landscape provides the next logical step in the sequence. Though he has less absolute power than Nemo, he has more relative power because the great collective entities against which Nemo had little chance have been destroyed. Their modest replacements are once again of a magnitude that individual action can alter. Nemo failed because his only alternative was to destroy, but in a postholocaust world the only alternative is to build.

Most contemporary mainstream fiction, it seems to me, fails to take this final step. Rooted in realistic despair or romantic escape—things as they are or things as we wish they were—it lacks the will to seek rational alternatives. The cuckoo may be found there, but not as a seeker. Jerzy Kosinski's *The Painted Bird* (1965), for example, reads like *Simplicissimus Redivivus,* although infinitely more cruel. Both works are autobiographical, both are episodic narratives of the horrors of war and superstition indigenous to Central Europe, and both protagonists are nearly identical cuckoolike wanderers who in their innocence make devastating indictments of the societies that persecute them, but neither character progresses even to passion or reform, far less seeking. Where, then, is the progression of thought in three hundred years? It may be that this very lack of progress is the most damning indictment of all against a culture that apparently lies dead in the water, but if that is true, then the progression represented by postholocaust narratives contributes even more to an understanding of the spiritual malaise of Western life.

In this progression and its contrast with contemporary fiction, we see, finally, the primary function of character in postholocaust literature. It may be unreasonable to believe that one man can build an entire new world, but it is not unreasonable to believe that he can create a myth. Science fiction is not prophetic, nor was it ever intended to be, so the literal actions of the postholocaust hero are indeed a fantasy. But as an analogue of contemporary life, postholocaust narratives are dramatizations of the revival of myth. "A given culture," writes Hayden White, "is only as strong as its power to convince its least dedicated member that its fictions are truths." This is what we can no longer do for ourselves, for our "sustaining cultural myths . . . have one by one passed into the category of the fictitious."[15] When we no longer believe in our myths, the only alternative is to create new myths, and it is this need that postholocaust heroes vicariously satisfy. In the vision and the quest of the cuckoo, we recreate myth as a foundation on which to build a new culture.

The ruins that litter the postholocaust landscape are the remnants not of civilization but of civilization's myths. The buried Statue of Liberty in the final scene of *Planet of the Apes* drives the hero to despair, not because of what it is but because of what it represents to him, a survivor from preholocaust America. Machinery, ruined cities, crumbled highways, Oxford's decaying towers, a buried cathedral, a postman's jeep, an unopened letter, books, names, even a grocery list—these are the distillate that remains after our "sustaining cultural myths" have evaporated from the distorted memories of the survivors. The "institutions" that remain after the holocaust—war, tyranny, superstition, and so on—are similarly the remains of sociopolitical systems that have degenerated following the loss or distortion of their guiding myths. When mythic vision is warped or rejected, enlightened religion becomes superstition and taboo, benevolent government becomes tyranny, and progressive science and technology become the power to annihilate. Without myth, the only thing left is reality, and reality is the disease that afflicts Western culture.

Science fiction itself is not the myth we need, for the narrative remains an analogue. Davy, John, David Strorm, Emmanuel (in Robert Merle's *Malevil*) are not the George Washingtons and Alexander the Greats of our future, for they are fictions, whereas myth is a transfiguration of reality. But their efforts are analogues for the actions of real people—real mythmakers—which Western culture so desperately needs. The heroic battle fought by the "road warrior" in George Miller's film to save the small colony of survivors, the resolute efforts of Emmanuel to assure the survival of Malevil, the almost obsessive journeys of Davy and Greybeard toward the East, the determination of Len Colter to reach Bartorstown, the dedicated quest of Brother Francis to preserve the precious relics of the holy Leibowitz, and the countless epic struggles simply to survive in postholocaust landscapes—these are the acts of mythmakers, men and women who live lives larger than those around them and thereby establish the ideals and traditions that sustain cultures. The prologue and epilogue to *The Road Warrior,* which reveal that the story is being told in flashback by the wild child who saw it happen, show that the warrior has assumed mythic proportions in the imaginations of the people he saved, and his legend will inspire and sustain the colony as it grows and matures. The pattern repeats in nearly all postholocaust narratives. Science fiction does not offer practical answers, but it does dramatize the need to search for answers.

As a variation on the stock figure of the wild man, the cuckoo places post-holocaust narratives in the tradition of cultural criticism which has been the conscience of the West since the twelfth century. As a descendant of Simplicissimus, Frankenstein's monster, Nemo, and other fictional outsiders, he is the culmination of a process of literary evolution which symbolizes the inner change and growth necessary to sustain the health of the cultural body—that is, the constant need for new myths as old ones age—and which reenacts the exercise of creative will required to counter the inevitable inertia that bleeds a culture if it does not continually revitalize its mythic dimension.

NOTES

1. William Golding, "Androids All," *Spectator,* February 24, 1961, p. 263.

2. James Gunn, "Heroes, Heroines, Villains: The Characters in Science Fiction," in *The Craft of Science Fiction,* ed. Reginald Bretnor (New York: Harper & Row, 1976), p. 164.

3. John Wyndham, *The Chrysalids,* in *The John Wyndham Omnibus* (New York: Simon & Schuster, 1964), p. 410.

4. Stephen Vincent Benet, "By the Waters of Babylon," in *Selected Works of Stephen Vincent Benet,* vol. II (New York: Farrar & Rinehart, 1942), p. 483.

5. Edgar Pangborn, *Davy* (New York: Ballantine Books, 1964), p. 7.

6. Russell Hoban, *Riddley Walker* (New York: Washington Square Press, 1982), p. 112.

7. Interestingly, postholocaust heroes frequently travel toward the East. The general drift of Western culture has, of course, been toward the West.

8. Scott Sanders, "Invisible Men and Women: The Disappearance of Character in Science Fiction," *Science-Fiction Studies* 11 (March 1977), pp. 14–24.

9. The following discussion is based on two excellent studies of the wild man: Richard Bernheimer, *Wild Men in the Middle Ages* (Cambridge, Mass.: Harvard University Press, 1952), and Hayden White, "The Forms of Wildness: Archaeology of an Idea," in *The Wild Man Within,* ed. Edward Dudley and Maximillian E. Novak (Pittsburgh: University of Pittsburgh Press, 1972), pp. 3–38.

10. Bernheimer, p. 116. See also Peter L. Thorslev, Jr., "The Wild Man's Revenge," in *The Wild Man Within,* p. 281.

11. Thorslev, p. 282.

12. Eric Bentley, "Preface," to H. J. C. von Grimmelshausen, *The Adventurous*

Simplicissimus, trans. A. T. S. Goodrick (Lincoln: University of Nebraska Press, 1962), pp. v–vii.

13. Milton Millhauser, "The Noble Savage in Mary Shelley's 'Frankenstein,' " *Notes & Queries,* 190, 12 (June 15, 1946), p. 248.

14. The time traveler is a typical cuckoo in that he is a brilliant scientist who has no name, about whom we know little, who apparently has no family, who cares little for social approval, and who chooses to leave his contemporary life to reshape a future postholocaust society. We find a similar figure, in more conventional form, in Sinclair Lewis's Martin Arrowsmith, who exiles himself to set up a utopian community of dedicated research scientists.

15. White, p. 6 (see note 9 for additional information).

6

INTELLECTUAL POWER IN H. G. WELLS' *THE WORLD SET FREE*

Nadine S. St. Louis

In 1913 H. G. Wells invented the atomic bomb. With it he started a world war, demolished most of the world's major cities, and set in motion the construction of a new civilization based on principles of equality and cooperation never before seriously considered by the nations of the world. *The World Set Free,* the novel in which he accomplished this remarkable feat—remarkable as much for its early date as for its magnitude—is often alluded to but seldom discussed.

Perhaps *The World Set Free* is so neglected because, despite its considerable length, it is more tract than novel. It does have characters, but they are seen only in glimpses, and many of them disappear almost as quickly as they are introduced. The novel's conflicts, more often global than personal in scale, tend to awe rather than involve the reader. As a result, when Wells' utopian vision emerges from his dystopian catastrophe, the reader's response is more likely to be one of surprise—"Good heavens! How did he manage that?"—than of sympathy.

Why, then, should we look at this novel of the first atomic war? For one thing, of course, it *is* the first. But more significantly, it raises questions that are even more important today than they were in 1913, on the eve of World War I: can conventional procedures be used to handle unconventional power sources? When humanity has such great energies at its disposal, must it inevitably turn them to destructive uses? And if it does, will it destroy civilization? What could be salvaged from the wreckage of such destruction? These are questions that we too must face if we are to maintain a secure future, and while Wells' specific answers may not be of much practical use, his controlling idea is one that deserves consideration.

The World Set Free is a novel about power. The narrator even begins by announcing: "The history of mankind is the history of the attainment of external power."[1] In the beginning he briefly traces the development of motive power from humanity's first use of fire to its discovery of atomic energy—"the snare that shall catch the sun"[2]—and merges fact into fiction as he surveys the impact of atomic power on twentieth-century commerce and society. Thereafter, he describes the war fought with atomic bombs that devastate the earth and threaten to destroy civilization. Even in the narrative of postwar reconstruction, he reintroduces atomic energy as a solution to several problems.

And yet, despite all this attention to motive power, Wells' dominant concern is power of another kind—the power of mind. He begins with the assumption that society's existing structure and values do not foster intellectual development or offer intelligent leadership; in such a climate, genius is isolated and the ordinary mind cannot cope with crisis. But with the optimism of his utopian vision, he goes on to argue that, if a crisis is drastic enough to shock people out of their preconceptions, it can produce not only a harmonious new world order but also the liberation and unification of the human mind.[3]

In the opening of the novel, a capsule history of civilization, Wells hesitates repeatedly over the image of the speculator, the dreamer, the storyteller, who alone observes the world around him and recognizes what it might become. This visionary's specific interests change over the ages, and he grows in sophistication, but his fundamental need to make others see his visions remains unchanged. At last, in the twentieth century, he appears in two guises, the first "a chuckle-headed, scrub-faced lad from the Highlands," sitting rapt at a series of public lectures on radium and radioactivity in Edinburgh; the second a physicist, one Professor Rufus, the lecturer. The professor, speaking, is fascinated by the potential for human growth that he foresees will emerge once the power of the atom can be controlled; the boy, hearing him, is enthralled by the possibilities suggested to his imagination.[4]

For the moment, Wells focuses dramatic attention on the passionate young Highlander, but for his own intellectual speculation in the novel, he is more deeply interested in the professor. He bases the fictional Rufus upon Frederick Soddy, one of the pioneers in atomic research and in later years Nobel laureate, acknowledging his debt to Soddy's *The Interpretation of Radium* in the dedication of the novel.[5] Soddy's book, which began as a series of public lectures at the University of Glasgow in 1908, explains in lay terms the work done in radium to that time. In the eleventh chapter, to which Wells refers specifically, Soddy examines the significance of the discoveries he and his coworkers had already made, concluding that, if the rate of atomic disintegration could be controlled, humanity could achieve both transmutation of elements and unlimited energy. Soddy first expresses the idea with which Wells begins, reflecting that the "struggle for physical energy is probably the most fundamental and general aspect of existence in all its form."[6] Soddy goes further, however, contending that humanity has reached a plateau; before it rise heights of apparently limitless physical power inconceivable so far in human history. These heights, he says, can be gained in the same way humanity has always won its goals, "by the labour of the collective brain of mankind guiding, directing, and multiplying the individual's puny power."[7] Soddy originates the topic and message of Professor Rufus' lecture, as well as Rufus' image of humanity striving toward the summit—an image that will take tangible form in a hospital built high in the Himalayan wastelands at the end of Wells' novel. And Soddy emphasizes the importance of the collective mind at work, a concept that provides the focus of the final third of the novel.

Working backward, perhaps, from this idea of a universal intellect—or perhaps thinking of the intellect of the scientist who has inspired him—Wells demonstrates the effects of crisis on the power of the mind at three levels in *The World Set Free*.

He first introduces us to the intellectual mind in isolation in the person of Holsten, a chemist who, in 1933, discovers how to release the energy of the atom and knows at the time that he is turning over to the world a power that it may not be smart enough to keep in check. On the day following his discovery, Holsten wanders through London, looking at passersby, eavesdropping on strangers, seeing himself as an alien among them come to destroy their security. " 'Felt like an imbecile who has presented a box of loaded revolvers to a Crêche,' " he later writes in his diary,[8] and he begins to wonder whether he should publish his results. When he tries to tell an acquaintance what his experiments have yielded, the man rushes away to find his dog.[9] Holsten has no one with whom to share his moral dilemma. At last, reasoning that change has always been as much a part of life as has stability, he sets aside his doubts: his discovery has been made now, and even if he were to eradicate all traces of his work, someone else would be sure to repeat it in a few more years.[10] Nonetheless, as an isolated genius, Holsten feels terribly lonely in his moment of triumph.

Following this portrayal of the place of genius in the prewar world, Wells next offers dismaying pictures of the minds of ordinary people whose thinking, or lack of it, has also been shaped by the traditional world. Holsten's misgivings, it turns out, are well-founded. In another decade, the new technology has revolutionized transportation and industry.[11] Unfortunately, the world is unprepared for such sweeping change: outmoded industries suddenly collapse, and suicide and violent crime increase drastically until, says the narrator, an anonymous resident of the postwar world, "It seemed as though human society was to be smashed by its own magnificent gains."[12] The masses of the workers, inexperienced in actively using their minds to survive, do not know how to cope with this economic upheaval.

Wells demonstrates their bewilderment and confusion through a secondary narrator, one Frederick Barnet, a perceptive, humane young man whose autobiography, *Wander Jahre,* provides most of the details of the period just before and during the war. Shortly before the war, wandering uncertainly through London's West End looking for work himself, Barnet happens upon a procession of the unemployed, "a dingy, shabby, ineffective-looking multitude" whose behavior at first puzzles him: they are marching in utter silence, neither threatening nor complaining, merely moving through the streets in wordless testimonial of their displacement.[13] Suddenly Barnet realizes that these people, having been struck by unforeseen catastrophe, are making not a demand but rather "an appeal" to some abstract *"intelligence"* that they cannot even identify, but that can and will, they believe, solve their problems, if only it can be brought to realize that the problems exist.[14] Barnet, however, also sadly concludes that the mob's search is futile, because the kind of intelligence they need does not, "as yet," exist.[15]

With the onset of the war in 1958, soon after this episode, Wells shows once more the inadequacy of traditional thinking to avoid disaster. Paris is the first major city to fall beneath atomic bombs, even as a renowned French military strategist is making plans "upon the lines laid down by Napoleon and Moltke,"[16] and soon after the bombs destroy the dikes separating Holland from the sea.[17] Before long, the war has spread throughout the industrialized world; famine, cannibalism, plague, and revolution threaten survival. Within a year, nearly every country has lost several cities, the toll including Moscow, Tokyo, Chicago, Berlin, the east half of London, Toulon, Kiel, and 218 others;[18] those cities not destroyed physically have been destroyed economically.

In the midst of this devastation, Wells again demonstrates the incapacity of the ordinary mind, this time outside Paris, where Barnet encounters a "man-milliner" along the road. The man will not believe when Barnet tells him that Paris no longer exists and that it probably will not exist again for scores of years. " 'I am a costumier,' " the man insists. " 'All my connections and interests, above all my style, demand Paris.' "[19] The man is utterly unable to conceive of another way of life, and when Barnet tells him that all the cities are gone, he replies: " 'It is impossible. Civilisations do not end in this manner. Mankind will insist . . . [on] Paris.' "[20] Barnet finally leaves him standing in the rain, " 'gazing wistfully, yet it seemed to me a little doubtfully now, towards Paris.' "[21]

The ordinary people, unused to applying their minds, are stunned by crisis, as Wells shows in the preceding episodes. But from the devastation of the war he draws out another level of mind, one manifestation of the intelligence Barnet's marchers have been seeking. The designated leaders of the world, although horrified by what has occurred, are by no means incapacitated. In fact, they are inspired to unparalleled action and provide the ideological center of the novel. Two of them, key figures in the reconstruction, are representative of the group.

The first is the French ambassador to Washington, Leblanc, an "impassioned humanitarian" but not in fact a heroic figure; he is characterized as an "ingenuous" man who would surely have remained in virtual obscurity had it not been for this "sudden simplification of human affairs" brought about by the war.[22] As it is, convinced that further conflict must be prevented and that a single world government is the only means to achieve that end, he urges the heads of existing governments to action, and a year into the war, on June 4, 1959, he brings together ninety-three of the world's leaders for a literal summit meeting in the open air on an alpine meadow overlooking the Italian town of Brissago.[23]

The second representative leader is Egbert, "the young king of the most venerable kingdom in Europe,"[24] through whose eyes we see much of the early work of the Brissago conference. Egbert at first seems an odd choice for spokesman—an enthusiastic, somewhat comic young man who clearly does not know himself very well. The narrator wryly comments "In theory—and he abounded in theory—his manners were purely democratic,"[25] and yet he repeatedly shows by the subservience he takes as his due that he has not achieved his goal.

As the work of the conference progresses, however, and we see the effectiveness with which Egbert and Leblanc perform, we come to understand the point of Wells' contention: successful leadership does not require genius; it does require an active mind, imagination, recognition of the problem, and willingness to join with others of like mind in seeking solutions.[26]

Like Egbert and Leblanc, Wells notes, most of the other participants in the conference are men in the middle—not intellectual giants, but practical men of vision for whom the reconstruction of the disintegrating civilization takes top priority.[27] They agree almost at once that what is needed is a single world government where everyone will contribute without any thought of personal gain or advancement. Their first action, therefore, is to renounce their leadership of sovereign nations and proclaim a World State.[28] Their next action is to find and confiscate all the world's Carolinum (the radioactive element from which the bombs are made), along with all its production facilities.[29] For the most part this is a simple matter, since the presidents, kings, and prime ministers of most of the major powers are participating in the conference. When the king of a minor Balkan state refuses to comply with the leaders' demands and proposes to make himself "the new Caesar, the Master, Lord of the Earth"[30] by maintaining an atomic arsenal, Egbert, with an inspection force, tracks him down and executes him and his henchmen on the spot.[31] The scene is in fact a rather shocking one, since several of the men are trying to surrender at the time they are shot. Clearly, however, in having the conference leaders support such action, Wells is saying that the new World State is too important to allow this kind of rebel to survive, possibly to start new trouble.[32]

Through the subsequent work of the world governing council, Wells defines the kind of thought he finds crucial to a stable civilization. The council recognizes only two alternatives, a return to "agricultural barbarism . . . or the acceptance of *achieved science*" on a massive scale to develop a society in which humanity will never again wish to wage such a war.[33]

To accomplish the latter end, the council moves first to impose "social stability" by raising all to the same level of civilization and requiring their active participation. Virtually overnight, government and law are reduced to a minimum.[34] The new system will function not by politics and statutes but by the unified activity of a society whose members are all achieving their full potential.

Thus the narrator describes his own time, some years after the formation of the World State: "Every good thought contributes now, and every able brain falls within that informal and dispersed kingship which gathers together into one purpose the energies of the race."[35]

To liberate the minds of the country people, agriculture is reorganized into what are essentially collective farms. All members of the resultant "cultivating guilds" live in newly built, modern towns—since atom-power transportation is virtually cost-free—where they can have contact with books and ideas and avoid the isolation and stultification of rural and village life.[36] By the narrator's time, this reorganization is almost complete.[37]

Because the atomic bombs have turned the demolished cities into seething firepits, great numbers of people are homeless. Resettlement is therefore carried out by a redistribution committee which oversees the building and populating of new towns. Since the most desirable parts of the world, previously chosen for city building, are now no longer habitable, the committee must supervise expansion into the world's wastelands.[38]

To enhance communication and minimize points of controversy, numerous other changes are made. The council introduces a universal language, a greatly simplified form of English, which is firmly established worldwide by 1970.[39] The metric system is introduced,[40] and all the world's calendars are standardized.[41] A new monetary system based on energy units is initiated.[42] And concurrent with all this innovation, commercial and even religious divisions begin to disappear. According to the narrator, the devastation that displaced people from every other familiar aspect of their lives also altered their thinking and drove away such "lightly held beliefs and prejudices" as religious sectarianism,[43] so that they have learned tolerance and cooperation almost spontaneously.

Necessarily, the educational system is changed significantly. Under the guidance of the council's education committee, schools are built or rebuilt worldwide to teach about war in general and about this atomic war in particular, the common curriculum emphasizing "that the salvation of the world from waste and contention was the common duty and occupation of all men and women."[44] This salvation, as Marcus Karenin, a renowned member of the education committee, explains, is to be achieved by the complete abnegation of self.[45] How Karenin himself embodies this characteristic will be seen shortly.

These sweeping changes, designed to stabilize society, have an unexpected side effect, a phenomenon called "Efflorescence"—the flowering of the creative imagination.[46] It has already been noted that resettlement of the country dwellers in towns is intended in part to give farm people new access to intellectual stimulation. Efflorescence affects the entire population. Once released from the limitations of their traditional roles and provided with the things they need to survive, people begin to display an intense desire to create, particularly things of beauty. Indeed, by his time, the narrator says, in a world in which subsistence is no longer a problem, most people have become artists, applying their energies not to "necessities, but [to] their elaboration, decoration, and refinement."[47]

Thus the world council creates utopia out of chaos by imposing uniformity upon a stunned and willing humanity. The stabilizing intelligence that Barnet found so lacking in the prewar world has been forced out of dormancy by the threatened destruction of civilization, and the drive to find "external power" noted at the beginning of the book has been channeled into the application of atomic—and intellectual—power to social progress. In the process, the stultified minds of the masses have been stimulated to previously inconceivable activity.

Having begun his story of the atomic age with one figure of great intellectual power, Wells concludes with another. The first, the chemist Holsten, remains in shadow most of the time after he makes his initial impact on the world, although we do learn that he is a valued member of the Brissago conference and the world governing council. The second, education committee member Karenin, enunciates the social message of the book and therefore receives greater attention in the final chapter.

Wells presents Karenin primarily through a series of conversations held in a research hospital built in a newly settled region high in the Himalayas. Intellectually brilliant but congenitally crippled and frail, Karenin is awaiting vital surgery and so passes the time chatting with his companions about the world that has been born out of the ruins of the old civilization. Their conversation ranges through political history and the new respect accorded science to the changing role of the individual. Karenin exults in the opportunities only beginning to be realized by the new society, observing that the old had to be razed to allow the new to emerge.[48]

He shows the originality of his mind when he states a strong feminist position, seeing sexuality and sex-role stereotyping as a distraction from intellectual fulfillment[49] and admonishing the two women in the group to perceive themselves not as sexual beings, women among men, but as "intelligent beings" who are a part of the universe: " 'You have to cease to be our adventure . . . and come with us upon our adventures,' " he concludes.[50]

Knowing that he will probably die from his surgery, Karenin savors his reflections on the many ways in which the world is improving. Echoing Frederick Soddy, he foresees in humanity limitless capability for progress. He describes life as an endless series of beginnings through which the human mind will be able to realize magnificent achievements.[51] Hearing that genetic research presently being done may eventually eradicate the kind of physical limitation that is destroying him, he feels himself to be emerging from a sort of spiritual cocoon, " 'like a wet, crawling, new moth that still fears to spread its wings.' "[52] Throughout the evening, Karenin questions his companions, building upon their responses ever greater assurances that the human mind and spirit have only begun to discover their capabilities. By the time his guests are ready to leave, Karenin has begun to think of himself not as an individual facing death but as an ongoing part of a larger entity. The act of exchanging ideas—what he describes as " 'the test and winnowing of expression' "—has, he says, freed him from the confines of a single identity and united him with them all. He perceives his guests to be

" 'as much me as this hand that beats the arm of my chair. And as little me,' "
because for him all of them are a part and a manifestation of the immortal spirit
of human achievement.[53]

Thus Karenin, official proponent of the submersion of the individual into the
collective, finds his own peace in his certainty that, even though he ceases to
exist, the "common mind" of which he is a part—the "informal and dispersed
kingship" of which the narrator has already spoken[54]—will go on. And indeed,
although the surgery is successful, Karenin dies about a week later of a blood
clot brought on by his immobilization.[55]

Wells ends his novel optimistically even though his protagonist dies. He has
begun by recognizing the persistence of the speculative mind throughout human
history, at the outset showing it isolated from most of humanity. The isolation,
portrayed most vividly in Holsten, is, Wells argues, inevitable so long as most
minds are oppressed by the need merely to survive. Benumbed by such oppres-
sion, the common people are scarcely able to perceive what happens to them,
much less to respond effectively. But these people rely on their leaders—leaders
who are not, in the ordinary course of things, great thinkers themselves, but
practical, active people with a strong sense of public duty. Crisis, Wells contends,
forces the visionary potential of these people to emerge. Working together with
others of like mind, they can not only resolve the crisis but also revive the
deadened intellect of those they lead, if they are willing to take action drastic
enough and if the crisis has been terrible enough to jar their followers into
receptivity. And when such revivification of mind occurs, the intellectual is no
longer isolated but can take his or her place in humanity as a part of a common
mind far stronger and more self-assured than that of any single individual.

NOTES

1. H. G. Wells, *The World Set Free: A Story of Mankind* (New York: Dutton, 1914),
p. 11. Subsequent citations refer to this edition. Because of the frequent complexity of
distinguishing Wells himself from his primary narrator in this novel, for brevity's sake
I shall normally speak only of Wells himself. Portions of this chapter appear in "The
First Atomic War: H. G. Wells' *The World Set Free*," *Wisconsin Dialogue*, Spring 1985,
and are included here by permission.

2. Ibid., p. 15.

3. In a radio broadcast from Australia in 1939, Wells admitted the extravagance of
the utopian vision, contending that the "Utopian writer . . . is not a realist, no, but he is
serious. His 'If only—if only you would' is wistful" (H. G. Wells, "Utopias," ed.
Robert M. Philmus, *Science-Fiction Studies* 9 [July 1982], p. 118).

4. Wells, *The World Set Free*, pp. 33–39.

5. Ibid.

6. Frederick Soddy, *The Interpretation of Radium, Being the Substance of Six Free
Popular Experimental Lectures Delivered at the University of Glasgow, 1908* (London:
J. Murray, 1909), p. 253.

7. Ibid., p. 252.

8. Wells, *The World Set Free*, p. 44.

9. Ibid., pp. 44–45.

10. Ibid., p. 50.

11. Ibid., pp. 52–53.

12. Ibid., p. 56.

13. Ibid., pp. 78–79.

14. Ibid., pp. 79–80.

15. Ibid., p. 80.

16. Ibid., pp. 95, 100–106.

17. Ibid., pp. 131–32.

18. Ibid., p. 222.

19. Ibid., p. 218.

20. Ibid., pp. 224–25.

21. Ibid., p. 226.

22. Ibid., p. 150.

23. Ibid., pp. 171, 176.

24. Ibid., p. 156.

25. Ibid., p. 157.

26. Many years later, in his autobiography, Wells verifies this point, observing that history is not the creation of "Great Men," but that their greatness, such as it is, is a product of the times that spawn them. *Experiment in Autobiography: Discoveries and Conclusions of a Very Ordinary Brain (Since 1866)* (1934; reprint, Philadelphia: Lippincott, 1967), p. 554.

27. Wells, *The World Set Free*, pp. 214–16.

28. Ibid., p. 173. For a comprehensive examination of the complex components of Wells' world state, see W. Warren Wagar, *H. G. Wells and the World State* (1961; reprint, Freeport, N.Y.: Books for Libraries Press, 1971).

29. Ibid., p. 173ff.

30. Ibid., p. 191.

31. Ibid., pp. 206–7.

32. In *Autobiography*, Wells supports this inference in speaking of his disillusionment with World War I: "the only way to universal peace is through the defeat and obliteration of every minor organization of force" (p. 579).

33. Wells, *The World Set Free*, pp. 210–11.

34. Ibid., pp. 244–48.

35. Ibid., p. 248. In *Autobiography*, Wells states, "[I]n 1900 I had already grasped the inevitability of a World State and the complete insufficiency of the current parliamentary methods of democratic government" (p. 556), a conviction which helps account for the remarkably abrupt eradication of all existing forms of law and government here.

36. Wells, *The World Set Free*, pp. 234–35.

37. Ibid., p. 236.

38. Ibid., pp. 240–42.

39. Ibid., pp. 236–37.

40. Ibid., p. 237.

41. Ibid., p. 238.

42. Ibid., pp. 238–39.

43. Ibid., p. 254.

44. Ibid., pp. 256–57.

45. Ibid., pp. 258–59.
46. Ibid., p. 249.
47. Ibid., pp. 249–50.
48. Ibid., pp. 277–78.
49. Ibid., pp. 289–99.
50. Ibid., p. 299.
51. Ibid., p. 288.
52. Ibid., pp. 302–3.
53. Ibid., pp. 305–6.
54. Ibid., p. 248.
55. Ibid., p. 308.

7

WEINBAUM'S FIRE FROM THE ASHES: THE POSTDISASTER CIVILIZATION OF *THE BLACK FLAME*

Edgar L. Chapman

1.

Stanley Weinbaum achieved the status of a legendary figure in science fiction histories and folklore largely because of the promise displayed in "A Martian Odyssey" (1934) and some other short stories and because of the poignancy of his early death. Isaac Asimov expresses this conventional view in his introduction to *The Best of Stanley G. Weinbaum* (1974),[1] ranking him with E. E. "Doc" Smith and Robert Heinlein as innovators who had stunning impact on the field of pulp science fiction. He bases Weinbaum's case largely on two premises: he was the first writer to treat aliens sympathetically, and he had a major influence on the young Asimov.[2] The second of these is obviously beyond dispute; the first, though a critical commonplace by now, seems to be equally well-grounded. C. S. Lewis, for instance, contended that his *Out of the Silent Planet* (1938) began to reverse a trend as old as Wells when it presented Martians who were different from humans.[3] But Lewis published his novel four years after "A Martian Odyssey" appeared with its lovable alien named Tweel, and it is possible that Lewis had read Weinbaum's story, since he often confessed to reading American science fiction in the 1930s in his spare time.[4] Whatever the truth about this may be, James Gunn presents much the same view as Asimov in a brief introduction to "A Martian Odyssey" in his important anthology *The Road to Science Fiction: 2*.[5] Despite this, Weinbaum's work has not been viewed very clearly in other respects, both in its strengths and its defects, and I suspect that Weinbaum remains a misunderstood author.

No doubt Weinbaum's death at the age of thirty-three, after a beginning which displayed a certain originality of vision, will always make him a fascinating figure. It is an enjoyable game to speculate about what he might have written had he lived as long as John W. Campbell or Robert Heinlein, but this sort of thing is rather pointless, just as it is in the case of C. M. Kornbuth. Weinbaum's career has been viewed all too readily through the lenses of a familiar myth: that of the boy genius or prodigy stricken before he could flower. While there may be some truth in this, it is also a very romanticized picture. Weinbaum was scarcely a great verbal artist who would have revolutionized literature, a Keats for instance, and probably even his influence on science fiction would never have equaled that of Campbell, Heinlein, or Asimov.

Some of the published comments about Weinbaum support the romantic mythology. He was, for instance, a chemical engineer who apparently liked the romantic possibilities of science, but he avoided the daily drudgery associated with such a job. Moreover, he liked popular literature. He is known to have written conventional romances for newspapers, and one of these at least was published.[6] He also managed a string of movie theaters and not only was attracted to the cinema but probably was influenced by the romanticism of certain films.[7] In what seems to me the most helpful essay on Weinbaum I have read, Robert Bloch comments that Weinbaum was able "only in his longer works" to draw "full-scale portraits of romanticized human beings."[8] Bloch also provides some other useful information. Weinbaum, for instance, was attracted to Farnsworth Wright's gothicism in *Weird Tales;* he enjoyed James Branch Cabell's urbane and satirical fantasy; and since he was attracted to the legend of Faustina, possibly because of Swinburne's poem, he planned a novel on the theme.[9] This latter fact should not surprise readers of *The Black Flame.* One conclusion drawn from these revelations and from a reading of Weinbaum's longer works is that he was a romantic of a special kind: he was attracted to Byronic or even Nietzschean attitudes. He may have had a weakness for gothicism, he was probably susceptible to the more juvenile kinds of romantic excess and wickedness of the kind associated with the neopaganism of Swinburne, and judging from the plots of two projected and never written novels he outlined for Bloch, he was strongly interested in sexuality. Finally it is clear that Weinbaum, given his work at a regular job, his productivity in his short career, and the number of posthumous stories later printed, was not only an ambitious writer but a driven one.

A close look at his longer works reveals his obsessions as well as the larger-than-life characterizations to which Bloch refers. *The New Adam* (1939), a full-length novel, is a somewhat bitter tale about the maturation of an alienated and unappreciated genius, a kind of Nietzschean superman who scorns society and conventional success. Not only does a watered down understanding of Nietzsche appear to be present, the influence of Olaf Stapledon appears as well.[10] But these influences are not very significant in the end because the novel, while sporadically interesting, is ultimately tiresome. The hero is not very likable, and the style is pretentious and seems to rely on a forced rhetoric. The theme is worth exploring, but A. E. van Vogt's treatments of it at least have the virtue of some lively action sequences.[11]

When we examine the stories usually printed together as *The Black Flame,* we find something different: we come to the heart of Weinbaum's vision. Both stories were published posthumously—"Dawn of Flame" in *Thrilling Wonder Stories* in June 1939, and "The Black Flame" in *Startling Stories* in January 1939; not until 1948 were they together as a novel, and it is hard to see them as such, although combining them in a single volume as chapters in a future history is acceptable enough.[12] Together they build the portrait of a future world, though taking place several hundred years apart. They also have some common characters because three of the main figures in the stories are "immortal," thanks to a longevity treatment. Nevertheless, the two stories function as prelude and full-scale statement of a theme rather than as a unified whole.

In terms of their literary worth, they have debatable value, although they have at least two memorable characters. But they are important because of their imaginative extrapolation of a postdisaster civilization and because of their significance for understanding and evaluating Weinbaum's contribution to the genre.

2.

When we examine the postdisaster world created in the stories, two distinct pictures emerge. In "Dawn of Flame," we find a technologically advanced society, recently emerged from the savagery of a new dark age, whose technology is largely controlled by a single genius who is in the ruling elite. In "The Black Flame," we find a utopian world established by a benign but coldly rational emperor who, like Napoleon, was once a "man on horseback" and who uses a scientific elite to maintain his power. "Dawn of Flame" shows the emergence of Joaquin Smith, Weinbaum's "man of destiny," as he extends his conquests. "The Black Flame" pictures Smith's rule over the entire world about seven hundred years later. Both stories also deal with the loves of Margaret, Smith's half sister and the "black flame" of the title. She is a fascinating character, a darkly ambiguous woman. She is an archetype of romantic eroticism, the "fatal woman" or "diamonic female" of romantic tradition. But if the stories are read carefully, the figure of Joaquin Smith, "the Master" of this new civilization, looms just as large as his sister's.[13]

In "Dawn of Flame," Smith rules a small empire around New Orleans but is in the process of enlarging his territory. According to the oral tradition— provided mainly by "Old Einar," who turns out to be one of his former allies— Smith was originally an adventurer who came out of Mexico, along with his half sister, Margaret, who has Spanish or Mexican blood. Although he is a natural leader, his power began to wax after his meeting with Martin Sair, a scientific genius, and another figure named Olin (who turns out to be "Old Einar," the keeper of folk legend). Not only has Sair developed weapons that make Smith's professional army invincible, he has administered an immortality treatment to himself, Smith, and Margaret. Since the aging process has been arrested for Smith and he is immortal—unless killed by a bullet—he has a luxury denied to Napolean and other conquerors: he has "world enough and time" to extend his rule over the entire globe.

"Dawn of Flame" takes place about three hundred years after a devastating war struck civilization in the middle of the twentieth century. According to Weinbaum's characters, competing nationalisms were responsible for it.[14] Nuclear weapons are mentioned, but it is hinted that biological warfare may have been the most destructive force. (Weinbaum is somewhat vague about this.) Nonetheless the effect of the war is clear: governments collapsed, barbarism ensued, books were destroyed, and a new dark age followed. The "Dark Years" last only about two centuries, however, and are followed by a new "enlightenment"—generated mainly by Martin Sair's revival of science rather than by some new philosophy.

Though a "dark age" of only two hundred years may seem optimistic to today's readers, the world of "Dawn of Flame" is far below the technological level of our time. Rather, it is a pastoral and neomedieval world of small towns and leagues dominated by city-states, much like Greece on the eve of Alexander's rise, and it is ripe for Joaquin Smith's war of conquest. Smith has already conquered the rural confederation of "Ozarky" and is marching on the "Selui" league, which appears to dominate the Mississippi Valley. We first see him when he and Margaret arrive on horseback (a symbolic image, one suspects) at the head of their army of professionals at Ormiston, a village (apparently) in the Missouri River Valley. Despite the best efforts of the hero, Hull Tarvish, an Ozark mountaineer, his sweetheart Vail, and the men of Ormiston, Smith easily overcomes the town and sweeps on irresistibly toward Selui.

Selui and its confederation are supposed to form a strong city-state, although its domination ends somewhere near Bloom'ton (the old Bloomington, Illinois), thanks to a disastrous defeat at the hands of an army from Chicago at Starved Rock. (Here Weinbaum, a resident for much of his life in Milwaukee, shows his own sympathies, as well as his knowledge of regional history: legend has it that one Indian tribe inflicted a crushing defeat on another at Starved Rock, a rocky eminence overlooking the Illinois River near LaSalle.) But since the city-states are constantly at war with each other, they deserve to be conquered, according to Smith, a man who dreams of establishing a peaceful and centralized world order.

Smith's easy conquest of Ormiston is achieved by using advanced technology, organized professionals, and enlightened despotism. His "Erden detonators" destroy the metal weapons of his adversaries and permit a virtually bloodless battle. He harms no one except the local "eldarch," or mayor, whose property he confiscates. His typical pattern when encountering a conspiracy is to execute the leader or leaders but pardon the rest. Such firm and ruthless but rational and pragmatic methods make it easy for defeated citizens to accept his rule. In his genius for replacing local rivalries and antagonisms with a strongly centralized rule, one suspects that Weinbaum is showing a covert admiration for the strong federalism of Franklin D. Roosevelt's New Deal policies, although this point should not be pressed too far.

"The Black Flame," the novelette to which "Dawn of Flame" is merely a prelude, is set seven hundred years later—over a thousand years from the middle of the twentieth century. Joaquin Smith has now completed his conquest of the world and rules as absolute dictator from Urbs, his capital city. His sister, Margaret, is still the capricious "black flame" who has taken many mortal lovers, and Martin Sair still provides scientific support for him. Now, however, others who have achieved genius distinction in science or other intellectual pursuits are also rewarded with the gift of immortality, though the majority of people live only the usual life span of mortals.

In "The Black Flame," Thomas Connor, an engineer from St. Louis, awakes after sleeping a thousand years and gradually begins to discover the wonders of Smith's brave new world. Connor had been electrocuted for killing his unfaithful fiancée's lover but the act had been in a fit of rage and, given the circumstances, the punishment seems excessive. By a freak accident, the electric shock does not kill him, it merely freezes him for a millennium. Connor recuperates in the bucolic world around the village of Ormon (which the reader infers is the former Ormiston), is nursed by a gentle local girl named Evanie, and meets a mysterious woman in the forest with whom he falls in love. The reader of "Dawn of Flame" realizes immediately that the forest goddess is Margaret, the "black flame," enjoying a pastoral retreat from public affairs at the palace, but Connor does not learn this until later.

After the mysterious lady vanishes, Connor becomes involved in an abortive revolutionary conspiracy with Evanie and her friend, Jan Orm. The three journey to distant Urbs, try to overthrow Joaquin Smith, and are defeated. Connor and Evanie flee but are forced to return by Smith's electronic "messengers." Smith condemns Connor to death, but Margaret intercedes for him temporarily. Connor stays in the palace for a while, and a stormy romance develops. Eventually, Smith decides that Connor is a man of talent and offers him immortality in exchange for his knowledge of ancient mathematics, especially calculus and logarithms. (Why no high school or college mathematics texts containing this information have survived, or how the marvels of Smith's civilization could have been built without higher mathematics is hard to explain!)

An "atomic bomb," or fission bomb, explodes in the palace, though it is not a very effective one, and Margaret uses the ensuing fire to get herself killed; she believes her love for Connor is unrequited, not realizing that though he loves her he does not trust her. After she is revived by Martin Sair's medical wizardry, she and Connor pledge mutual love. It is agreed that the immortality process will be reversed long enough for her to bear children, and it appears that she and Connor will live happily ever after as immortals in Joaquin Smith's beneficent empire.

I will comment later on the merits of this plot; for now it is sufficient to note that the story provides ample opportunity for Weinbaum to describe the government and society of which Joaquin Smith is the architect and absolute dictator. Smith, called simply the Master, has taken as his symbol the Midgard Serpent of Norse legend, which represents his sway over the entire world. He rules this empire from a towering palace in Urbs, a city of thirty million in the Hudson Valley. (It is not, apparently, a revived New York, for that city is mentioned as a separate metropolis whose location is suggested by the fact that one of its suburbs is Kaatskill.) Smith maintains control over the more or less sophisticated citizenry by the clever use of advanced technology. For instance, nearly every citizen is monitored by television, an idea that anticipates Orwell's future but antedates *1984* by over a decade.[15] His guards are armed with ion beamers that suggest the electronic guns used in the *Star Trek* series and some recent films. His electronic "messengers" are capable of hunting down a fugitive and harassing him into returning to Urbs, as they do to Connor and Evanie. (It should be noted that there are devices of a similar nature in the early Jack Williamson.)[16]

Smith's control of the best scientific talent is assured by rewarding scientific advances with immortality, as well as by the difficulty of mounting a successful revolt. Apparently, the populace acquiesces in this policy, though in truth it would probably create enormous social unrest. To be sure, there are numerous revolts against Smith's rule, like the one Connor participates in, but the reason given for this is more general boredom than a sense of social injustice. Smith defends his policy on immortality by contending, with some logic, that immortality for all would cause a terrible overpopulation problem. On the other hand, he insists that humanity is destined for a glorious future if only he can guide it in the right direction.

Mature reflection suggests that Weinbaum is an elitist who not only would find it easy to accept the rule of a strong leader like Smith but would, like his hero, Thomas Connor, give such a regime his strong support if it would only recognize his own genius. It would appear that Smith does not consider the majority of the world's people to be worthy of immortality, and I suspect that Weinbaum might well have agreed with him.

At any rate, the average citizen is a rather passive individual under Smith's regime. Though he has taken some pains to employ sterilization and selective breeding to eliminate criminality, stupidity, and insanity, Smith acknowledges that daring and originality also seem to have been reduced by his efforts. Indeed, the people of Ormon with whom Connor first lives after awakening seem so passive that the reader is inevitably reminded of H. G. Wells' Eloi in *The Time Machine* (just as Connor's awakening may suggest Wells' *When the Sleeper Wakes*).[17] But Evanie and Jan Orm do have the energy to plan a revolution, and Evanie proves to be more dangerous than she looks, for not only does she experience the usual feminine jealously of Margaret but she plants the bomb that explodes in the palace.

Although Weinbaum envisions many technological innovations, including a rocket plane that Margaret flies beyond the earth's atmosphere, and although he actually seems to grasp the principle of a fission bomb, he has little idea of the effects of some of these things. For example, the plane would require a number of oxygen and other life-support devices that he does not provide, and an atomic bomb of any strength would surely have destroyed the entire palace, rather than merely incinerating the throne room. Of the radiation effects of atomic explosions he seems entirely ignorant, although his future world does contain two types of mutants which the reader at first assumes to have been created by radiation: amphimorphs, or aquatic humans, and metamorphs, or forest mutants. These species are treated sympathetically by Weinbaum, as we might expect remembering his characterization of Tweel, but they are definitely relegated to second-class status in the empire. A final defect is the absence of computers, unless the "messengers" qualify.

Weinbaum's postdisaster world is interesting and sufficiently imagined for us to forgive some oversights or mistaken extrapolations, although as we have noted, it is scarcely credible that it could have been developed without the knowledge of higher mathematics that Connor possesses. But there is one amusing social trend that Weinbaum anticipates, though he may have been inspired by wishful thinking.[18] He clearly likes short skirts, one of the symbols of the social liberation of the 1920s. Except on formal occasions, Margaret wears skirts that come to the knee or stop above it, and the women of Urbs are said to follow this fashion. Even in "Dawn of Flame," Vail Ormiston, the secondary heroine, a shy village girl who wears full-length dresses, suffers the indignity of having her gown burned off to the knees by an explosion. No doubt some feminists would disapprove of such social views, but Weinbaum would probably have enjoyed the 1960s vogue of the miniskirt.

Finally, it should be noted that in Joaquin Smith's world there is virtually no religion and, as Margaret complains, no very worthwhile art or literature. Weinbaum may have found the first condition desirable, but the second is clearly associated with the lack of initiative in a world dominated by a dictator and a small elite. Perhaps he intended to suggest that the peace and stability of such a society inevitably have their costs.

3.

A look at the stories as literature finds that, despite Weinbaum's considerable imagination, they are flawed. Though his narratives are well told and dramatically presented,[19] his style is often immature, his characterizations are overly romantic and theatrical, and his plots are heavily melodramatic. In this respect, of course, there is no difference in kind from most of the fiction written by his contemporaries; whatever differences are present are differences of degree.

In terms of style, for instance, Weinbaum insists maddeningly on his "black flame" image for Margaret, and he tends to wear us out with lurid references to her in terms of poison and demonism. Margaret is a "devil," a "sorceress," a "daughter of Satan," and so on. At one point, he implies that she is related to François Villon's "Black Margot," a prostitute the poet apparently loved.[20] He also exasperates the reader by repeatedly describing some aspect of Margaret's body—usually her feet—as "dainty," a sentimental adjective that contradicts the tone he habitually tries to establish.[21]

Weinbaum's characterizations can be equally as annoying as his style, although it should be conceded immediately that Joaquin Smith and Margaret are cut from the mold of romantic titans and that they are easily two of the more memorable creations in early science fiction. Smith is a surprisingly effective character, as some of my comments have already suggested: driven by dreams of personal destiny and the destiny of the species, he is a strong, rational, and pragmatic ruler, nearly always in control, and far above pettiness or malice. He comes far closer than the protagonist of *The New Adam* to defining Weinbaum's ideal of the superman or elitist hero, and he seems far superior to the supposed heroes that Weinbaum often puts at the center of his stage (like Hull Tarvish and Thomas Connor).

Similarly, Margaret is also memorable, although even Weinbaum seems somewhat ambivalent about her. She is depicted as a sultry temptress, who easily outshines such pallid ingenue heroines as Vail Ormiston and Evanie. She differs from the usual heroine of 1930s science fiction by having a good deal of sexual experience and by being a warrior who has both killed and ordered the deaths of many men. We do not, however, actually see her doing the latter; rather, she always seems to be granting clemency to some foolish character who has tried to assassinate her or interceding with Smith for someone's life. As for her sexual experience, as she argues in her own defense, a woman goes through several mortal lovers in eight centuries or so; thus her lack of innocence does not appear quite as reprehensible as some of the other characters, especially the female ones, like to think. (Margaret's real problem may be that she is in love with her half brother, Smith, and no man around is strong enough to stand up to him until Connor appears.) Moreover, her immortality not only produces boredom but deprives her of the chance to bear children, until Weinbaum fortuitously produces a reversal of this situation in his happy ending. Even though modeled after the fatal woman of romantic tradition, Margaret represents a lively improvement over the cardboard heroines and coquettes that appear in the science fiction of E. E. "Doc" Smith and other 1930s writers, despite her annoying aspects. She is depicted, for instance, as smoking black cigarettes, a notion that seems unbelievably silly today. Her love of theatrical gestures often becomes tiresome, as when she arranges competition, so that her beauty can be seen as superior to another woman's, or when she responds to boredom by attempting some daredevil stunt or by threatening suicide. At such times she seems all too much like the stereotypic bored, rich girl of the 1930s films that Weinbaum is reputed to have enjoyed.

Despite her excesses, however, she, like Joaquin Smith, evinces Weinbaum's originality. One must go back to Edgar Rice Burrough's Dejah Thoris to find a heroine in science fiction with anything like Margaret's vitality, and Dejah Thoris is a much shallower character.

Where Weinbaum's fiction is weakest, however, is in the plot action and the characters who support his "black flame." In "Dawn of Flame," Hull Tarvish, though a likable fellow, is finally only a simple mountain lad, viewed somewhat patronizingly by both Margaret and Weinbaum. And the sentimental heroine, Vail, is an insipid ingenue who serves as Margaret's foil. Her jealousy of Margaret seems rather petty and ignoble. Despite these faults, the story is entertaining and inoffensive.

"The Black Flame," on the other hand, is much more melodramatic, and its plot is frequently annoying. Thomas Connor is a rather Byronic and unsympathetic fellow, and his love/hate relationship with Margaret is a bit trying, especially when he seems fanatically determined not to reveal his feelings to her lest he be mocked or ridiculed. No doubt this love story seemed torrid to readers in the late 1930s. As a matter of fact, I recall thinking it quite exciting when I read it as a college freshman in the early 1950s. But, ironically, the courtship romances that one generation finds exciting seem rather puerile to another. The theme of "The Black Flame" is the familiar "taming of the shrew," but today's readers are likely to find it quite tame itself. (No doubt editorial inhibitions about sex have reduced the impact of the story; today Weinbaum might have told the tale much more explicitly.)

If Weinbaum's fiction in these stories seems in many respects flawed and dated, it nevertheless has certain enduring virtues. His portrait of a postdisaster world of peace and stability, under the benevolent despotism of Joaquin Smith, is quite fascinating.[22] In addition, his characterizations of Smith and Margaret, while overly romantic and often trying, are vital and memorable. Perhaps he should be remembered for creating three innovative characters: Tweel, Joaquin Smith, and Princess Margaret. If his major characters in *The Black Flame* fully express this, the conflict between Margaret and Connor displays his fascination with romantic love and the "daimonic woman," and his portrait of Joaquin Smith reveals his obsession with the romantic cult of Napoleonic individualism. If the evidence of *The Black Flame* is of any value, then Weinbaum should be remembered as a misunderstood romantic.

NOTES

1. Isaac Asimov, "Introduction," in Stanley G. Weinbaum, *The Best of Stanley G. Weinbaum* (New York: Ballantine Books, 1974), pp. vii-xii. This book also contains an "Afterword" by Robert Block, pp. 300–306.

2. Ibid., pp. ix-x.

3. C. S. Lewis in "Unreal Estates," a dialogue with Brian Aldiss and Kingsley Amis, recorded at Magdalene College, Oxford, U.K., 1963. This dialogue first appeared in *SF Horizon,* 1964, and has been reprinted in *Spectrum 4,* ed. Kingsley Amis and

Robert Conquest (New York: Berkley, 1966; New York: Harcourt, Brace, 1965). The dialogue is more accessible today in C.S. Lewis, *Of Other Worlds: Essays and Stories,* ed. Walter Hooper (New York: Harcourt, Brace, 1966), pp. 86–96. The specific comment about changing our attitudes toward aliens is on pp. 90–91, although there are also specific comments about it in Lewis' novel *Out of the Silent Planet.*

4. Speculation on influences is often pointless, but Lewis' interest in science fiction in the 1920s and 1930s is established in several places. See, for instance, "On Science Fiction," in *Of Other Worlds,* pp. 59–73.

5. James Gunn, ed., *The Road to Science Fiction: 2* (New York: New American Library, 1979), pp. 236–38. Gunn's point of view is also expressed in Isaac Asimov, *The Foundations of Science Fiction* (New York: Oxford University Press, 1982), p. 29, where he attributes stylistic excellence and realistic characterization to Weinbaum and considers such traits handicaps to his success. To some extent, my essay disputes Gunn's view of Weinbaum, at least in *The Black Flame.*

6. Ibid., p. 237.

7. Ibid.

8. Robert Bloch, "Stanley G. Weinbaum: A Personal Recollection," in Stanley G. Weinbaum, *The Best of Stanley G. Weinbaum,* pp. 300–306. The quotation is from p. 302. Bloch also provides evidence of Weinbaum's deep interest in films. Of course, his operation of movie theaters is in itself indicative of more than a passing interest with the movies, although the fact is not sufficient to establish him as a discerning critic.

The best critical analysis of Weinbaum, in my opinion, is that of Brian Stableford, in E. F. Bleiler, *Science Fiction Writers: Critical Studies of the Major Authors from the Early Nineteenth Century to the Present Day* (New York: Scribner, 1982), pp. 145–49. Even so, this essay is very cursory in discussing the stories in *The Black Flame* and not specific about Weinbaum's indebtedness to the darker side of romanticism; Stableford's notion that *The New Adam* is Weinbaum's "best work" might be difficult to defend. Other critical essays on Weinbaum, including Stableford's brief comments in Peter Nicholl, *The Science Fiction Encyclopedia* (Garden City, N.Y.: Doubleday Dolphin, 1979), p. 646, take a more conventional line. Robert Scholes and Eric Rabkin in *Science Fiction: History, Science, Vision* (New York: Oxford University Press, 1977), pp. 40–41, are perceptive but tend to consolidate the image of Weinbaum as an early science fiction realist. Neither Stableford nor Scholes and Rabkin give much recognition to the more romantic inclinations of Weinbaum's work.

9. Ibid., pp. 303–5.

10. Influences are, as I have already suggested, often difficult to trace, and Stapledon's *Odd John* may not have appeared in America until 1936, the year after Weinbaum's death, but earlier Stapledon novels like *Last and First Men* (1930) might have influenced both *The New Adam* and *The Black Flame.* More information is needed about Weinbaum's early reading and about his interests during the period when he was composing his longer stories and novels.

11. I refer of course to *Slan* (1940) and *The World of Null-A* (1945).

12. Stanley G. Weinbaum, *The Black Flame* (New York: Avon, 1969). This reprint is the first mass market, paperback edition. Subsequent quotations and references are from this edition. The first hardcover version was published by Fantasy Press in New York in 1948. It is worth mentioning that both "Dawn of Flame" and "The Black

Flame'' were frequently reprinted in various pulps during the 1940s and 1950s. I recall reading them in this format in 1954, but where seems beyond recall.

13. The ''fatal'' or ''demonic'' or ''daimonic'' woman is a staple of romantic characterization, dating at least from the appearance of Keats' ''La Belle Dame sans Merci,'' or Coleridge's Geraldine in ''Christabel.'' Mario Praz discusses this aspect of romanticism in his classic study *The Romantic Agony* (New York: Oxford University Press, 1933; 2d ed., 1951; reprinted, New York: Meridian Books, 1956). Chapter Four, ''La Belle Dame sans Merci,'' pp. 187–286, treats the many incarnations of the ''daimonic'' woman.

14. Weinbaum, *The Black Flame*, pp. 19–21.

15. The idea of electronic scanners occurs more than once in 1940s science fiction, so Orwell, if he had read any pulp science fiction, may well have been indebted to sources other than Weinbaum. Weinbaum's use of television monitors, however, is their earliest use in science fiction that I know of.

16. In Williamson's early and immature novel *The Green Girl* (1929), the metal tyrant—a sentient monster perhaps inspired by his reading of A. Merritt—uses metallic bars to control his slaves, but these are strapped on the backs of his victims rather than sent flying through the air. In Weinbaum's story, Smith's ''messengers'' attach themselves to the neck or head and reduce the victim to impotent slavery.

Similar devices appear in some of the stories collected in Jack Williamson, *The Early Williamson* (Garden City, N.Y.: Doubleday, 1975); notably, for instance, ''Doom from Planet 4'' has a device that seeks out its target by remote control, but instead of forcing its victim to march back to headquarters it simply blows him up. *The Face in the Abyss* (1931), one of A. Merritt's worst novels (Merritt was one of Williamson's favorite authors and also possibly influenced Weinbaum), uses a somewhat different device that enables the ruler of a hidden country in the Andes to enslave ordinary people, including Merritt's slow-witted hero, Nicholas Graydon.

17. Connor is first mistaken for a ''sleeper'' by the citizens of Ormon; we are told that ''sleepers'' were people who chose to be put to sleep for centuries by electronic shock. Risking the chance of never awakening against the chance that their investments would grow, ''Sleepers'' who survived would awaken wealthy. As for the influence of Wells, it appears to be rather strong at the opening of ''The Black Flame,'' but it is not a very profound influence on the story as a whole or on Weinbaum in general, I think.

18. Of course, in a sense, Weinbaum was merely echoing the rebellious spirit of the 1920s. Moreover, science fiction of the 1920s and 1930s abounds in ladies with abbreviated skirts, as the illustrations collected in various nostalgic anthologies and histories of the genre reveal.

19. Asimov says Weinbaum was not a ''born writer,'' Asimov, p. ix. Bloch, however, says that Weinbaum not only told his stories well in writing, but that he ''told his stories almost as well in person.'' See Bloch, p. 302. Bloch's view seems closer to the truth, in my opinion.

20. Weinbaum, *The Black Flame*, p. 57. Margaret herself explains that a poet who once loved her and knew Villon's work gave her the name. The references to poison, Satanism, and ''daughter of hell'' are so frequent throughout both stories as to require no documentation. Not only Vail Ormiston but even Hull Tarvish and Thomas Connor apply such epithets to Margaret, not to mention Evanie and Jan Orm.

21. Ibid., p. 54. We even find the description of her eyebrows as ''dainty.'' Clearly

new status quo, and rumors persist that a secret hideaway exists out west where the old ways and knowledge are preserved. The stories about this place, Bartorstown, impel two adolescent boys, cousins Len and Esau Colter, to run away from their home in northeastern Ohio to find this technological El Dorado. Their odyssey takes them first to the Ohio River town of Refuge, where they settle for a short time. There they encounter a man named Hostetter, whom they had known in their hometown of Piper's Run. They suspect (and rightly so) that he is in some way connected with Bartorstown. Eventually, Len and Esau get caught up in the various conflicts of Refuge and are forced to leave along with Hostetter and Esau's bride, Amit Taylor.

During their journey west, Hostetter tells the boys about Bartorstown and warns them that it might not live up to their expectations. He also makes it clear that when they reach their destination there is absolutely no going back. Finally, the trek ends at the small mining town of Fall Creek, which is the cover for Bartorstown. Esau and Len are then taken into the mountain refuge where the real Bartorstown is hidden. There, they find an atomic power plant complete with posters of the victims of nuclear warfare. They also see the most complex computer ever built, with the incongruous name of Clementine. The computer's main function is to find a defense system that can "control the interaction of nuclear particles on their own level so that no process of either fission or fusion [can] take place whenever that force field [is] in operation."[2] Joan Wepplo, who becomes Len's wife, tells him about the so-called Solution Zero—which is a proof that the mathematical solution Clementine's operators are looking for does not exist. Without the defense system, atomic power may never be revived. The entire community knows about Solution Zero, but the topic is never, ever discussed. Joan, who is disillusioned with Bartorstown because of Solution Zero, wants to escape from there. She talks Len into leaving with her, and together they begin the long journey back east to Piper's Run. But their freedom is short-lived when Hostetter and his men catch up with and return them to Fall Creek. Len becomes resigned to the fact that it is better to "try and chain the devil up than to try keeping the whole land tied up in the hopes he won't notice it again."[3]

One of the major themes of *The Long Tomorrow* is the battle between science and its opponents (here in the guise of religious fundamentalism), and although this book is set in earth's near future, it is really universal. It is also clearly an analogy for the various times in history when new ideas that ran counter to accepted orthodoxes were condemned as being "evil" or "immoral." There have always been doomsayers who decried revolutionary theories as being "against God's will." As an avid student of history, Leigh Brackett knew this, and whether or not she intended it, it comes through in the story. There are, for example, those who would kill to prevent any hint of the old knowledge from becoming widely known and accepted again. Some of their arguments sound suspiciously like those of earlier eras which spoke out against such ideas as the sun-centered universe, the possibility of space flight, and Darwin's theory of evolution. One of the best examples of this comes early in the book at a revival meeting in Piper's Run. The preacher rails against the "wickedness and blas-phemies" of the atomic era, where the people "went a-whoring after strange gods."[4] During the course of the meeting, William Soames, a trader suspected of expounding the glories of the past, is murdered by the stirred-up mob—the idea being that if the person is killed, the beliefs will mercifully remain hidden.[5] This is not new. Even now there are those who feel that burning books will do away with ideas they find unsettling.

Which side Brackett supports, however, is clearly evident. Those who oppose any talk of Bartorstown or the old ways are characterized as being narrow-minded and intractable. Yet the heroes, Len and Esau, who are curious about the past which they know only from their grandmother's stories about the pre-Destruction world, steal old books and hide them in a tree even though they know that if they are caught they will be punished for more than petty theft. Len's father discourages any talk of the past and of Bartorstown, which he maintains is only "folklore." Finally, the boys must leave Piper's Run when they are discovered with a radio which Esau "copped" from Soames' wagon. Later, Len and Esau flee Refuge when an angry mob burns Mike Dulinsky's warehouse because it believes that he wants to revive the cities. The boys, who work for Dulinsky, try to defend him, but despite their efforts he is murdered. The mob accuses Len and Esau of being from Bartorstown and wants to kill them too, but they are saved by Hostetter and a ready getaway boat. In the author's eyes, those who would suppress the truth are dangerous fanatics—far more dangerous than those who might upset the status quo with their passion for knowledge.

This is not to say that Brackett views the Bartorstown people as being faultless, holy, or all-wise. Hostetter even admits that he and his people are also fanatics. They are as dedicated to preserving the past knowledge as their opponents are to obliterating it. They have no qualms about silencing anyone they feel may be a danger to them. This is why once a person learns the secrets of Bartorstown, he or she can never leave. Neither Len nor Esau is trusted because it is feared that they will reveal the location of Bartorstown if they return home. Such a revelation would end the community and Clementine because the Establishment could not tolerate their survival. Nonetheless, Brackett's sympathies are with the Colter boys, Hostetter, and Bartorstown. They are like Diogenes with lantern in hand searching for the truth.

What is interesting about *The Long Tomorrow* is that those who are trying to suppress the past and any knowledge of it are religious zealots. Brackett herself was very uncomfortable with any kind of organized religion. She was reared High Church Episcopal, although her mother ignored those portions of Holy Writ she disagreed with and always exchanged heated words with clergymen over their sermons. Brackett stated that as a child she had a difficult time reconciling the attitudes in Bible stories with the exact opposite ones expounded in non-Bible stories. Later on, she read a good deal of mythology and comparative religion which further served to confuse her. The more things were explained to her, the more she doubted the explanations. The upshot of all this was that Brackett decided that she would never *really* know the truth until she got to the "Great Beyond," and added, "I came to clearly understand why Adam was forbidden the fruit of the Tree of Knowledge."[6] Her study of history led her to detest organized religion, and this undoubtedly generated her attitude toward the zealots in the novel.

Though Brackett always stated that she did not write *The Long Tomorrow* to propound her religious beliefs, it is clear from the story that she greatly admired the Amish way of life. A native Californian, she did not have contact with the Amish until the 1950s when she and her husband, science fiction author Edmond Hamilton, bought and restored an 1830s farmhouse. Hamilton was a native of Youngstown, Ohio, and, at the time, his family resided in the area. The house was in Kinsman, which is about forty miles north of Youngstown. There are many Amish in northeastern Ohio and western Pennsylvania, and Brackett became fascinated with their ability to function without the accoutrements of modern living, such as electricity and automobiles. She came to feel that if a nuclear war did come, they would be the best suited to survive the destruction.[7] Thus, in *The Long Tomorrow*, society is led out of the chaos of the Destruction by the Amish and their fellow travelers, the New Mennonites.

There is an ambivalence in Brackett's treatment of the New Mennonites, however. On one hand, she admires their ability to cope in a world turned upside down. For example, before the war they are seen as quaint anomalies, but "when the cities ended, and men found that in the changed world these of all folk were best fitted to survive, the Mennonites had swiftly multiplied into the millions they now counted."[8] On the other hand, she felt that their religious fundamentalism was anathema to a free-thinking society. Brackett's New Mennonites are as narrow-minded as they come; they are people who use God to justify doing away with anyone deemed to be a threat. Not all of the New Mennonites are that way, as Len's father points out, but many are, and they will stop at nothing to keep the cities and science from ever rising again.

Her portrayal of the New Mennonites, however, is mild compared to Brackett's portrayal of the New Ishmaelites, a group of religious zealots that Len and Esau encounter on the trek west. While the former attack only when provoked, the latter exist by and for their fanaticism and "served it without rhyme, reason, or thought."[9] They were mainly misfits and deviants who went west originally to avoid established society. Living little better than wild animals, they adhered to self-flagellation and were prone to attack anyone who offended their somewhat warped sensibilities in one way or another. The New Ishmaelites contributed an ultraradical reaction to the kind of cities and science that had led to the downfall of the pre-Destruction way of life. Brackett is telling her readers that anything carried to extremes is bad—be it religion, science, or whatever. Self-righteousness of any kind is self-destructive and tends to make its victims highly intolerant. That is the worst crime—intolerance of other peoples' ideas and beliefs. Both the New Mennonites and the New Ishmaelites are guilty of this; one group is just more extreme than the other.

Not only is *The Long Tomorrow* a vehicle for Brackett's ideas about religion, the Amish, censorship, and freedom, it is also an allegory for the westward movement in American history. The author had long been interested in the history of the American West. She was a member of both the Western History Association and the Western Writers of America. She liked to read westerns and even wrote them. Her only western novel, *Follow the Free Wind,* won a Golden Spur Award from the Western Writers of America as best novel of 1963. All except two of the films she scripted for Howard Hawks were westerns: *Rio Bravo* (1959), *Rio Lobo* (1970), and *El Dorado* (1967).[10] It is thus no surprise that the West plays a significant role in the setting of *The Long Tomorrow*.

Len and Esau represent the restless spirit of the hundreds of pioneers who left comfortable homes in the East to seek their fortunes because they heard fantastic tales about exotic places out west where fortunes could be made overnight. This was also true of many of the people who first came to America seeking some mythical treasure trove. In most of these cases, the reality seldom lived up to the expectations, and the same is true about the Colters. They hear stories about the place called Bartorstown and come to believe it is a fantastic city where technology reigns supreme. Grandmother's stories about the way things were before the Destruction encourage them to look for the city, but when they finally arrive, it disappoints them. Like so many pioneers before them, Len and Esau must come to grips with reality or be swallowed up by it. Len especially comes to understand the truth, but both do and this permits them to survive.[11]

The Long Tomorrow is more than a thoughtful postholocaust novel. It is also a warm, sensitive coming-of-age story. When the book opens, Len and Esau are innocent, happy adolescents who enjoy basking in the simple delights of a county fair. By the end of it, they are married men who have, like their creator, "tasted the fruit of the Tree of Knowledge." Throughout, they are confused by all that happens to them, especially with things that run counter to what they have been brought up to expect. It is a particularly wrenching experience for Len. He wants desperately for the myth of Bartorstown to be true and thus finds it particularly difficult to cope with once he gets there. The harsh realities of life cause him to question the cherished teachings of childhood. These dichotomies prompt a crisis of faith, which permits Joan to convince him to escape from Bartorstown. By the end of the story, Len realizes there is no escape from knowledge. He understands that even if he led the way back to Bartorstown and it was destroyed, the knowledge would not die. He comments about the New Mennonites' fierce desire to limit information and freedom:

They call it faith, but it is not faith. It is fear. The people have clapped a shelter over their heads, a necessity of ignorance, a passion of retreat, and they have called it God, and worshipped it. And it is as false as any Moloch. So false that men like Soames, men

like Dulinsky, men like Esau and myself will overthrow it. And it will betray its wor-
shippers, leaving them defenseless in the face of a tomorrow that will surely come.[12]

In 1955, when *The Long Tomorrow* was published, the United States was
enmeshed in a Cold War with communism. That plus the pervasive effect of
Hiroshima and Nagasaki and a growing concern over the power of the Soviet
Union led other writers to voice their fears of all-out nuclear war in such excellent
postholocaust studies as Walter Miller's *A Canticle for Leibowitz,* Nevil Shute's
On the Beach, John Wyndham's *The Chrysalids* (or *Re-Birth),* and Wilson
Tucker's *The Long, Loud Silence.* And it was probably the ever-present threat
of nuclear war that spurred Brackett to write *The Long Tomorrow* rather than
just her avowed interest in Amish culture. Like many other Americans in the
Eisenhower 1950s, she felt that a holocaust might come given the "balance of
terror" existing among the superpowers at that time. Although she did not state
this directly, it is evidenced by the fact that she built a fallout shelter in her own
backyard. The 1950s was the "golden age" of the fallout shelter, and it is
perhaps fitting that two science fiction authors were in possession of such a
structure (although the Hamiltons were the first, last, and only residents of
Kinsman to build one).[13] It is clear that Brackett and her husband feared the
worst and wanted to be prepared come what may, and it is this impetus, more
than any other, that prompted *The Long Tomorrow.*

In this novel Brackett has penned a work that is quite different from her
beloved "space operas." Instead of outer space, she deals with the inner space
of peoples' hearts and minds, and although *The Long Tomorrow* is not exciting
in the sense that her space swashbucklers are, it is an insightful piece of literature.
Brackett was essentially a humanist, and this is evident here. Her story is about
people—who they are, what they do, what makes them tick. Strongly delineated
characters moving through rich, three-dimensional settings have always been a
hallmark of her style. It is through this technique that the reader comes to know
and understand the Colters, Hostetter, and even the New Mennonites. Brackett's
love of people is obvious. And it is her knowledge of human nature that creates
the timeless quality of *The Long Tomorrow* and makes it one of the best of the
postholocaust genre.

The Long Tomorrow offers no solutions to current world nuclear problems
(which are not unlike those existing in the 1950s). However, Brackett does feel
that, if an atomic war were to occur, we must make sure that knowledge does
not die. She knows that sweeping the knowledge away, hiding it, will not make
it disappear. As Len concludes, "The knowledge will exist. Somewhere.
In some book, some human brain, under some mountain. What men have found
once they will find again."[14] Knowledge brings with it the responsibility of
careful and wise usage.

It is interesting to note that Brackett always decried what she disdainfully
referred to as "think pieces." Yet she produced a novel that is, in the best sense
of the term, a "think piece." As a reviewer for the *New York Times* stated, *The*

Long Tomorrow is a thoughtful, provocative examination of "the ever-recurring clash between action and reaction in human thought and feeling."[15]

NOTES

1. Leigh Brackett, *The Long Tomorrow* (New York: Ballantine Books, 1955), epigraph. Additional citations are from this edition of the novel.

2. Ibid., p. 203.

3. Ibid., p. 260.

4. Ibid., p. 17.

5. Ibid., pp. 17–25.

6. Paul Walker, ed., *Speaking of Science Fiction* (Oradell, N.J.: Luna, 1978), pp. 374–75.

7. Ibid. Additional material on Brackett can be found in Rosemarie Arbur, *Brackett, Bradley and McCaffrey: A Primary and Secondary Bibliography* (Boston: G. K. Hall, 1982); Rosemarie Arbur, "Leigh Brackett: No 'Long Goodbye' is Good Enough," in *The Feminine Eye: Science Fiction and the Women Who Write It*, ed. Tom Staicar (New York: Frederick Ungar, 1983); and "Leigh Brackett," personal interview by Hugh G. Earnhart and Juanita Roderick for the Youngstown State University Oral History Program, October 1975.

8. Brackett, p. 4.

9. Ibid., p. 164.

10. "Leigh Brackett," personal interview by Earnhart and Roderick.

11. For a detailed examination of *The Long Tomorrow*'s relationship to American myths and literary tradition, see Diane Parkin-Speer, "Leigh Brackett's *The Long Tomorrow:* A Quest for the Future America," *Extrapolation* 26, 2 (Summer 1985).

12. Brackett, p. 259.

13. "Adeline Hamilton Sherwood," personal interview by Donna DeBlasio for the Youngstown State University Oral History Program, February 1983. Adeline Sherwood was Leigh Brackett's sister-in-law, with whom Leigh lived after Edmond Hamilton's death. Mrs. Sherwood died in 1984.

14. Brackett, p. 259.

15. J. Francis McComas, review of *The Long Tomorrow, New York Times,* October 23, 1955.

9

TO PLAY THE PHOENIX: MEDIEVAL IMAGES AND CYCLES OF REBUILDING IN WALTER MILLER'S *A CANTICLE FOR LEIBOWITZ*

Thomas P. Dunn

O Fortuna, velut luna statu variabilis,
semper crescis aut decrecis; vita detestabilis . . .
sors immanis et inanis, rota tu volubilis

O Fortune, fickle in character
as the moon; you are always increasing or decreasing;
life is detestable . . .
destiny enormous and empty,
you are a revolving wheel

—Anon. 14th c. Fortuna Imperatrix Mundi

1.

Walter Miller's great novel *A Canticle for Leibowitz* (1960) is one of the richest, most abundant texts in all of science fiction literature.[1] The book is alive and crawling with grotesque horror—mutant cannibals, a two-headed woman, and the brutal horrors of a postnuclear-holocaust world—but at the same time and to the same degree alive and on fire with the intelligent dialogue of witty allies and adversaries, gentle humor and tough-minded optimism, incredible strength of faith and nobility of character, and the beauty of dedication, right action, and self-sacrifice, under the most adverse conditions imaginable. Heroic in its rejection of despair, *Canticle* is the living proof that science fiction can be a vehicle for the discussion of important issues and a medium for speculation about future societies and situations.

Canticle is, moreover, the quintessential science fiction novel for a variety of reasons. First, it is for many the single most important example of the postholocaust tale, giving us one of the fullest pictures of rebuilding within the covers of a single volume. And alongside this there is the notion, so often treated comically here, of a "lost past," with the characters knowing less than we readers about their true history. Two classic works on this theme are Robert Heinlein's *Universe* (1964) and H. G. Wells' *The Country of the Blind* (1911). Stories in which characters wander in the darkness and the flickering shadows of Plato's cave seem naturally to attract us, and they are constantly being written.[2]

Miller also includes, as we shall see, some comment on future scientific developments which surpass our own, notions of robot technology and the "cyberneticizing" of our society. Space travel, scientific discovery, politics, and anthropology are all fused in his vision, as are the terror of book burning as depicted often in science fiction, perhaps best in Ray Bradbury's *Fahrenheit 451* (1953), and the erasure of history, as in George Orwell's *1984* (1949). But transcending and including these elements is Miller's depiction of the human condition and his derivation from that of our human purpose.

This study will argue that *Canticle,* while presenting human history as arduous, painful, and cyclical, is not an invitation to cynicism or despair but a presentation of earthly life as a testing ground against which humanity must struggle mightily for sainthood. *Canticle,* then, is a futuristic, mostly realistic, profoundly didactic work sharing many of the values and even some of the formal elements of the medieval Christian apocalypse.[3]

In a carefully patterned, three-part format, *Canticle* tells of America's future to the year 3781. Its sections, really three short novels, titled *Fiat Homo, Fiat Lux,* and *Fiat Voluntas Tua,* tell respectively the vicissitudes of the Albertine Order of St. Leibowitz some six, twelve, and eighteen centuries in the future. We also learn something of our near future and the nuclear devastation that awaits; hence the novel develops a picture of human history over the next two millennia all based around a single monastery and its relationships with the world—and later the cosmos—at large.

Told very briefly, the story is as follows. In the dim past, which is our near future, the nuclear powers went ahead with their long-feared exchange, leaving large chunks of the earth a radioactive ruin and plunging America into a barbaric, primitive state. A nuclear physicist, one Isaac Leibowitz, joined the Cistercians, then founded a Catholic monastic order of "bookleggers" and "memorizers" to hoard and preserve the written treasures of our day until civilization returns to normal. At the same time, there sprang up a know-nothing movement of thugs to carry out the "Simplification"—that is, the destruction of all wisdom, all political and scientific figures of rank, and finally of anything that smacked of any learning whatsoever. In this second holocaust, Leibowitz himself was martyred.

In the first of the book's three sections, some documents of the (now Blessed) Leibowitz are brought to light by Brother Francis Gerard. Although the purpose of these documents is misunderstood, they are lovingly preserved and studied and serve to aid the final effort to have Leibowitz canonized by "New Rome," a new Vatican somewhere in the upper west. In the second section, a Renaissance movement spawns some brilliant scholars including "Thon" Taddeo, a mathematician and theoretical physicist who uses the abbey's documents to reinvent material and technological civilization, bringing scientific knowledge out of darkness once again. But then in the final section we see that the very knowledge preserved by the religious devotees has once again spawned a terrifying nuclear buildup which threatens to engulf the earth in a second "Fire Deluge" more horrible even than the first holocaust. The response of the abbey of St. Leibowitz is to outfit a starship and send a daughter cell out to the Centaurus star system, which has by this time been partially colonized. It leaves with minutes to spare, and in the book's final pages the current abbot, Dom Zerchi, who has remained behind, spends his final days fighting against a government-sponsored euthanasia center which is quietly killing radiation victims. A final all-out nuclear exchange puts an end to all life on earth except that remaining in the deep ocean currents.

This, then, is the background against which Miller paints a picture of humanity which, if not rosy at all, at least gives some cause for hope. The book brings humanity full circle from one major destruction to the next and implies in many different ways that such cycles of destruction have occurred in the past and will recur in the future. This single fact has inspired the first generation of *Canticle*'s critics and scholars to see the work as rather gloomy, even though nearly all regard it as a masterpiece. And so *Canticle* routinely appears on lists of the best novels in science fiction, often the short lists as well, and it has earned scholarly attention by the most astute critics in the field.

Brian W. Aldiss, veteran scholar as well as major science fiction writer, says, "*Canticle* has the dryness, toughness, and nutritional value of *cordon bleu* pemmican. All science fiction writers are astonishing, but some writers are more astonishing than others. *Canticle* appears to be the rocky summit of Miller's brief writing career."[4] Harold L. Berger in his important monograph *Science Fiction and the New Dark Age* (1976) regards Miller as despairing of man and displaying a strongly proclerical feeling vis-à-vis science.[5] Robert Scholes and Eric S. Rabkin see Miller as amalgamating science and religion into "a modern humanism," which transcends distinctions between Jew and Christian and which ends the antagonism between science and religion which, among many others, C. S. Lewis dramatized in his work.[6] Gary K. Wolfe makes the significant point that *Canticle* asserts scientific knowledge as a secular *logos* which even nuclear destruction cannot erase: "Nuclear holocaust is a weakness of culture, not of science; the wasteland is the ruins of mankind's works, not its understanding."[7] Willis E. McNelly notes that *Canticle*, as regards nuclear destruction, is both admonitory and premonitory and he stresses the concluding debate between Zerchi and Dr. Cors as crucial to an understanding of Miller's novel. McNelley also underlines the idea expressed in *Canticle* that by seeking to minimize suffering and to maximize security, we find only their opposites: maximum suffering and minimum security.[8] W. Warren Wagar, whose *Terminal Visions* (1982) studies hundreds of end-of-the-world narratives, is surely correct to see an Augustian worldview in *Canticle;* he asserts that Miller's theme is "the cyclicism of orthodox Christianity, neither hostile nor friendly to science, but contemptuous of all utopianism."[9] And in *Fantasy and Mimesis* (1984), Kathryn Hume saw Miller as offering a work in the "literature of revision," a book which provides humankind with a program for changing reality for the better. In Miller's view, Hume argues, this depends upon our acceptance of personal responsibility, our willingness to say, "The trouble with the world is me."[10]

As these many comments show, *Canticle* is both lucid and complex in its portrayal of a future world and hence is illuminated best by a wide variety of critical comment. This is especially so in the case of a work that features a rich subtext of thematic images and echoes and which, unlike many science fiction novels, presents depth of character as well. But before discussing these elements, let us examine more closely the parts of the work: four stories of growth and change, victory and discovery, set in an overall structure of stasis, devastation following devastation.

The first story, that of Leibowitz himself, is one of cunning and self-sacrifice.[11] From facts presented, the reader is able to piece together that Leibowitz worked until his death among the bookleggers and memorizers to leave acquired knowledge to the future. When the "Fire Deluge" was upon him, he tried to save his wife, Emma, by tricking her into taking shelter, telling her that a box of random junk was an important treasure that had to be preserved.[12] As luck would have it, she died just the same, and Leibowitz carried on alone, until the "Simplifiers" caught up with him and killed him with fire and strangulation. (The saint is always depicted with faggots at his feet and a noose around his neck.) As Scholes and Rabkin point out, it is entirely fitting that Leibowitz, a Jew, should be regarded as a Catholic saint. Before the novel's end, far more important distinctions will be overlooked in the effort to preserve something of the past. But in the novel's first section, his Jewishness is a running gag, with generations of Dark Age Catholic monks pondering such documents as *"Pound pastrami . . . can kraut, six bagels—bring home for Emma."*[13]

In the next major development we watch Brother Francis Gerard on a lonely penitential vigil discover the Leibowitzian documents in a place labeled in pre-Deluge English: "ALLOUT SURVIVAL SHELTER Maximum Occupancy: 15." Miller uses such occasions for ironic comedy:

Brother Francis visualized a Fallout as half-salamander, because, according to tradition, the thing was born in the Flame Deluge, and as half-incubus who despoiled virgins in their sleep, for, were not the monsters of the world still called "children of the Fallout."[14]

Francis endures punishment and a long wait for the priesthood because of the nature of his discoveries, but he sticks to his goals and is eventually vindicated before his abbot, Dom Arkos. Francis is given the chance to take a wiring diagram and his magnificently illuminated copy to New Rome and there witness for himself the canonization ceremony of St. Leibowitz. Our sadness at his death shortly thereafter is mitigated by the fact that he dies fulfilled and at peace. Later he is granted the title of ''Venerable,'' the first step on the stairway to sainthood.

Six centuries further in the future, the monastery's abbot, Dom Paulo, must struggle with the many issues raised by the documents—the ''Memorabilia'' they are called—and the wonders they make possible. One of his own monks, Brother Kornhoer, by studying the Memorabilia succeeds in making an electrical generator and using it to light a lamp. By that lamplight, ''Thon''—the title apparently means ''scholar''—Taddeo studies the Memorabilia for the sake of advancing theoretical knowledge of science. This section of *Canticle (Fiat Lux,* it will be remembered) culminates in a wonderful scene in which Dom Paulo watches with apprehension as Brother Kornhoer directs a work gang of robed monks busy turning the shaft of a monstrous electrical generator to light the way for the secular scholar. The scene is emblematic of the entire age in which knowledge moves again beyond the monastery walls and out of monastic control.

There are similarly emblematic scenes in the final book, called when first published ''The Last Canticle.''[15] Dom Zerchi, the current abbot, is the Moses who will stay behind while the new Joshua (named, appropriately, Joshua) is sent forth to lead a Holy Remnant of religious zealots and children to the stars. When Joshua objects that he is not ready, not able to be a priestly leader, Zerchi upbraids him:

Listen, none of us has been really able. But we've tried, and we've been tried. It tries you to destruction, but you're here for that. . . . What are you made of, son? What's to be tried?[16]

Another powerful scene finds Dom Zerchi and his monks under arrest for picketing a ''Mercy Camp'' near the abbey. Besides the religious and moral issue of euthanasia, Zerchi raises the interesting point that the government is operating these death camps so that those in the terminal pain of radiation sickness will not foster a rebellion against the established military order. Zerchi tries to the last gasp to get a young mother to refrain from taking her desperately ill and suffering child to the camp.[17]

The final scene is an extremely complex and symbolic action tying together many themes of the novel. In it, Zerchi, himself dying, tries to baptize a hideous old woman, a tomato vendor, whose deformity consists of an extra homuncular head. The head, suddenly awake, rejects baptism, parrots the abbot's words, and offers him a communion wafer. Zerchi is transfixed: he dies with the knowledge that he has seen and touched one who, like the Blessed Mother, is a creature of preternatural innocence. He whispers the Magnificat and weeps in gratitude— he has witnessed a certain promise of resurrection. Although there is not space to discuss the scene in detail, the following is a brief list of some of its many resonant chords.

- It is a sacrament of Communion with "Mrs. Grales," the tomato vendor as celebrant.
- It is a miracle of the Virgin, in which both function as the Mother of Mercy.
- In its studied grotesqueness, it shows graphically that the body is not the person. As Zerchi had said earlier, we don't *have* souls, we *are* souls. We *have* bodies.[18]
- It is a miracle of new life, perhaps even of a new life form.
- It parallels the end of Section I in which Francis dies reciting a rosary, and that of Section II, another queerly inverted sacrament in which a poet mistaken by a dying officer for a priest murmurs *"Ego te absolvo"* then stabs the officer (an enemy) in the heart.
- It is a sign, in lieu of a rainbow, that something will continue despite the general destruction.
- It features Mrs. Grales/Rachel as a type of Janus figure looking backward (Mrs. Grales) on destruction and forward (Rachel) on the new world.
- As the phoenix of legend rises beautiful and young from its own ashes, so Rachel may be regarded as the reborn Mrs. Grales and hence a symbol of the Resurrection and an emblem of immortality.[19]
- It presents a literalization of a thorny theological dilemma (shall an extra head be baptised?), evoking an image of medieval scholastic debate.
- It echoes the first book of the Bible with the old "tummater woman" as a reverse type of Eve, offering repentant man the fruit of divine knowledge.
- It is a monument to Miller's skill, which is able to transform the ugly and grotesque into something moving and powerful.

2.

Now let us look at the entire novel in profile to see what patterns and literary strategies emerge from this welter of events and images. One clear formal principle emerging from this reading of the three books—or the four stories—of *Canticle* is that the actions of all are in many ways parallel. Consider the following:

- Each is a story of an abbot and a younger man whose objectives are at odds with each other.
- Each is a story of the flickering light of civilized moral vision amid the ruthless decadence and darkness of the surrounding, apparently hopelessly corrupt, world.
- Each asks and answers the question, "What's to be done with the Memorabilia?" In all three cases, the decision is made to preserve and open the knowledge contained therein, first to New Rome, then to the world at large, then to the star colonies of Centaurus.
- All pit people of firm purpose and religious conviction against others of unbridled egoism and cunning treachery.
- A mysterious figure, an ancient Jewish man vaguely identified as the Wandering Jew of legend, moves through the background of each story searching, like Lazarus, for

the one who called him forth from the dead. One major significance of this character is that he never finds what he is looking for. America is not, apparently, the new Jerusalem, nor is the Messianic promise yet fulfilled on earth.[20]

• The question of the value and purpose of life is raised repeatedly.

• The conflict of church and state is a constant concern.

• Each tale pivots on cruel ironies, comic squabbles, grotesque problems, horrid bloodshed and torture, buzzards feasting on human flesh, brilliant and befuddled minds working against all odds to put together and maintain a little truth and light.

This partial list should be sufficient to show that Miller wants us to regard these stories as, in many ways, congruent and illustrative of a cyclical pattern operating in human affairs. In every age, it seems, some will strive, some Holy Remnant will obtain for humanity a measure of saving grace; saints will appear, bear witness, work selflessly, and if required give the ultimate sacrifice. Greed and cruelty will surround them at every point and interfere to pervert and thwart every human step out of darkness. Finally, these cycles of growth and progress will bring not a return to Eden but another monstrous cataclysm whose arrival is insured by the wickedness in most human hearts. As God promised Noah, fire, not flood, will arrive to sweep nearly all before it, erasing the gains won at terrible price.

In the context of *Canticle* it takes eighteen centuries for this cycle to be completed, and we see readily that it has happened before. Most obviously, there is the comic parallel between these two millennia and the two behind us (the readers). We see Dark Age monks huddling behind stone walls while barbarian hordes rape and pillage. There is at the monastery a "Venerable Boedullus" which should call to mind the Anglo-Saxon historian the Venerable Bede. Then we have Renaissance times, Renaissance men, a burgeoning of new light and beauty. But the darkness drops again, and just as in Yeats' poem "The Second Coming" a new monster after "twenty centuries of stony sleep . . . slouches toward Bethlehem to be born." Finally both epochs end in nuclear devastation.

And yet, while there are great and sweeping changes occurring throughout *Canticle*, the overarching structural principle is an utter stasis in which the natural order is wasteland, with earth formless and void, and darkness upon the face of the deep. To dust we will return, collectively as well as individually. There is strong evidence that Miller wants to show us *plus ça change, plus c'est la même chose*. The first devastation, the one awaiting the readers, is called the Flame Deluge, recalling Noah's escape amid the wreck of the sinful world. The escape to the stars is viewed as a new Exodus. And toward the end of his life, Zerchi asks a bitter rhetorical question:

Listen, are we helpless? Are we doomed to do it again and again? Have we no choice but *to play the Phoenix,* in an unending sequence of rise and fall?[21] (Emphasis mine)

The answer to this rhetorical question, as Wagar states, is meant to be a resounding "Yes!"[22] We must endure not only the hardship of trying to build in our own time but the certain knowledge that nearly all will be swept away because of our fumbling ignorance and ungovernable destructive passions. Indeed, the fact that all human life is decisively erased from earth suggests that there may be even larger cycles operating. Lucifer will fall and Eden will be lost yet again.

Thus the image most consistently evoked in *Canticle* is the constant, inexorable churning of a massive wheel, the great *rota* of the Goddess Fortuna, carrying people up in hope, then dashing them to the ground in despair, all under the divine sanction of a God who provides for humanity a world in which all is mutable and unenduring, a world in which we humans have no continuing place.[23]

Bearing all this in mind, let us take up the question of pessimism in *Canticle*. Perhaps one reason why many readers have seen this cyclic vision as pessimistic is that important characters in the novel, indeed its ethical agents, view it as hopeless. Dom Zerchi has his moment of despair, as we have seen, when the process appears to him as "mad clockwork" to which humankind is forever chained.[24] But there is another way to view cataclysm: nations and epochs of history, and even planets and stars, have each their "Arkos and Zerchi" or Alpha and Omega. We must not despair simply because we are seeing the death of a world: faith provides a final proof against despair, especially when the life cycle of a planet or of a society is viewed as analogous to our own life cycle, with which each of us, it is to be hoped, has come to some, at least, provisional terms. Later, as Dom Zerchi fights to prevent euthanasia, he seems to have arrived at a more optimistic view. When the mother protests she cannot comprehend a God who is pleased with pain, Zerchi responds, " 'No, no! It is not pain that is pleasing to God, child. It is the soul's endurance in faith and hope and love in *spite* of bodily afflictions that pleases Heaven. Pain is like negative temptation. God is . . . pleased when the soul rises above the temptation.' "[25]

There is literary precedent for the worldview that Miller seems to be recommending. Thornton Wilder's play *The Skin of Our Teeth* is a fanciful "Story of Mankind" which witnesses the human race, represented by the Antrobus family, three times saving themselves and little else from the wreckage of civilization. The third time, Sabina, a mistress of Mr. Antrobus whom they always take along, complains bitterly, "That's all we do—always beginning again! Over and over again. Always beginning again." Mrs. Antrobus turns on her, not for her relationship with Mr. Antrobus, but for her whining desperation: "Sabina, I've let you talk long enough. I don't want to hear any more of it. . . . Stop arguing and go on with your work," she says. "I could live for seventy years in a cellar and make soup out of grass and bark, without ever doubting that this world has a work to do and will do it."[26]

Further reinforcement for this cyclical, generally medieval view are images linking microcosm and geocosm. As Joshua and Zerchi walk out into the night to cross the highway to reach the refectory, the highway provides an eerie sight of a larger life form pulsating. Trucks become great lumbering "mindless" animals that moan and whine and "watch" the road with their dish antennae. Apparently robotic, they guide themselves along with magnetic feelers that take direction from guiding strips built into the roadbed. The road itself is a "pink, fluorescent river" of oiled concrete, and the trucks remind the monks of "economic corpuscles" in the arteries of humanity.[27]

But to carry the thought one step further, there is evidence within *Canticle* that the cycles of destruction are necessary precisely because we insist on trying to make for ourselves a heaven on earth. It is because of our constant striving to attain utopia that we reach a point of despair and then of destruction. Brother Joshua, agonizing in the monastery garden over the cup which Zerchi would hand to him—to leave earth forever for the stars—has this moment of insight: "Too much hope for Earth had led men to try to make it Eden, and of that they might well despair until the time toward the consumption of the world"[28] The picture is pessimistic only in secular, agnostic terms. Joshua correctly foresees that building Eden will be impossible in the struggling off-earth colonies: "Fortunately for them, perhaps," Joshua thinks, "the closer men came to perfecting for themselves a paradise, the more impatient they seemed to become with it, and with themselves as well."[29] Only when the world is in darkness, Joshua realizes, can people yearn for the light; when the light finally is restored, or nearly so, by reason, discontent sets in.

Joshua sees full well that humankind will again tear the earth apart, "this garden Earth," so that "Man might hope again in wretched darkness."[30] Viewed as such, the process is no more hopeless than is the individual life merely because it must end inevitably in death. The end of a society or even the end of a world is no more tragic than the end of each individual life. If nuclear catastrophe—even annihilation—is a horrifying inevitability, is it worse than a world in which the "Simplifiers" are forever victorious? Is it not better to have learned and lost than never to have learned at all?

At the very end of G. B. Shaw's *Saint Joan,* Joan asks a question of God: "O God that madest this beautiful earth, when will it be ready to receive thy saints? How long, O Lord, how long?"[31] If this study has read Miller correctly, the world may never be ready to receive its saints, but in its very ugliness it makes a fine environment for their development. Eden is never again to be mortal man's home, but for man's perfection, one by slow painful one, the struggle to reach it must go on, *per omnia secula seculorum. Deo Gratias!*

NOTES

1. Walter Miller, *A Canticle for Leibowitz* (London: Weidenfeld & Nicholson, 1960). Portions of the novel appeared in the *Magazine of Fantasy & Science Fiction* and in various anthologies from 1955 to 1957.

2. Ursula K. Le Guin's chilling tale of martyrdom in the service of truth, "The

Masters,'' for example, features a benighted scientific aristocracy which condemns those who insist on experiment and speculation instead of blind obedience to authority.

3. For a good overview of the medieval apocalypse, see Morton Bloomfield, *Piers Plowman as a Fourteenth-Century Apocalypse* (New Brunswick, N.J.: Rutgers University Press, 1962). Although there is not space here to explore the question in detail, it would be well to explore at some future time the possible parallels between the ''Do-well, Do-bet[ter], and Do-best'' sections of *Piers Plowman* and the three books of *Canticle,* as well as possible parallels between William Langland with respect to the story of the apocalypse and Isaac Leibowitz with respect to the *Memorabilia.*

4. Brian W. Aldiss, *Billion Year Spree: The True History of Science Fiction* (Garden City, N.Y.: Doubleday, 1973), p. 279.

5. Harold L. Berger, *Science Fiction and the New Dark Age* (Bowling Green, Ohio: Bowling Green University Popular Press, 1976), pp. 151–55.

6. Robert Scholes and Eric S. Rabkin, *Science Fiction: History, Science, Vision* (New York: Oxford University Press, 1977), pp. 221–26. Quotation from p. 226.

7. Gary K. Wolfe, *The Known and the Unknown: The Iconography of Science Fiction* (Kent, Ohio: Kent State University Press, 1979), pp. 137–46. Quotation from p. 146. This work achieves the fullest and most penetrating analysis of *Canticle* to date by centering attention on the many significant oppositions within the work. Wolfe cites as well several examples of the way history corrupts knowledge during its transmission.

8. Willis E. McNelly, ''A Canticle for Leibowitz,'' in *Survey of Science Fiction Literature,* vol. I, ed. Frank N. Magill (Englewood Cliffs, N.J.: Salem Press, 1979), pp. 288–93. McNelly lists eleven reviews and two earlier articles including an analysis by Walker Percy.

9. W. Warren Wagar, *Terminal Visions: The Literature of Last Things* (Bloomington: Indiana University Press, 1982), discussion from pp. 189–190, quotation from page 190. For further information about the intricacies of publication and construction of *Canticle,* see David N. Samuelson, ''The Lost Canticles of Walter M. Miller, Jr.,'' *Science Fiction Studies* 3 (1976), pp. 3–26.

10. Kathryn Hume, *Fantasy and Mimesis: Responses to Reality in Western Literature* (New York and London: Methuen, 1984), pp. 120–23.

11. This story is not part of the running narrative but rather is presented in bits and pieces throughout Book One.

12. Miller, p. 33.

13. Ibid.

14. Ibid., pp. 24–25. This kind of amalgamation, which seems humorous to us in the twentieth century, actually reproduces rather faithfully the kind of blurring of the past which occurs any time a culture looks backward over centuries. Ernst R. Curtius discusses the concept in detail, showing how the medieval artist reproduced antiquity as he saw it, blurring distinctions which Roman poets and Homeric Greeks would have considered fundamental. See his well-known study *European Literature and the Latin Middle Ages* (New York: Harper Torchbooks, 1963) (first published in German, 1948; in English, 1953), pp. 17–35.

15. *Magazine of Fantasy and Science Fiction,* February 1957.

16. Miller, pp. 271–72.

17. Ibid., pp. 297–306.

18. Ibid., p. 281.

19. For an explanation of the phoenix as Christian symbol see J. C. J. Metford,

Dictionary of Christian Lore and Legend (London: Thames and Hudson, 1983), p. 198; for a retelling of the legend, see *Physiologus*, trans. Michael J. Curley (Austin and London: University of Texas Press, 1979), pp. 13–14.

20. When Dom Paulo of Book Two meets with him in his incarnation as Benjamin, the latter tells him, " 'I don't much expect Him to come, but I was told to wait, and—' he shrugged 'I wait.' " Miller, p. 172.

21. Ibid., p. 255.

22. Wagar, p. 190.

23. For a full iconography of this important medieval image, see Howard R. Patch, *The Goddess Fortuna in Medieval Literature* (Cambridge, Mass.: Harvard University Press, 1927; New York: Octagon Books, 1967). Indeed, the wheels which Brother Kornhoer and his work gang turn push the world and themselves toward their destiny.

24. Miller, p. 255.

25. Ibid., p. 300.

26. Thornton Wilder, *The Skin of Our Teeth,* in *Three Plays by Thornton Wilder* (New York: Harper & Row, Bantam edition, 1958) (play copyright 1942 by Thornton Wilder), pp. 65–137. Quotations from pp. 128–29.

27. Miller, pp. 258–59, and see the description coming shortly after this of the community of monks as a single organism, p. 263.

28. Miller, p. 273.

29. Ibid., p. 274.

30. Ibid.

31. George Bernard Shaw, *Saint Joan: A Chronicle Play in Six Scenes and an Epilogue,* in *Nine Plays by Bernard Shaw* (New York: Dodd, Mead, 1935), pp. 981–1147. Quotation from page 1147.

10

THE DEATH OF THE HEART IN
LEVEL 7

Carolyn Wendell

Mordecai Roshwald's *Level 7* (1959) has at least two distinctions: after the initial reviews and a British television drama based upon the story, it has been almost unanimously ignored—perhaps because it is surely the bleakest of the Cold War period's speculations about the devastation of a nuclear holocaust. And that is its second claim to a unique position. Of all the tales of World War III, most left a few likeable survivors after the bomb was dropped. Only Nevil Shute's *On the Beach* made it clear that the world would be empty of life shortly after the last page (and one reviewer commented that *Level 7* made *On the Beach* "look like giddy optimism").[1] *Level 7* projects a world where not only are there no people left, there are no animals, no plants, no landscape that even looks earthly. Nothing is left but layers of ashes and some pavement aboveground and some rotting corpses in a "shelter" below. Its apocalyptic vision seems more in keeping with a contemporary vision projected by the films *Testament* (1983) and *Threads* (1984). The much discussed *The Day After* (1983) seems much less grim.

Also, as literature, *Level 7* is less than totally successful: the literary reader expects character, and there is very little here. Even the narrator is only marginally and occasionally sympathetic, and he is certainly never very interesting as an individual. The leisure reader expects action and suspense, but even the war is boring—the narrator pushes some buttons, sees some colors on a screen, and then it is over (no mushroom cloud, no screams, no panic in the streets). While there is reason for this lack of drama, the novel does not make for stimulating reading. To the audience of 1959, *Level 7* may well have seemed a didactic extreme (Damon Knight thought so and even concluded that it was not

science fiction).[2] But by now, a quarter of a century later, given weapons technology vastly improved in both quantity and quality (so much so that terms from
science fiction are used to describe it by a president from the film world), as
well as scientific agreement about such probable results as nuclear winter, the
nightmarish vision of *Level 7* seems realistic, even reasonable. It is worth another
look for its inexorable, moral reasoning: the preparation for, and waging of, a
nuclear war requires a reversal of traditional human values and emotions that
amounts to a spiritual destruction of the individual. The earth can be destroyed
only when we have already destroyed ourselves. *Level 7* shows us the requirements: total subservience to authority, placid tolerance and flexibility that is
really emotional vacuum, surrender or negation of individual traits and passions,
and finally a complete loss of selfhood.

The novel takes the form of 116 journal entries that span some eight months
from spring to fall (the entries begin thirty-seven days after the narrator's experience starts, so they date only from March 21 to October 12, although the
content covers eight months). The writer, X-127, a military technician, tells of
his and others' descent to a shelter 4,400 feet below ground where they are
sealed in to launch atomic missiles and then of their creation of a society of
underground survivors. Not much happens: the entries describe day-to-day activities (mostly conversations among the inhabitants), analyze the writer's reactions to his surroundings (and his reactions are consistently low-key), and
recount what few events occur (the war, the depression and suicide of a coworker,
the writer's marriage and divorce). Also X-127 condenses for us a series of
recorded lectures that inform Level 7 inhabitants about other levels of the shelter.
And he tells us about the reports made by a couple who dug their way out, so
we hear about the surface of the planet. Eventually, people begin to die of
radiation leaked from the atomic reactor that provides energy for Level 7. As
the journal writer, X-127 apparently (and necessarily) lasts longer than the others,
but his last entry makes it clear he too is dying.

Roshwald's novel answers ingeniously two questions central to any story about
nuclear war: who would commit such a horror, and what would happen to the
survivors? With admirable economy, this story contends that those who would
cause such a holocaust would also be well-enough protected to survive. While
there is no portrait of the decision-makers and we do not even know what
countries are involved, some conclusions can be drawn about the nature of those
ultimately responsible from the arrival of X-127 and his coworkers. Before his
descent to Level 7, X-127 recalls being told by his commanding officer that he
will be given a promotion to major, a raise in pay, and two weeks' leave, after
he has spent "a day or two" underground.[3] Since his stay underground is actually
to be permanent, a fact his commanding officer (C.O.) must have known, the
apparent rewards (bribes?) are lies, exacerbated when X-127 and the others are
told the truth shortly after they arrive and receive this assurance about their
situation, "You need not worry about your friends and relatives outside. They
will be notified that you have been killed in a painless accident and that you left

no remains." The irony hardly needs comment, particularly when it is followed by, "We regret this, but your disappearance must remain absolutely secret."[4] The lies, callous and cruel though they may be, are justified by the logic that ends justify means: the people must be moved underground without protest from them or from those they know aboveground. (And in ways no doubt unintended by the announcement, these people are already dead.) But any heartbreak or anguish they or people who love them suffer is secondary to military strategy.

Similarly, the later "Know Other Levels" series explains that Level 2 is designated for "peace-mongers, extreme oppositionists, critics of society and other cranks."[5] Military/governmental attitude toward disagreement is clear from diction—the "and other cranks" says it all. Since Level 2 is only 100 feet deep and holds provisions for just six months, the shelter is totally ineffectual, another fact that the government must know—but the lie will appease those who might make trouble. The end (people behaving as the government wants them to, docilely) justifies the means (deadly lies that people will be protected when they will not be).

The subservience required by a brutal and dishonest leadership is revealed by X-127's comments on the commanding officer who promises his promotion, raise, and leave.

As the administrative apex of a highly trained unit of military technicians, he was our superior in rank but inferior to us in technical education, in I.Q. and—so we thought— in his indispensability for modern warfare. So he was always obeyed, but seldom respected; and never treated as a friend.[6]

He explains that the C.O. quite often called in his subordinates to discuss "important matters," to make "political inquiries" about activities and contacts, or to indulge in "a friendly-seeming chat without any apparent purpose."[7] Regardless of what the subordinates thought or felt about the superior or his motivations, he was always obeyed. Since *Level 7* appeared thirteen years after the Nuremberg Trials for war criminals, the world was well aware by that time that horrors could be inflicted by subordinates "just following orders." X-127's acquiescence results in part, no doubt, from a given personality that has been selected because of its passivity, but it also comes from conditioning that has become habit. The whole process is mechanical and impersonal. Nuremberg had shown such a thing was possible. Given this possibility, any horror is possible: the Holocaust—or the total destruction of an entire planet.

Also quite obvious in the novel is the mechanical and impersonal nature of Level 7's inhabitants. Throughout, X-127 and the others confined with him are portrayed as emotionally shallow, even emotionless. From their arrival at Level 7, even after a descent of 4,400 feet (and the trip was unusual, even stressful, down tunnel, elevator, corridor, and escalator, each narrow and ever-descending), we note their peculiar lack of response or even curiosity. No one refuses to descend, no one so much as asks a question, and once they are all seated at a table at their destination (having immediately and unquestioningly followed the order to sit down, before they have even so much as looked around), they do not even introduce themselves. Rather, they start a patter of small talk that is either amusing or annoying in its inanity—such as wondering what will be served for lunch![8] Worse, it is three whole days later before the narrator talks to his roommate.[9] X-127 explains both these situations, where silence rather than curiosity and reaction is the norm, as the result of preoccupation with other matters, but even he admits that he and his companions suffer a ''curious lack of interest in other people.''[10] He says he senses resentment of their situation in himself and others, but there is never any expression or display of that resentment (thus it is difficult to see it as very real).

Level 7 inhabitants do not even comment on, much less object to, their names, which are not names but assigned letter and number combinations, based on location and profession. Our names (and nicknames) signal difference, uniqueness, individuality; theirs signal similarity, likeness to others. The first letter tells what role or work the person is assigned: P for psychologist; N for nurse; T for teacher; AE for atomic energy officer, and even (perhaps with some slight humor) Ph for philosopher and Ch for (a yet-to-be-born) child. All designations end in 7, probably because they live on Level 7. The middle two numbers remain unexplained. And why the narrator and his roommate have the letter X rather than Bp (button-pusher) is a mystery. It may be that once the war is over the button-pushers have no apparent roles to play. Since their jobs are short-term, their names and, by extension, themselves are as well.

Their lack of response makes it difficult to know or feel much for the characters, who seem very nonhuman, especially when pairing-off time reveals their lack of even rudimentary emotions. Courtship usually generates passion and drama, but not for these people. While X-127 is enthusiastically pursued by P-867, he is attracted to N-527 but does ''not feel too cut up''[11] when he learns she will marry someone else. Next he enjoys the company of T-747, with whom he creates myths for future subterranean generations. But in the end, he decides to propose to P-867, even though he does not care for her. In fact, he reasons with admirable upside-down logic that since married couples can spend very little intimate time together, it is best if married couples do not care for each other. Thus, P-867, whose bossiness and know-it-all attitude severely annoy X-127, makes an ideal mate for him. Drama becomes account book. Later, X-127 is divorced by P-867 with even less fuss than when he married her.

Ironically (or inconsistently) P-867, the psychologist who explains to X-127 repeatedly the folly of emotion, betrays more feeling than he does (despite his analysis of his sensitivity and worry about his lack of feeling). She quite obviously ''sets her cap'' for him and, as the saying goes, chases him until he catches her. She frets about his moods (albeit in her shrewish way), even angrily tears up a chunk of his diary when his mood changes from depression to detachment, and has tears in her eyes when they divorce. If Level 7 dwellers have indeed been chosen for ''stable disposition,'' as X-127 is told by the loudspeaker,[12] surely a miscalculation was made with the selection of P-867. Or—and this is more likely—Roshwald fell victim to female stereotypes unquestioned in the 1950s, even if they interfered with literary consistency.

The citizens of Level 7 remain nonentities to us with no names, no person-alities, no passions. Even X-127, whom we know best, is a bit of a bore. His dreams, all of which foreshadow imminent destruction, are more vivid than he is. One of them reveals an awareness of what he and his companions are. He dreams he is with many people when the bomb is dropped. All of them gaze at "flat, dead ground" afterward and remain silent, looking at one another and the scene before them. Then the people slowly and horribly change into lifeless rubber dummies, and the dreamer sees his own hands begin to change.[13] X-127 interprets this as prophecy, but he fails to recognize it as judgment of the people of Level 7—silent, inactive, physically alive but morally and emotionally dead, conditioned to be "rubber dummies" manipulated into position where they will stay forever because they have no will or power to change themselves. The real horror of this dream, and of Roshwald's vision, is not the destruction done by the bomb, but the destruction that has already been done—the dead hearts and souls that allow the bomb.

P. Schuyler Miller, in his review of *Level 7*, noted that it follows the tradition of both Zamiatin's *We* and Orwell's *1984:* Roshwald "wants only to show us the horrors of the regimented society that can plan in this way, and of the made-over, brain-washed people who can live in it contentedly."[14] Or, as Damon Knight put it, "the nightmare is the socialist nightmare of numbers; the suffo-cating sense that individual personality is being crushed; that everybody above you is deceiving you, and himself being deceived in turn."[15] Roshwald takes this horror of a politically rigid, authoritarian society a few steps further to its final result: the total annihilation, of people, of planet.

The impersonal war is conducted by pushing buttons, in fact, by automatic button pushing. Level 7 learns two days after the war has destroyed the world that "in all probability the war *did* start by accident. The retaliation *was* auto-matic."[16] No human being made a decision (this alone means that X-127's exalted status of button-pusher has been as much a farce as his promotion and raise and as the assignment of one million people to Level 2). Button pushing is part and parcel of this nightmare world of rubber dummies, to the point where it becomes an appropriate metaphor for the society and its dwellers, who neither act nor feel. Instead, they push buttons to communicate, to propose marriage and to marry, to ask for help when ill, to vote on world affairs. X-127's one pleasure is music, which must be switched on, and he and T-747 plan didactic stories for future generations of Level 7 children who will push buttons to hear story tapes. Automatic people live in an automatic world.

Knight's review compared the descent to Level 7 with Alice falling down the rabbit hole.[17] However, once there, the people inhabit a world far more like the one Alice found when she walked through the looking glass: topsy-turvy. Au-tomated dummies live by codes far different from ours. Some of the sharpest ironies in the novel come from this reversal. For instance, the romance of X-127 and P-867 can make sense only in the context of a society where space is so limited that marital partners cannot live together and can be assigned only one hour a day of privacy. As X-127 puts it, since "restricted privacy is a necessity . . . the less a person cares for his mate, the better."[18] In our world marital love is assumed to be good, even necessary; in Level 7 loving one's spouse can only cause problems.

When X-127 and his friend write myths for children, they agree on certain self-evident principles: open spaces, great distances, and variety are negative values; confinement and monotony are positive ones. Level 7's first marriage, performed in the laundry room, occurs as the classical music tape is cycling through Chopin's "Funeral March." The treat of chocolate that P-867 shares with X-127 at their wedding feast makes him ill. After the war, the operations room is to be converted into a maternity ward. Life in bomb shelters turns upside down all traditional human values.

The one exception to the personality types and values of Level 7 is, of course, X-127's roommate, X-117, who serves as foil to everyone else. Because of his fear of destroying life, the psychologists diagnose him abnormal and neurotic. "Normal" in Level 7 means pushing buttons without thought or feeling. After being "cured" and partially participating in the three-hour war, he cries and calls himself a "hangman" who "did what a robot told me to do."[19] He shows an awareness of the horror both of the results of his actions and of the automatic, unthinking cause of them. X-127's response is a Level 7 rationale, "I feel better than I did before. Not that I enjoyed pushing those buttons particularly, but doing it made me feel rather important"[20] (and that "rather" is grimly chilling). To match X-117's unbearable guilt, which leads to his suicide the following day, X-127 can offer only "the chilly feeling I had when I saw the black screen in the Operations Room."[21] X-127's response to X-117's suicide is a baffling attempt to distinguish between killing with one's bare hands and killing by pushing a button on a "typewriter": "smooth, clean, mechanical."[22] He concludes that X-117 could not distinguish between the two and that was the source of his problem. In fact, X-127's inability to see any difference between the two makes him a callous killer.

The value system demonstrated by this line of thought is part of the upside-down world of Level 7, which the inhabitants believe is preferable to all others. Besides the Kafkaesque nightmare and the Orwellian repression, there is also a Panglossian idiocy in the outlook of Level 7 citizens who can rationalize anything: "Level 7 is the best of all possible levels, the best of all possible worlds."[23] At least Candide was able to turn from moral judgments about his dreadful world to his garden. X-127 can only turn his face to the wall and die.

After the death of X-117, the narrator appears to be starting to develop a conscience. When the couple from Level 3 report on the surface destruction, he writes, "Only now do I realize how *cold* I was inside. How dead. Now I can understand X-117. He must have had a lot of that warm feeling."[24] The novel teeters on the brink of becoming a tale of character transformation. Roshwald, however, avoids that: P-867 tears up journal entries for about ten weeks, thus wiping out whatever evidence there may have been for change in X-127. The novel ends with X-127 as a detached reporter of events who only on occasion expresses bitterness. While this weakens the novel severely as literature, it may have been the only possible choice if Roshwald wanted to finish his story.[25] As demonstrated by X-117's fate, a moral, feeling person in Level 7 can be only mad or bent on suicide. X-127 must live if we are to hear the whole story of Level 7.

As he dies at the end of the last entry, he writes the words that have come to represent the values made abnormal in the subterranean society: "friends   people   mother sun   I   I"[26]—human love, warmth (both literal and metaphorical), and a recognition of the individual, too, have died.

Level 7's picture of World War III is possibly the most terrifying of any yet envisioned, and not only because of the pain and destruction that will result. The vision portrayed, of a world already dead before the bombs fall and little changed afterward, suggests a connection between this death of the heart and the button pushing. And that is the final nihilism, the ultimate nightmare. As apathy and impersonality grow, Roshwald's novel argues, the closer we come to annihilation.

Level 7 shows us the end, the extreme by which we can measure our own passions, commitment, and individuality. The more like the rubber dummies of Level 7 we become, the better our chances of losing hearts and lives—and world.

NOTES

1. Phoebe Adams, "The Atlantic Bookshelf," *Atlantic Monthly,* April 1960, p. 112.

2. Damon Knight, "Books," *Magazine of Fantasy and Science Fiction,* July 1960, p. 78.

3. Mordecai Roshwald, *Level 7* (New York: Signet, 1959), p. 7.

4. Ibid., p. 14.

5. Ibid., p. 87.

6. Ibid., p. 6.

7. Ibid.

8. Ibid., p. 10.

9. Ibid., p. 22.

10. Ibid., p. 23.

11. Ibid., p. 56.

12. Ibid., p. 22.

13. Ibid., p. 65.

14. P. Schuyler Miller, "The Reference Library," *Analog Science Fact and Fiction,* November 1960, p. 62.

15. Knight, p. 77.

16. Roshwald, p. 101.

17. Knight, p. 76.

18. Roshwald, p. 69.

19. Ibid., p. 110.

20. Ibid.

21. Ibid.

22. Ibid., p. 22.

23. Ibid., p. 31.

24. Ibid., p. 122.

25. Also, Roshwald has gone on record with his priorities. He has commented that *Level 7* was written "out of concern for the future of humanity. The extinction of mankind described here is an educational ploy. The automation and dehumanization of Level 7 is the expression of another concern" (Mordecai Roshwald, quoted by R. Reginald, "Mordecai Roshwald," *Science Fiction and Fantasy Literature: A Checklist, 1700–1974 with Contemporary Science Fiction Authors II* [Detroit: Gale Research, 1971], p. 1054). Another source quotes him as saying that "science fiction is for me a *form* of expression rather than an objective in its own right. In this sense I would classify *Level 7* with such books as Swift's *Gulliver's Travels* or Huxley's *Brave New World*," whose value he feels is in their meaning as parables rather than as literature (Mordecai Roshwald, quoted by E. R. Bishop, "Roshwald, Mordecai [Marceli]," *Twentieth-Century Science-Fiction Writers,* ed. Curtis C. Smith [New York: St. Martin's Press, 1981], p. 455). In short, Roshwald perceives himself as educator and persuader rather than as artist. The literary medium is secondary to the message.

26. Roshwald, p. 143.

11

NOT WITH A BANG BUT WITH A WHIMPER: ANTICATASTROPHIC ELEMENTS IN VANCE'S *DYING EARTH*

Gregory M. Shreve

And all the world's a stage,
and all the men and women merely players:
They have their exits and their entrances;
. . . Last scene of all,
that ends this strange eventful history,
Is second childishness, and mere oblivion,
Sans teeth, sans eyes, sans taste, sans everything.[1]

Catastrophe is change. Derived from the Greek *kata,* meaning "downwards," and *strephein,* meaning "to turn," it originally referred to the change which produces the denouement of a drama, quite literally the "turning upside down" of the beginning of the plot. Man is a creature of such inversions and changes. His birth is catastrophic, thrusting him, abruptly, onto the world's stage. It is a violent coming forth, the culmination, itself, of a small explosive catastrophe of passion. A man's death is his final, private catastrophe, a "turning upside down" of his birth, as his birth was an inversion of his conception. It does not seem strange therefore that man, a creature of such eventful history, should view his world and his universe as an unstable and violent place. Man has conceived of world's end, quite characteristically, as a sudden and violent change; world's end is an equivalent but inverted form of the world's turbulent and fiery birth. Birth and death are reflections of one another. Which is beginning and which is end?

Authors and poets have conceived of the world's end in a variety of forms:

in deluge; in holocausts of consuming, nuclear fire; in all-encompassing plagues; and in freezing glaciers. These visions of the end share many elements common to the modern conception of the word "catastrophe." There is the presence of extreme violence and destruction and of the sudden, radical overturning of order, calm, and stability. World's end is always momentous, laden with significance. Our phenomenology and cultural history place upon the word "catastrophe" burdens of portent, alteration, and purgation. Since the great catastrophe may be both death and birth, the hope of resurrection burns bright. Thus does the phoenix arise from its own ashes.

There is a genre of science fiction that explores the forms of planetary catastrophe and the resurrections of human life that, inevitably, occur in their aftermath. In Edwin Balmer and Philip Wylie's classics *When Worlds Collide* (1933) and *After Worlds Collide* (1934), the catastrophe is followed by a rebirth. Man escapes the destruction of his ancestral home and begins life anew. In Sterling Lanier's *Hiero's Journey* (1973), life continues, albeit changed, after global holocaust. There is a tendency for authors to see the great catastrophe as simply the demarcation of an old life from a new, more exotic, more dangerous, and presumably more interesting life. Catastrophes are often seen as turning points, junctions in larger and more cosmic cycles, perhaps therefore both inevitable and natural. The catastrophe is viewed millennially or, more exactly, apocalyptically, as the prelude to a resurrection.

There is also a tendency to view holocausts from a human perspective. Fictional catastrophes threaten man with extinction; his civilization and his known ways of life are endangered. The players may be catastrophically uprooted, almost destroyed, or dissipated. They are always altered by the extremity of the great catastrophe. New players take their cues and block their places upon brand new stages. Thus in Walter Miller's *Canticle for Leibowitz* (1960), there is a new social schema, but man continues, altered, against the backdrop of the earth. In Stanley Weinbaum's *The Black Flame* (1948), the rules of life on earth are altered and the scenery has changed, but life, albeit more exotic, goes on.

In the aftermath of the great catastrophe, the old is broken down, burned, or washed away. Authors have taken two views of life in the aftermath, one as liberation, the other as bondage. Life may be more difficult and dangerous, but there is the feeling that there is renewed purpose to life, that the challenges of life have reappeared. The breakdown of order and stability have, in a sense, liberated the individual and prepared the foundations for new and more vigorous societies. Thus in Leigh Brackett's *The Long Tomorrow* (1955), the atmosphere of challenge and purpose is the dramatic focus of the novel. On the other hand, in Peter Dickinson's *The Weathermonger* (1968), the aftermath is indeed a new beginning, but one founded on conservatism and retrogression. Nevertheless, even in these accounts the narrative focuses on liberation, a tossing off of the remnants of the past. In some, the great catastrophe is a cleansing or a purgation where the new order is purer and more rarified than the old.

In other examples of the genre, the focus is on the reconstruction of the past.

The great catastrophe has wiped out the best of civilization, usually the literature and art and technology, and the narrative focuses on the rebuilding of the past, though even here there is a winnowing. Only the best is rebuilt. The societies are new ones, discarding the restrictive elements of the old. There is always a sense in most of the narratives of an increased vigor, as if the great catastrophe had renewed the soil of old earth and enriched the fertility and resourcefulness of its inhabitants. Life is, to be sure, more difficult, almost always more dangerous and uncomfortable, but of such challenges is fiction made.

There are many possible scenarios in the "catastrophe/postcatastrophe" literature of science fiction, but the primary underlying themes of this subgenre seem to be resurrection, alteration, purgation, liberation, vigor, purpose, or challenge.

All of these parallel human experience, and generally speaking they are tied closely to the concept that catastrophe is not final, that there is something beyond. To deny this would be to deny that catastrophe is significant, that events of such violence and impact are not also meaningful in some way. Thus the conceptualization of the postcatastrophic in science fiction and its fertile speculation on the rules of life on a new and resurrected earth play upon themes that most closely touch the human spirit.

In most conceptualizations of world's end, the perspective is catastrophe-focused. In many, the catastrophe is impending; the ambience of the novel depends on the approach of the catastrophe, its signs and portents. This perspective is apocalyptic. Catastrophe looms, approaches, appears, and man wins through. Other views are postcatastrophic. In them, the catastrophe is past and the precatastrophic era is evoked by images of the past and traces of precatastrophic life: abandoned roads, ruined cities, Liberty half-buried in the sand.

Jack Vance's conception of world's end, as conceived in "The Dying Earth" trilogy, however, is quite different and totally unique. It follows none of the typical patterns. It is both noncatastrophic and antiapocalyptic. It is noncatastrophic because there is no violent overthrow of the established order; there are no cataclysms or holocausts. It is antiapocalyptic because there are no new vigorous "remade worlds" to come—the earth is old; there is to be no second coming. Catastrophes are sudden and violent. Much of the fictional power of the catastrophe, as used in science fiction's postcatastrophe genre, lies in its violation of mundanity, its complete departure from the world as we know it. Vance's earth, however, has undergone no violent, sudden changes. The earth has, instead, slowly and in the minutest increments declined and faded. This is clearly shown in "T'sais," one of the six short stories comprising *The Dying Earth,* when the Wizard Pandelume appraises the planet:

Once it was a tall world of cloudy mountains and bright rivers, and the sun was a white blazing ball. Ages of rain and wind have beaten and rounded the granite, and the sun is feeble and red.[2]

In the place of catastrophe is a long but inevitable decline, a slow and final "petering out." "The Dying Earth" trilogy is an inversion of the postcatastrophe genre; Vance has substituted graduality and the slow, eroding passage of the eons for the suddenness of catastrophe; he has substituted decay, erosion, and decadence for violence and upheaval; he has substituted the finitude and stark symmetry of a linear universe for the implicit periodicity of a resurrected one.

The trilogy is a spectacular, fictional canvas covering three books: *The Dying Earth* (1977), *The Eyes of the Overworld* (1977) and *Cugel's Saga* (1984). It is a lustrous and finely detailed account of earth in its latter days. At this world's end there are no futures to be plotted and no resurrections possible. Vance's technique is effectively to invert all of the major presuppositions of the postcatastrophe genre and to display subtly the ironies and the futilities of the human preoccupation with dreams of resurrection.

Vance's earth occupies a linear, symmetrical universe; there are no eternal cycles of birth and rebirth. Resurrection and rebirth, common themes of the postcatastrophe novel, presuppose a nonlinear universe, a universe of eternal and recursive cycles, where the progeny of a resurrection may be more magnificent than its catastrophic source. Indeed, the legend of the phoenix rising from its own ashes gains its power from the asymmetry of the image; from base ash arises that most rare and excellent of birds. The six short stories that make up the first volume of the trilogy are in reality six little parables, each a discourse on linearity, symmetry, and finitude. In the story "Turjan of Miir" the lesson is a basic one: the life of a man, of a planet, of a universe is finite and is bounded by its symmetry and temporality. There is a beginning point and an ending point. Before and after stretch into nothingness. There are, Vance tells us, true endings and beginnings. Beginning and ending are twins, bound inexorably together. T'sais, the tragically flawed twin of the beautiful T'sain, illustrates this when she challenges the wizard, Turjan, to kill her. "Do as you please," she says, "Life and Death are brothers."[3] There are boundaries; when we reach the end, life is over. The sudden overturnings and renewals of the apocalypse are not for Vance. Indeed, as Pandelume observes, "The universe is methodized by symmetry and balance, in every aspect of existence is this equipoise, observed."[4] Thus, for growth there is decline; for every birth, a death; for every good, an evil. And, of course, for every world's beginning, a world's ending.

In *Eyes of the Overworld*, the sage, Pharesm, tells Cugel that the Law of Equipoise demands a counteract for every act.[5] In a universe based on Equipoise, the idea of resurrection is excluded, as is the hope of a remade, renewed world. Although for millennia religions have flourished on evocations of the remade world—what is a paradise but a particular manifestation of the "remade world"?—Vance would caution us about belief in resurrections. In the short story "Guyal of Sfere," Guyal's father tells him frankly:

Death is the heritage of life; a man's vitality is like air in a bladder. Point this bubble and away, away, away, flees life.[6]

One must be fair and point out that Vance is not just antiresurrectionist but also antiteleological. Antiteleology is one of the major unifying elements of the trilogy. Cugel, the protagonist of the last two books, is a true trickster character. Relying on the trickster's well-defined role as a debunker, Vance uses Cugel to underscore the futility of man's grand schemes. In comic and sometimes unintentional ways, Cugel debunks man's grand preoccupation with cosmic purposes, first causes, and final truths. In *Eyes of the Overworld,* for example, he meets the magician, Pharesm, who has toiled five hundred years to discover the essence of life. After Cugel mistakenly lunches on the object of Pharesm's search, the creature called Totality, Cugel informs the mage: "its flavor, even after careful grilling at the brazier, was not distinctive."[7] In *Cugel's Saga,* Vance introduces us to the Order of Solar Emosynaries, a group dedicated to restimulating the vitality of the sun through a complex arrangement of mirrors and lenses which are trained upon the sun with ritual precision and punctuality. After hearing them claim responsibility for the continued daily appearance of the sun, Cugel naively suggests: "Conceivably the sun has waned beyond all possibility of regulation, so that your efforts, though formerly useful, are now ineffective."[8] Similarly in the villages of Vull and Tustvold, in the city of Lumarth, and at the Black Obelisk of Erze Damarth, Cugel contributes with blithe abandon to the dismantling of ideology and religion. While Vance's lack of faith in the likelihood of resurrection and renewal is part and parcel of a wry skepticism that permeates the trilogy and is best personified in the person of Cugel, the skeptic's viewpoint is also well displayed in the short story "Ulan Dhor" where the lessons of the parable are the futility of religion, the transitory nature of power, and great plans brought low by time. It is of a cloth with Vance's perception of a finite universe.

One of the most common features of "remade world" stories is a dramatic alteration of the postcatastrophic landscape. The new landscape and its denizens are frequently exotic and dangerous, but provides powerful new images for the writer to use, the images helping to highlight the contrast between the old and the new. Catastrophe, by its radical nature, is presumed capable of the profound transformations that follow in its wake. The alteration is, in effect, a second "creation," and the author's perspective is essentially creationist. Vance's dying earth is also an altered landscape, but it is not the product of either creation or re-creation. Rather, it is the product of evolution. Its inhabitants, several thousand "strange souls," are not the products of a remade world but hybridizations and distillations, the progeny of untold years of ferment and infusion. The altered landscape of the classic remade world is the product of abrupt and radical transformations. Change is sudden, and the alteration, by definition, is catastrophic in nature as well as source. *The Dying Earth,* on the other hand, is not remade—there is only one making—its landscape and its creatures are evolutionary. There is, in the contrast between the remade world and the dying earth, a contrast between the creationist and the evolutionist.

There remain, nonetheless, powerful images to be evoked by Vance's ancient landscape. Among the sharpest evocations are the myriad weird creatures that

populate latter-day earth. It is interesting to note that most of Vance's creatures—
the deodands, asms, gids, grues, erbs, and leucomorphs—are odd hybrids of
man and other beasts. It is as if the author were saying we need no catastrophes
to populate the earth with a weird menagerie; time and man's endless experimentation will suffice.

Another characteristic of the "remade world" is that it emerges, cleansed and
liberated, from the ashes of its past. Indeed the larger theme of resurrection is
inextricably linked with the notions of purgation, cleansing, and forgiveness.
One of Vance's most powerful inversions of the "catastrophe" genre is his
inversion of the theme of purgation. His attitude is most clearly revealed in
"Guyal of Sfere," one of the stories in *The Dying Earth*. There, Kerlin, curator
of the Museum of Man, answers Guyal's questions about the motives and nature
of the demon Blikdak:

Consider him! . . . He is nothing else but anthropoid, and such is his origin. . . . Blikdak
is from the mind of man. The sweaty condensation, the stench and vileness, the cloacal
humours, the brutal delights, the rapes and sodomies, the scatophilac whims, the manifold
tittering lubricites that have drained through humanity formed a vast tumor; so Blikdak
assumed his being.[9]

It is clear that Vance's earth is not only an old one but is one with a burden;
there has been a cumulation over time of untold layers of good and evil. So
much time has passed, so much evil committed, that an entire demon-world has
been created, a malignant cohort to the dying earth. The Law of Equipoise, a
dictum of Vance's own creation, would explain the peculiar state of the earth.
Every good act and every bad act has left a residue; over twenty thousand or
more eons, the earth lays under an ethical burden of its own making. In the
short story "T'sais," the wizard Pandelume says of it, "There is evil on Earth,
evil distilled by time."[10] Man has lived on earth a long, long time, and it appears
that, in the balance, there has been more evil than good. Demons and other
peculiar cumulations of human sin seem more populous than their angelic coun-
terparts. Earth is in its twilight. What is the sense of hope for renewal in an
earth so run down, so tired, bearing such a burden? Forgiveness is not as simple
as a sacrifice or a confession. A holocaust, in its original sense as a burnt offering,
is not sufficient to exorcise the malignancy.

Vance's Law of Equipoise has an ethical manifestation in a strict concept of
justice. This is best exemplified, again in "T'sais," where T'sais and her lover
Etarr are restored and their disfigurements banished, not by magic or by sacrifice
but by a Divinity of Utter Justice who says to them: "To each who comes,
justice is done!"[11] Global purgations and cleansings are not possible in a world
of Equipoise; we are each as individuals responsible for our own actions. There
is a universal balance sheet of good and evil which each of us as individuals
writes upon. If we, as a race, fail to create the perfect world, there will be no
second chance.

In most postcatastrophe stories, the global holocaust, in its sacrificial sense, brings about a liberation. After all, purgation is about freedom—a lifting of sins, a sloughing off of the mistakes of the past. We drown our sins in water, as in baptism, or burn them in fire, but there is no such liberation in Vance's cosmos. We carry with us through life the sum total of our experiences, our actions and inactions, our good deeds and bad. We are, in Vance's cosmology, all that we have done. His is a world well used. There is nothing new or likely to be new about it. Too much has transpired on this globe over too long a time for us ever to be free of it. Turjan, in "Turjan of Miir," muses as he surveys the air of ancient earth: "How many times had this air been breathed before him? What cries of pain had this air experienced, what sighs, laughs . . . ?"[12]

It would be remiss, however, to presuppose that Vance is an utter cynic, denying all hope or any chance at liberation. He does, in fact, uphold a philosophy he has espoused elsewhere, most noticeably in the novel *To Live Forever* (1956). There, Gavin Waylock, an immortal of the Amaranth class, must flee to the stars to live a life unfettered and free. Similarly in "Guyal of Sfere," the concluding story of *The Dying Earth* anthology, the young lovers, Guyal and Shierl, wonder what to do after they have received the keys of the Museum of Man from its curator. Guyal comments as he looks up at the stars: " 'Knowledge is ours, Shierl—all of knowing to our call. And what shall we do? . . . What shall we do?' "[13] The story is an intriguing conclusion to the first volume for the very reason that it hints at a liberation and a freedom that the rest of the volume has denied. Explicit in the story is the idea that the museum is the earth in microcosm; it is a place of relics and fossils. The earth is no place for the young, for the untrammeled freedom required by new ideas. In answer to their question, Kerlin, the curator, urges the lovers to flee: "Attend, the stars are bright, the stars are fair; the banks know blessed magic to fleet you to youthful climes."[14]

Vance is not, strictly speaking, a pessimist, although his landscape leads us to believe that he is. It is just that unlike other authors he disdains the device of the remade world. The vigor and vitality of life arise not from the ashes of a planetary holocaust but from less global, but perhaps more cosmic, things such as simple acts of human love. It is interesting to note that in "T'sais," the most upbeat and ultimately optimistic of Vance's parables in *The Dying Earth,* young lovers are featured quite prominently. T'sais, the beautiful protagonist, is fatally flawed. The wizard Pandelume created her from his vats, but he wrought carelessly: "what we hold to be beautiful seems to her loathsome and ugly, and what we find ugly is to her intolerably vile."[15] Unhappy with her condition after seeing her perfect twin, T'sain, T'sais escapes to earth to, as she puts it, "search for love and beauty."[16] There, after many adventures, she meets and falls in love with Etarr, whom the witch, Jevanne, has cursed with a demon's face. Yet in the end, as they stand before the god of Justice, they are restored. Although Justice is the agent, it is clear that love has been their true salvation. They were restored from the moment T'sais confesses to Etarr "that which underlies my brain . . . that which is me loves you, the you underneath the mask.''[17] In an old and tired world we can expect no planetary miracles of vitality and vigor; the world cannot be remade, but we can remake ourselves. Vitality lies in the youth that love brings. Guyal and Shierl, at the Museum of Man, gaze at the white, bright stars; Etarr looks down into T'sais' face, into ''the eyes glowing with such feverish joy that they seemed afire.''[18] The message is clear; we alone, through love, renew ourselves.

There are, ultimately, no great purposes in Vance's world. The great challenges of the classic postcatastrophe novel with its grand rebuildings and noble struggles are not for him. It is clear that in such an old world one monumental task, more or less, is insignificant. All deeds, unimaginably monstrous and exhilaratingly noble, fade and are ultimately forgotten. The passage of time, inexorable and slow, erases all mementos and monuments. In Vance's finite and symmetrical universe, governed by the universal Law of Equipoise, all things come to an end. It avails us naught to ignore the inevitable. In the story ''Lliane the Wayfarer,'' a darkly beautiful allegory of death, Vance reminds us that even the young and vital, like Lliane the Wayfarer with his golden eyes and all unthinking and careless in his rash bravado, will not avoid death. Chun, the Unavoidable, says when he hands the witch Lith two golden threads for her unfinished tapestry, ''it is two long threads for you. Two because the eyes were so great, so large, so golden.''[19]

All that is or can be significant in our transitory passage are the simple things like love, which in the short span of two lives leaves an indelible mark.

NOTES

1. William Shakespeare, *As You Like It, The Complete Works of Shakespeare,* ed. Hardin Craig (Glenville, Ill.: Scott, Foresman and Co., 1961), II, l. vii.

2. Jack Vance, *The Dying Earth* (New York: Pocket Books, 1977), p. 42.

3. Ibid., p. 11.

4. Ibid., p. 12.

5. Jack Vance, *Eyes of the Overworld* (New York: Pocket Books, 1977), p. 101.

6. Vance, *The Dying Earth,* p. 108.

7. Vance, *Eyes of the Overworld,* p. 101.

8. Jack Vance, *Cugel's Saga* (New York: Baen Enterprises, 1984), p. 253.

9. Vance, *The Dying Earth,* p. 150.

10. Ibid., p. 42.

11. Ibid., p. 66.

12. Ibid., p. 9.

13. Ibid., p. 156.

14. Ibid., p. 155.

15. Ibid., p. 13.

16. Ibid., p. 49.

17. Ibid., p. 60.

18. Ibid., p. 67.

19. Ibid., p. 79.

12

J. G. BALLARD: WE ARE THE SURVIVORS

Judith B. Kerman

What are we to make of J. G. Ballard's apocalypse? The question is implicit in much of the critical response to his early work, providing the title of a major essay by H. Bruce Franklin. Critics are divided between those who see him as a major literary force whose importance transcends science fiction and those who find him intriguing but finally unsatisfying, his characters "hopeless," his plots unconvincing, and only his peculiar landscapes sometimes worthy of appreciation.

Ballard's work is most commonly divided into two major phases: four early novels of global apocalypse, written in the 1960s and later novels which might be called obsessive or even pornographic, technological dystopias. But there are also numerous short stories resembling both types, and critics have noted that,

Despite some deceptive differences in casts of characters, the stories all seem to be part of some larger story or parable, being seen from different points of view.[1]

Readers note a constant repetition from book to book of situations, character types, physical artifacts, themes, and images. In the typical Ballard catastrophe story of the 1960s, the protagonist, an English physician or biologist, is caught up in a global catastrophe, which may or may not be a result of human technologies but which results in the immediate collapse of normal society. He wanders through the dramatically changed landscape, interacting with various other characters in a way which has been called "affectless"; the reader feels that this lack of affect is typical of him and not a result of the disaster.

The protagonist is obsessively drawn to the epicenter of the disaster, respond-

ing to it as his true home, the set of conditions under which he will become
what he truly must be. Ballard often suggests that this changed world has resulted
from an alteration, particularly a reversal, in the flow of time and that the
protagonist is the character who is most sensitive in responding to it.

Among the other characters, he meets beautiful women whom he perceives
as projections of his own fantasies, as well as cripples, consumptives, lepers,
or other diseased individuals. His antagonist is invariably a rich madman who
attempts to defy the new conditions and reestablish dominance. The madman
often executes a major architectural or engineering feat, such as a pyramid or
dam.

When critics speak of the Ballardian "landscape," they note his persistent
use of water, sand, dust, dunes, drifts, crystals, and concrete. Crystals invariably
"deliquesce," tall buildings are partly submerged in sand or water, and sometimes layers of debris form geological strata. Fossils and beaches are important
transitional symbols, marking the boundaries between two times (past and future)
and two states of being (water and sand, life and crystal). Dwellings are usually
hotels, clinics, chalets, or beach houses.

The landscape is often called a desert and is littered with the debris of technological civilization. David Pringle's list of Ballard's "properties" includes:

concrete weapons-ranges, dead fish, abandoned airfields, radio telescopes, crashed space-
capsules, sand dunes, empty cities, sand reefs, half-submerged buildings, helicopters,
crocodiles, open-air cinema screens, jewelled insects, advertising hoardings, white hotels,
beaches, fossils, broken juke-boxes, crystals, lizards, multi-storey car parks, dry lake-
beds, medical laboratories, drained swimming pools, mannequins, sculpture gardens,
wrecked cars, swamps, motorway flyovers, stranded ships, broken Coke bottles, bales
of rusting barbed wire, paddy fields, lagoons, deserts, menacing vegetation, high-rise
buildings, predatory birds, and low-flying aircraft.[2]

While no story contains all of these, most appear repeatedly. Franklin
comments,

Ballard is a poet of death whose most typical fictions are apocalyptic imaginings, beautiful
and ghastly visions of decay, death, despair. His early novels . . . are science fictions of
the wasteland.[3]

Ballard was a particularly eminent founding member of the 1960s "New
Wave," so his treatment of the catastrophe theme is important in the history of
science fiction and, by extension, in the literary eschatology of our scientific
era. Typical of the "New Wave," he opposed the view of science fiction which

will admit to the genre only those motifs which have celebrated science . . . the optimists,
enthralled by the transformations being brought about in everyday life by a vibrant
technology.[4]

Although the first four novels were ambiguously futuristic, Ballard declared:

"I wanted a science-fiction of the present day. I am interested in the technology of the present of this world . . . the only alien planet is Earth."[5]

Ballard's repudiation of far-future and alien-world stories seems related to the pessimistic view of technology that arose from the political counterculture of the 1960s, its sense of impending nuclear and ecological doom.

Internally [to the New Wave] the charge was made that science fiction actually was dead—because the future was no longer credible. The crises of the twentieth century . . . were obviously insurmountable. We would never make it into the twenty-first century. This being so, these dreams of interplanetary colonies, of technological things to come, of galactic empires and so on were reduced to the status of pure fantasy . . . [their scientific credibility] cancelled out by the coming end of civilization and the world.[6]

Ballard responded to this situation by making a distinction between extrapolation or prediction, the underpinnings of the optimistic "hard" science fiction, and prophecy based in more visionary modes. He complained:

It's unfortunate for the writers of science fiction that they have to perform their task of describing the symbols of transformation in a so-called rationalist society, where scientific, or at least pseudo-scientific explanation is *required a priori* . . . the true prophet never deals in what may be rationally deduced.[7]

Is human society remade or renewed in Ballard's catastrophes? By and large, he does not seem interested in the question. In *The Burning World* (1964), for example, a new society evolves on the beach under the conditions of the drought. People form small communities, combining aspects of robber baronies and primitive tribes, ruled by ruthless madmen, and they compete for fish and water. However, the descriptions of the physical situation are patently impossible; for instance, distillation of seawater (energy source unspecified) has over a few years created miles-wide salt beaches; the sea has receded in spite of the fact that nothing can evaporate from it; and people capture fish and seawater in basins they dig in the salt dunes and bring the captured water home by driving it across the surface of the dry salt flats with brooms!

This is part of a larger disdain for verisimilitude, leading one critic to comment that the reader's belief "tends to crumble when certain prosaic questions are asked, such as why the police were not on hand to prevent the worst excesses."[8]

In the other three catastrophe novels, society is either shown in immediate and abject collapse (as in *The Wind from Nowhere*) or depicted as far away from the action (as in *The Crystal World*, set in a jungle colony; and *The Drowned World*, set in the ruins of London, far from the main society hunkered down in the Arctic). In fact, there seem to be very few people in the world of the early novels, with the single exception of the first gathering of refugees on the beach of *The Burning World;* in the next chapter, which takes place considerably later, the beach appears depopulated. In the few short stories that depict major populations, catastrophic overpopulation is the problem, and one gets little other sense of the character of society.

Far from depicting a remade society, Ballard does not seem interested in whether human society even survives. Two of the novels and many of the short stories suggest the ultimate likelihood of total destruction of life as we know it (one novel shows the beginning, one an advanced stage); while two (generally considered the weaker two) suggest a sudden and unexplained reduction in the destructive conditions just as the novel ends, leaving a devastated world and a destroyed social order. Ballard's interest appears to be in the process of catastrophe rather than in the long-term outcome, leading Fallowell to charge that

Prophets of doom are prophets in no useful sense, even if their predictions are true. They do nothing but gluttonize on disaster and encourage us to do likewise.[9]

Ballard's lack of any significant "pretence that his fantasies of the death of the world or the human species are scientific, plausible, or even possible,"[10] provides an important clue to his purpose. In both fictions and essays, he states that the landscape of his works is an externalization of the human psyche, and he has several times declared that

We live in a world ruled by fictions of every kind . . . inside an enormous novel. . . . The fiction is already there. The writer's task is to invent the reality. . . . The most prudent and effective method of dealing with the world around us is to assume that it is a complete fiction—conversely the one small node of reality left to us is inside our own heads.[11]

Ballard purposely undermines the reader's ability to rest comfortably in verisimilitude, a strategy linked to his repeated claim that our nonfictional reality is itself a fiction created by technology and advertising. Even when he was writing the four superficially nontechnological novels of catastrophe, he insisted that he was not interested in mystical eschatologies but in the implications of technological society. Ballard is a conscious surrealist who

clearly sees his own imaginings as only ostensibly caused by an unnatural quirk of nature. The world of his fiction already exists in the imaginations of a decadent society [for instance, in the paintings of Delvaux and Max Ernst].[12] He comments approvingly that Dali splits up the elements of reality and assembles them to constitute a kind of Freudian landscape. We entertain certitudes about the subject of reality which permit us to live. . . . The work of Dali and other surrealist painters is to undermine these certitudes.[13]

By emphasizing the fictional character of the world readers consider "real" and presenting the inside of the writer's head, even at its most fantastic, as more real than the culture we experience daily, Ballard emphasizes the role of his fiction, of all fiction, as symbolic expression and simultaneously as itself part of the real.

Ballard's eminence grows from his willingness to tackle two major issues involved in implementing such a theoretical position. First, he struggles to establish a distinction between prophecy and scientific extrapolation or prediction. Whatever we may think of his style, he is much more successful as a surrealist poet than as a creator of plot, character, or even, in a realistic sense, setting. He reintroduces poetic vision. His disdain for rationalist credibility makes it impossible for the reader to pretend that his book is "realistic" in the naive sense of verisimilitude.

He uses his reader's resulting alienation, as he says, to undermine the quasi-scientific, extrapolative relationship many readers want to assume between today's nonfictional reality and the possible futures portrayed in science fiction. Instead, he reestablishes the biblical role of the prophet as one who describes things as they are now through the medium of visionary language.

In doing so, and by his "constantly reiterated reminder . . . that the external landscapes are merely projections of an inner landscape,"[14] Ballard takes the second decisive step: he declares the boundary between "real life" and his fictions to be illusory.

To the extent that most readers see science fiction as predictive, I believe they tend to see it in a "naively realistic" mode. Science fiction stories seem to tell us how life could be if some particular real event occurred. As Ballard observes, readers expect scientific credibility from their "thought experiments." On the other hand, in such stories the boundaries between the fiction and our "real" world are firm. While an apocalyptic work tells how things will be *if* some catastrophe occurs, that future-oriented *if* is the main place where the boundary between book and life can be dissolved. Until the *if* occurs, we are safe to enjoy the vicarious terrors of the story, all the more so because the extrapolative method encourages us to believe they are both possible in the future and nonexistent in the present.

Of course, critics have long departed from "naive realist" modes of reading, but in the 1960s Ballard was addressing a large and growing popular audience for science fiction, whose relationship to the question of verisimilitude is more problematic. Science fiction appears to be, for many readers, a quasi-religion of a peculiarly fundamentalist kind, "a unique kind of story whose purpose is to teach and propesy."[15] While critics generally consider it a category of fantasy literature, fans of "hard" science fiction often disdain "sword and sorcery" and develop elaborate theories differentiating "true" science fiction from fantasy. The messianic age predicted in the science fiction story is expected to come, if not in its details, at least fully in its implications; readers take "faster-than-light travel" literally. And, indeed, the technological triumphs and disasters of our civilization tend to support such expectations, leading Ballard to comment:

Everything is becoming science fiction. From the margins of an almost invisible literature has sprung the intact reality of the 20th century.[16]

Ballard took the radical step of writing books that are unsatisfying if read literally. His novels ask implicit questions about verisimilitude and simultaneously about our culture, while his essays make his purposes explicit. No wonder the fans disliked his work; he wants to undermine their comfort not only in science fiction but in everyday reality as well. Ballard's main claim to prediction, as opposed to prophecy, is on the psychological level; he is talking about the world we live in, not the one we imagine. But he shows us that the world we live in *is* a world we have imagined and then realized: "The terrestrial and psychic landscapes were indistinguishable, as they had been at Hiroshima and Auschwitz, Golgotha and Gomorrah."[17]

This is made most clear in his views of landscape and of catastrophe. The stunningly successful short story "The Terminal Beach," set on an atomic bomb test atoll, bridges and conflates the early catastrophe and the later technological novels. Perry and Wilkie write:

Eniwetock . . . is not only the world of Ballard's characters; it is *the* world for all of us, but only the Ballard characters can perceive it accurately. The biologist and his female assistant [who] help Traven . . . represent the "normal" human being, doing an "acceptable" job of work. . . . But their response to the island—and what the island represents—is clearly inadequate. The dead Japanese who has committed suicide recommends to Traven a philosophy of acceptance . . . but Traven finds great difficulty in reconciling himself to that position. The [blockhouses in the atomic bomb target], he confesses, stand in his way. The blocks are technology. . . . [To] soothe his inner compulsion he has to place the corpse between himself and the blocks as protection. . . . [T]o move towards the right response to a world represented by Eniwetok is difficult and can only be achieved by drawing upon the experience and wisdom of ways not normally accepted by technological society.[18]

The corpse of the dead Japanese places the story in the context of myth: the corpse is the angel with the flaming sword, which Traven places as both prohibition and protection between himself and the Eden of thermonuclear noon.

Not only does Ballard describe landscapes literally created as projections of the human psyche, "synthetic landscapes" like Eniwetock or a resort hotel, but he also sees landscape as an inherently psychological entity in our time. Discussing his experimental "novel" *The Atrocity Exhibition,* he wrote,

when I evoke the suicide of a Marilyn Monroe . . . it's because it doesn't appear to me simply as the death of a woman, but as a kind of space-time disaster, a catastrophe which created a rupture in our perception of time and space. . . . In effect, Marilyn Monroe, the Kennedys, the astronauts, are part of our mental landscape with as much right as the streets and houses that we frequent.[19]

This perception, as well as his description of automobile accidents as "a pandemic cataclysm institutionalised in all industrial societies,"[20] links the four early catastrophe novels firmly to the later technological books such as *Crash!* (1973) and *High-Rise* (1975), in which the disasters are restricted to one individual or a small group and are presented as growing out of the inherent nature of our technology.

Thus Ballard's stories written in the 1970s as "views of the present are not less dreadful than the previous view of the future, but more so."[21]

The connection between landscape and human psychology also explains the importance of biologists and physicians, who appear in forty-eight stories and four novels, often as the protagonists. Living things are the last and most crucial objects upon which we humans might project our fantasies and make them real, simultaneously appropriating all life to the psyche. Ballard's protagonists study viruses and the effects of radiation on natural flora and fauna. Ballard equates genetic charts and the record-selection charts on jukeboxes; he describes genetic experimentation gone awry.

In an ironic act of true prediction, in the 1960s Ballard prophesied the moral and psychological issues arising from genetic engineering. (In the light of his obsession with consumer products, a current joke about "designer genes" is particularly resonant.) True to his prophetic mode, he asked questions not only about practicality but about human values and purposes, the psyche and the soul. His biologists and physicians are both the individuals most able to note and track the changes in the biosphere and those most responsible for the experiments that make molecular biology a true technology in our time, capable of changing the world as well as describing it.

Another of Ballard's techniques for suggesting the problematic character of the relationship between fantasy and reality is the way he deals with female characters. Some critics have been disdainful of them as "listless biodegradable people, magazine archetypes . . . they have strayed here from the genteel de-odourised suburbs of the novelette."[22]

Others, such as David Pringle, see them as "lamias," which sometimes seems an accurate description for characters such as Miranda Lomax in *The Burning World*. Yet, often, while stressing the role of particular women in his protagonists' view of the world (Suzanne Clair and Louise Peret in *The Crystal World*, the young woman in "The Terminal Beach," Coma in "Voices of Time"), Ballard subtly hints that the women have a reality apart from the protagonists' projections, just as Marilyn Monroe had a reality apart from her place in the media landscape. In the essay "The Wounded Land," Brian Aldiss discusses one example of this as proof of Ballard's "wit,"[23] although I think the technique serves more urgent purposes. In Ballard's stories, as in too much of our culture's fiction, the woman is "the other," but she may also be human in her own right.

Much has been made of the evident desire of Ballard's characters to stop or reverse history, the time-related nature of his catastrophes, his pessimism (which he has both affirmed and denied in the same essay),[24] and his mysticism. Although he has called science fiction "the apocalyptic literature of the 20th Century,"[25] he has also sneered at the efforts of Lois and Stephen Rose[26] to find religious meaning in his works, insisting that "science fiction is totally atheistic" and that "if Mother Nature has anything in science fiction it is VD."[27]

H. Bruce Franklin has written brilliant and, on the whole, convincing analyses linking Ballard's obsession with the end of the world to the collapse of the British Empire.[28] But there is something more subtle and important going on.

Ballard has indicated that the most important aspect of the twentieth century is the "fact" of unlimited possibility. He believes that science and technology have not only made the past irrelevant, perhaps even killed it, but have also made limitless alternatives available to the present.[29]

Note that he does not say that they are available to the future. Ballard vividly describes the twentieth century as the "Pre-Third . . . suspended from the quivering volcano's lip of World War III."[30] He insists that "the future is a better key to the present than the past."[31] He writes, as Franklin has noted, stories in which the main character strips everything of its meaning, locking himself into solipsism by "reducing all objective reality to an appearance of his own mind."[32] Franklin's description of the alienated person, reduced by solipsism and commercial values to an "automaton of mindless consumption,"[33] is full of the resonances of Traven in "The Terminal Beach": hiding from his rescuers in a ditch full of partially melted, plastic mannequins, a horrific echo of the survivors hiding among the victims of Nazi massacres and simultaneously a projection of the dead of atomic war, melted like discarded toys.

Ballard questions whether contemporary writers can still make use of the conventions and perspectives of the nineteenth-century novel, especially its linear narrative and characters who live grandly in ample domains of space and time. He questions whether the writer has any longer the moral authority to create self-sufficient and self-enclosed worlds and to preside over them, knowing all the answers in advance.[34]

Ballard declares that this approach in fiction has been made impossible by science and technology, which have revised our concepts of past, present, and future. He points out that just as, in social and psychological terms, the past was a casualty of Hiroshima, the future is also being lost, annexed into our present as merely one possible option among many. The present has become all-voracious, an infantile place where almost any demand—whether for identity, travel, sexual role, or life-style—can be immediately satisfied.[35]

It is enough to give you vertigo, "a marriage of reason and nightmare . . . the spectres of sinister technologies and the dreams that money can buy."[36] Both the perception of the imminent end of time, implicit in the real possibility of nuclear war and the prospect of instant gratification change our relationship to the past as well as the future. We become unable to see time as a continuum in the mode of the nineteenth-century religion of progress which spawned the science fiction of future technology and space travel. The projected outcome, the mirage toward which "progress" progresses, is no longer credible.

One possible response is a cyclical sense of time; another is timelessness, stasis or Eden, eternity; a third is the perception of devolution, which permits us to hold to a linear time sense while explaining the disappearance of hope. Ballard experiments with all of these.

In this kind of world, boundary issues become critical. Ballard can sensibly describe a character in *The Atrocity Exhibition,* a later book, as

reacting against . . . the specific and independent existence of separate objects and events. . . . [F]or Traven science is the ultimate pornography, analytic activity whose main aim is to isolate objects from their contexts in time and space. This obsession with the specific activity of quantified functions is what science shares with pornography.[37]

This preoccupation with separation, with boundaries, explains both the microstructure and the larger function of Ballard's works.

At the level of imagery, he works constantly with boundaries and phase changes. His crystals, symbols of eternity, deliquesce. The river, "the great moderator," dries up, leaving each individual "an island in an archipelago drained of time."[38] Beaches, the boundary between the past of water and the future of sand, are settings in at least twenty-five stories; "The Terminal Beach" itself is made of concrete, "preeminently the symbol of *now in Ballard's fiction.*"[39]

Again and again in his stories we find the shapes of things dissolved by water or buried in shifting sands. Again and again we find concern with mutation; most strikingly, in *The Crystal World* it is with leprosy, the biblical disease of sin, a disease of dissolving fingers and noses, explicitly linked to the crystallizing phenomenon which simultaneously stops and multiplies time. And the fossil, the living, mutable thing become crystalline and eternal, is a talisman in several stories.

But Ballard's work is also concerned with the boundaries between life and art, as I have suggested. He wishes to create "an open narrative in which the act of reading itself becomes part of the creation process, or rather, the process of investigation."[40] If life is fiction, his fiction is life. Eric Rabkin and Robert Scholes note:

"Apotropaism" is the magical or religious art of warding off evil charms, incantations, or ritual performance. Whether that is what Ballard is up to, his fiction is clearly a fiction of extremities, in which the horrible is commonplace.[41]

This is more than a matter of cautionary tales. The New Wave attacked the implicit belief of previous science fiction in the religion of progress, with its European, superman-style hero and its implications of inevitable material reward for scientific rationalism. Ballard also accuses other science fiction writers of placing their stories in outer space or the far future in order to avoid understanding the psychological realities of their own civilization. He considers the hero of mainstream fiction (and implicitly the science fiction hero as well) guilty of the isolation and rationalism which the nineteenth century promulgated as the (masculine) ideal, "the man of action and power who seeks to master nature, to subject the natural and human worlds to his own will and pride."[42] Ballard calls this "Crusoeism," and each of the catastrophe novels features a madman of this type, who is clearly the double of the obsessed protagonist.

Ballard's protagonists are not, as some have suggested, simply passive. They are as isolated and self-directed as the madman, at least in terms of social norms, and they plunge into all kinds of perilous physical action with great intrepidity. They are not so much passive as obsessed, no longer "captains of their fates." They are heroes because they follow the logic of the landscape.[43]

But they are clearly doubled by the other half of the madman; the mad antagonist, the superman, is the avatar of Western man imposing his psyche on the world, while the protagonists are having their psyches possessed by cosmic forces of time. Different stories take different angles to the hero/madman pair. Which one is the reader? Which is Ballard?

Ballard claims that the world we experience daily is already a fiction, a projection onto the physical world of our fantasies, made possible by technology. As human society becomes more and more technologically powerful, that claim becomes more credible, and indeed it is not ridiculous to claim that some phenomena of our lives are directly inspired by science fiction itself. If we accept this vision of things, there is no longer any point to questioning the verisimilitude of Ballard's catastrophes, their scientific basis, or the credibility of the odd characters and marooned, evanescent societies that result.

Ballard chooses to create relatively incredible narratives as a way of participating meaningfully in the fact that the "real" world in which we live is a creation of the human imagination, up to and including the likelihood of mass suicide. Caught up in the processes of our own mass psychology, we act as if it were a force of nature, an externally imposed catastrophe, our destiny.

In these circumstances, Ballard's writing may indeed be "apotropaic," serving both magical and cautionary purposes. It partakes of prophecy in a deeper and more meaningful way than the normal equivalence of prophecy and prediction would suggest, although it is very likely an "atheistic" prophecy.

We, his readers, are given the opportunity to participate in creating other outcomes. If, more and more, anything that the human mind can imagine will become real, then the society that survives the catastrophes of Ballard's imagination is the world outside the boundaries of the book, the one in which the reader lives. We, the readers, are the potential survivors of the Ballardian catastrophe in which we actually live. If there is to be a remade world, we must make it, by re-creating the possibility of a "real world" independent of our psychological projections. That would be the true Eden.

NOTES

1. William Atheling, Jr., *More Issues at Hand* (Chicago: Advent Press, 1970), p. 5.

2. David Pringle, *Earth Is the Alien Planet: J. G. Ballard's Four-Dimensional Nightmare* (San Bernardino, Calif.: Borgo Press, 1979), p. 16.

3. H. Bruce Franklin, "Foreword to J. G. Ballard's 'The Subliminal Man,' " in *SF: The Other Side of Realism. Essays on Modern Fantasy and Science Fiction*, ed. Thomas D. Clareson (Bowling Green, Ohio: Bowling Green University Popular Press, 1971), p. 200.

4. Thomas D. Clareson, "The Other Side of Realism," in *SF: The Other Side of Realism. Essays on Major Science Fiction Writers*, ed. Thomas D. Clareson (Bowling Green, Ohio: Bowling Green University Popular Press, 1971), p. 15.

5. J. G. Ballard, quoted in John Fletcher, "J. G. Ballard," in *Dictionary of Literary Biography: British Novelists Since 1960*, part I (A–G), ed. Jay L. Halio (Detroit, Mich.: Gale Research, 1983), p. 50.

6. Donald A. Wollheim, *The Universe Makers: Science Fiction Today* (New York: Harper & Row, 1971), p. 103.

7. J. G. Ballard, quoted in John Griffiths, *Three Tomorrows: American, British and Soviet Science Fiction* (Totowa, N.J.: Barnes & Noble, 1980), p. 31.

8. Fletcher, p. 55.

9. Duncan Fallowell, "Ballard in Bondage," in *Books and Bookmen*, March 1977, pp. 59–60.

10. H. Bruce Franklin, "What Are We Going to Make of J. G. Ballard's Apocalypse?" in *Voices for the Future: Essays on Major Science Fiction Writers*, vol. 2, ed. Thomas D. Clareson (Bowling Green, Ohio: Bowling Green University Popular Press, 1979), p. 83.

11. J. G. Ballard, "some words about *Crash!*" *Foundation* 9 (1975), p. 48.

12. Franklin, "Foreword," p. 200.

13. Ballard, "Crash," p. 53.

14. Franklin, "Apocalypse," p. 85.

15. Clareson, "Other Side of Realism," p. 2.

16. J. G. Ballard, "Fictions of Every Kind," *Books and Bookmen* 16, 5 (February 1971), p. 11.

17. J. G. Ballard, quoted in Nick Perry and Roy Wilkie, "Homo Hydrogenesis: Notes on the Work of J. G. Ballard," *Riverside Quarterly* 4 (January 1970), p. 100.

18. Ibid., p. 103.

19. Ballard, "Crash," p. 52.

20. Ibid., p. 49.

21. George Barlow, "J. G. Ballard," in *Twentieth Century Science Fiction Writers*, ed. Curtis C. Smith (New York: St. Martin's Press, 1981), p. 31.

22. Fallowell, pp. 59–60.

23. Brian Aldiss, "The Wounded Land: J. G. Ballard," in *SF: The Other Side of Realism. Essays on Modern Fantasy and Science Fiction*, ed. Thomas D. Clareson (Bowling Green, Ohio: Bowling Green University Popular Press, 1971), p. 119.

24. Ballard, "Crash," pp. 45–47.

25. Pringle, p. 17.

26. Lois Rose and Stephen Rose, *The Shattered Ring: Science Fiction and the Quest for Meaning* (Richmond, Va.: John Knox Press, 1970).

27. Ballard, "Fictions," pp. 11–12.

28. Franklin, "Foreword" and "Apocalypse."

29. Ballard, "Crash," p. 46.

30. J. G. Ballard, "The Terminal Beach," in *Chronopolis and Other Stories* (New York: Putnam, 1971), p. 52.

31. Ballard, "Crash," p. 47.

32. Franklin, "Apocalypse," p. 88.
33. Ibid., p. 100.
34. Ballard, "Crash," p. 48.
35. Ibid.
36. Ibid., p. 45.
37. Pringle, p. 31.
38. J. G. Ballard, *The Burning World* (New York: Berkley Medallion, 1964), p. 11.
39. Pringle, p. 26.
40. Ballard, "Crash," p. 52.
41. Eric Rabkin and Robert Scholes, *Science Fiction: History, Science, Vision* (New York: Oxford University Press, 1977), p. 89.
42. Franklin, "Apocalypse," p. 90.
43. Pringle, p. 21.

13

"ARGUMENT NOT LESS BUT MORE HEROIC": EPIC, ORDER, AND POSTHOLOCAUST SOCIETY IN PIERS ANTHONY'S *BATTLE CIRCLE*

Michael R. Collings

From one perspective epic represents stasis. During the Renaissance, for example, the epic defined the height of literary achievement, as epitomized by Virgil's *Aeneid*.[1] In that poem, it was argued, Virgil captured the essence of humanity. As recently as 1942, C. S. Lewis wrote that by symbolizing the destiny of humanity the *Aeneid* "is 'great' in a sense in which no poem of the same type as the *Iliad* can ever be great. The real question is whether any epic development beyond Virgil is possible."[2] Milton similarly reacted to Virgil's reputation and to the epic tradition;[3] although dealing with God, Christ, and fallen angels, *Paradise Lost* also attempted to incorporate into Milton's Christian universe the status accorded to the pagan Virgil. And in spite of the subsequent decline of the epic after Milton, as the epic became more form than functional worldview, it retained a sense of awe seldom attained by other genres. In a time when long narrative poems are seldom written and even more rarely read, the *sense* of the epic survives, applied (and frequently misapplied) to unusually long or complex works. In this sense, then, epic becomes literary stasis, a genre of ultimate performance; beyond Virgil and Milton lies emptiness.

From another perspective, however, epic implies tension, cultures in conflict. Achilles enacts his private tragedy against the backdrop of the fall of Troy. Virgil's *Aeneid* re-creates the transition from Troy to imperial Rome. *Beowulf* suggests the passing of an old order, not only in the death of the king but also structurally in the interpolated Christianity so frequently at odds with the poem's Anglo-Saxon vision. *Paradise Lost* takes as its subject the most critical transition of all: the fall of humanity.

It seems appropriate, therefore, that science fiction writers build upon the epic, particularly when dealing with postcatastrophe human society. Structure is necessary, and since the novels depicting postholocaust conditions posit a rapid, violent, and irrevocable removal of traditional supports, something else must be adduced to provide stability. Some writers turn to religion, as in Walter Miller's neo-Catholicism in *A Canticle for Leibowitz* (1960) or Dean Ing's social Mormonism in *Systemic Shock* (1981). Others rely on military, political, racial, or cultural structures. Piers Anthony's *Battle Circle* trilogy, however, builds upon a literary foundation, as the novels become a twentieth-century prose analogue to the poetry of Homer, Virgil, and Milton—in form and structure if not in impact and grandeur.

Before examining epic in the *Battle Circle* novels—*Sos the Rope* (1968), *Var the Stick* (1972), and *Neq the Sword* (1975)[4]—it might be helpful to define the word. *Epic,* like so many other genre-related terms (including *science fiction* itself) is ambiguous. Even the Renaissance critics disagreed frequently, resulting in a continuous stream of treatises delineating the nature of epic. Contemporary readers, for whom *epic* connotes multigenerational novels or a twelve-hour television miniseries, may see the word as even more slippery. C. M. Bowra defines an epic poem as

a narrative of some length [that] deals with events which have a certain grandeur and importance and come from a life of action, especially of violent action such as war. It gives a special pleasure because its events and persons enhance our belief in the worth of human achievement and in the dignity and nobility of man.[5]

Excluding the requirement that an epic must be a poem, Bowra's definition seems as appropriate to Anthony's *Battle Circle* as to the *Orlando Furioso* or the *Song of Roland*.

In addition, within the epic, "character," as John M. Steadman says in reference to Milton, "is Fate" and much more.[6] At the core of every discussion of epic lies the question of the hero. Thomas Greene cites Northrop Frye's criteria that the epic character is

superior in degree to other man but not to his natural environment. . . . He has authority, passions, and powers of expression far greater than ours, but what he does is subject both to social criticism and to the order of nature.[7]

While such a character is explicitly denied qualities associated with godhood, the result is that particular awe associated with epic, as we watch a limited human complete an extraordinary action.

The hero's actions complement the hero. Tradition requires that they be performed by an individual or small group, that they result from the hero's acting to benefit the community, that they make a difference to the hero and his community, and that they be objective and external acts which "certify [themselves] in the world of time and space."[8]

Each of these epic characteristics appears in *Battle Circle,* modified to meet the demands of the novel as form and of Anthony's contemporary readers. Additionally, each novel corresponds to a particular epic subgenre: the Iliadic epic of individual prowess, the Odyssean epic of wandering, and the Virgilian epic of sacrifice.

Joan Mallory Webber has noted that the epic forms a historical genealogy rather than a code of abstract laws. A work is considered epic when it demonstrates a family resemblance to that which has preceded it.[9] To the extent that epic has survived into this century, it manifests in forms most concerned with stasis and change, with conflict and resolution—among them science fiction.[10]

ILIADIC EPIC: *SOS THE ROPE*

Writing of the *Iliad,* E. M. W. Tillyard concludes that the poem created the epic as genre; after the *Iliad* all that remained was to modify the form.[11] In several senses, this comment might be directed to *Sos the Rope. Sos* defines what follows in the trilogy; Anthony's responsibility is not to create a postcataclysm worldview but to show it modifying through time. Epic as structural device appears fully developed in *Sos.* It only remains for Anthony to explore its possibilities in the remaining novels.[12]

The *Iliad* deals with war and politics. Its characters are fighters or statesmen attempting to gain external control over their world. "Subjective conquest," Greene argues, "may complement the objective in epic, but cannot replace it."[13]

Sos is similarly preoccupied with warfare and politics. Within three pages, the reader discovers a primitive world—made so by the near suicidal mistakes of civilized humanity—in which politics equals warfare. Warriors meet in battle circles, ritualized outlets for aggression in a world aware of the devastating results of uncontrolled warfare. The two men fight for a name, *Sol,*[14] and a weapon. Out of their neo-Homeric, hand-to-hand battle comes order, momentary and fragile but present nonetheless. The victor binds the "nameless one" (later to become *Sos)* to himself as a vassal, completing the first stage in his drive to create an empire. They exchange loyalties: for a year's service, Sol gives the other a name. By the end of chapter one, the movement of the novel is clear: Sol as Agamemnon figure, the *rex* of traditional epic, dedicated to creating civil order within a context of violence and strife; and Sos, the Achilles figure, against whose passions the remainder of the novel must be measured.[15] There is even a Briseis. Sol's wife takes a form of his name as her own and becomes Sola; yet she also loves Sos, and the sexual attraction between them stimulates the conflict in the novel. Underlying all of this is the ultimate fact of Sol's sterility (an aftereffect of the radiation released in the Blast) which dooms both Sol and his empire to barrenness.

After a year of service, Sos leaves Sol's nascent empire, returning to the school of the "Crazies" (a subculture dedicated to retaining the vestiges of pre-Blast learning) and mastering a new weapon, the rope. With it, he becomes a greater warrior, returns to the wilderness, and challenges Sol for possession of Sola and her child (Sol's legal daughter, but Sos's natural child). Sos disrupts the tenuous political structure Sol had established and takes the first step toward destroying battle-circle society itself.

Sos is defeated and journeys to Helicon, a slag heap generated by the Blast, where he must (according to tradition) die. His ascent of Mount Helicon parallels the epical ascent or descent leading to revelation. In the *Iliad,* the gods intervene in the struggle; in *Sos* the remnants of technological society inhabiting the mountain intervene to save Sos. In the ironically named "underworld" of Mount Helicon (ironic because it is both aboveground and controlled by the living, not the dead), Sos is surgically reconstructed as a figure of literally Olympian proportions. In his rebirth, he becomes a juggernaut composed of human tissue welded to plastic, metal, and nylon. He is a machine of destruction, intent upon dismantling Sol's empire in order to preserve an emerging social order. By defeating the empire, he will assure that it cannot swallow the individual[16] and lead to another Blast.

Anthony's characters, like Homer's, divide against themselves as their political aspirations diverge,[17] creating a satisfying complexity in both character and plot. In order to preserve a crucial structure within his society, Sos must destroy the structure Sol is convinced will alleviate the effects of the Blast. Civilization, Sos argues, brings devastation. It is better that the battle circles remain, with individuals meeting face-to-face in ritualized warfare, resolving problems personally rather than making them matters of national concern.[18]

The novel concludes with the same dual emphasis on individual prowess and larger political issues. Sos and Sol meet. Sol is defeated and leaves for the mountain of death, taking the child, Soli, with him:

Sos remained to be the architect of the empire's quiet destruction, never certain whether he was doing the right thing. He had built it in the name of another man; now he would bring it down at the behest of a selfish power clique [Helicon] whose purpose was to prevent civilization from arising on the surface. To prevent *power* from *arising.*[19]

As Tillyard concludes about Achilles, Sos seems "not a mere fighter; he draws into himself and unifies all the scattered references to the morality of his time. He is a man sinned against, sinning, and repentant."[20] As an exemplum of heroic fortitude,[21] Sos emerges as the master of the new order.

ODYSSEAN EPIC: *VAR THE STICK*

The *Odyssey* moves in radically different directions than the *Iliad.* It is, as Tillyard states, based on peace and domesticity, on local rather than national politics. Odysseus searches for domestic order.[22] The poem concludes with the restoration of order, but on a limited, personal scale.

Similarly, *Var the Stick* begins with an essentially different tone from *Sos.*

Where *Sos* began with ritual combat between two warriors for honor, name, and weapon, *Var the Stick* begins with a farmer protecting his cornfields. The warrior-armies of Sol's empire have become less nomadic, more sedentary. The empire has virtually disappeared, along with many elements of battle-circle society.

Into this world comes an intruder, an outsider: Var the mutant, a physical reminder of the Blast. Sos of No Weapons must deal with the intruder individually, since the search for the monster with an armed party would invalidate the lingering concept of hand-to-hand combat. The mutated boy has no chance against the cyborg Sos; yet when Sos suffers radiation poisoning in the Blast-wasted Badlands, Var helps him. Enemies become friends. Finally, Var joins Sos, receiving in the battle circle his name and a golden bracelet symbolizing, in good epic fashion, his manhood.

Having been forced by the "techies" of Mount Helicon to destroy Sol's empire, Sos vows to remove their influence as a vestige of the scientific community responsible for releasing the Blast. Var accompanies the army into Sos's version of the "war to end all wars."

The confrontation diminishes into a battle between champions, an Iliadic meeting on an isolated mesa between Var and Soli—who is the Heliconian champion, Sol's legal daughter, and Sos's natural child. Caught between conflicting loyalties, Var and Soli flee, beginning an odyssey of search and discovery. George Slusser has noted that many of Arthur C. Clarke's heroes move outward into the unknown, toward a conflict with whatever lies beyond themselves, then back again, altered almost beyond recognition.[23] This is precisely what Anthony begins in *Var,* and, although the return is not completed, Var and Soli create a domestic order within the larger context of unrestrained violence. Their adventures include encounters with Amazons, with a mutated neo-Minotaur in New Crete, and with the inhabitants of China. Along the way Soli becomes Vara as she accepts Var's bracelet; the essential family unit forms in spite of their wanderings. And her legal and biological fathers, Sol and Sos sacrifice themselves to save their daughter and her mate.

Var the Stick does not complete the Odyssean pattern, however. The two wanderers do not return; they only decide to do so. Vara realizes through her travels in alternative cultures that the battle-circle society is the best possibility. It must not be destroyed. She and Var resolve to return, rebuild Helicon, abolish guns, and disband the nomad armies. And with that resolution the novel ends.

Var is not a comfortable book to read; it is violent, as befits a representation of a violent world. Death in multiple forms lurks as a constant threat. The characters' wanderings expose them to incessant peril, yet only through these wanderings can they realize their political goal: to define the system best suited for post-Blast society. As Tillyard has argued, the search for order cannot be separated from the freedom to wander and to experience change.[24] Anthony's version of the mutant child, Var, is first hunted as a beast, then integrated into human society; first used as a weapon against Helicon, then pursued as a traitor; first accepts his physical ugliness and mutated clumsiness, then finally earns the love of Soli/Vara. And in this portrait we perceive the restoration of order and stability. When Var and Vara decide to return, the quest is completed; armed with love and unity, with experience and knowledge, they can attempt to restructure society following the destruction of Helicon.

VIRGILIAN/MILTONIC EPIC: *NEQ THE SWORD*

The question of whether the *Aeneid* or *Paradise Lost* is the "greater" poem has stimulated much debate; in large measure, however, the question is moot simply because of the historical relationship between the two. As Bowra indicates, Milton and the other Renaissance epic poets frequently modeled their art on Virgil; thus "Virgilian" seems the best term for this third division within epic, particularly since Milton's achievement rested in part on blending Virgil's literary heritage with his own sense of Christian history. Since Anthony's trilogy is unconcerned with matters of overt religious truth, depending more upon social questions and political structures, it seems most promising to investigate *Neq the Sword* in terms of Virgilian epic.

Neq begins in a moment of crux, marking the change in one man's status. Neq must prove himself in the battle circle by meeting his first opponent. He receives his name and his manhood bracelet, but shortly thereafter he meets Sol of All Weapons, is defeated, and becomes part of Sol's empire. For a chapter or two Anthony recapitulates portions of *Sos the Rope* and *Var the Stick*, particularly those portions dealing with the empire.

Yet Anthony soon indicates that Neq's world is changing. By the age of twenty-four, Neq "had no present and no future, like the empire."[25] Like Aeneas before him, Neq gazes over the ruins of what had once symbolized order and stability: both Sol's empire and the battle-circle code. The fragile social order that followed the Blast, the Iliadic battle circle, had been fractured and Neq faces a lawless, confusing world. The destruction of Helicon in *Var,* intended to restore freedom to the nomadic tribes, had paradoxically upset the entire structure, resulting in roving bands of renegades.

Neq begins his own odyssey, which leads him to the "Crazies' " school. He meets Miss Smith, who persuades him that Helicon must be restored to reestablish balance among the nomads, the "Crazies," and the technological remnant still surviving in the ruins of Helicon. Neq and Miss Smith (who accepts Neq's bracelet and becomes—briefly—Neqa) set out for Helicon but are captured by outlaws. Neq is forced to fight outside the battle-circle code; the renegades rape and kill Miss Smith/Neqa. And in a denial of all that the circle code had meant, the outlaw leader severs Neq's hands at the wrists, destroying not only Neq's skill with a weapon but his chances of surviving the barbaric world that has evolved in place of the battle-circle society. Neq is left to die.

But he does not. Nursed to health by a "crazy," he vows vengeance, recapitulating Achilles' response to the death of Patroclus. He has swords affixed to the stumps of his arms and becomes a killing machine, striking by stealth as he hunts down every member of the outlaw band, regressing to the status of an Iliadic character obsessed with his own loss and desperate for retribution.

His society, however, is inimical to such a character. As with Rome in the time of Virgil, individual action has become virtually useless. "The great prince," Bowra writes of Augustan Rome, "was not the warrior who defeated his enemies in hand-to-hand encounter but the organizer of victory and the administrator who imposed his will on other men."[26] Much the same is true of Neq and his development. He realizes the futility of revenge, since the guilt he sought to punish lies not with the individuals who murdered Neq and maimed him but with the collapse of the system. In order to have meaning, his vengeance must be constructive rather than destructive, and that would mean dedicating himself to rebuilding Helicon. Like Aeneas, Neq has lost everything: his place in a stable society, his wife, his livelihood as a warrior. In their place, however, he has gained something greater—responsibility. The Iliadic hero was noteworthy for his desire for glory and his respect for sacrifice; often, in fact, the hero attained the latter through death in battle, assuring himself of the former. The Virgilian hero, on the other hand, discovers a "new field both for glory and for sacrifice. The cause which deserves the one and inspires the other [is] not an ideal of individual prowess but of service to Rome."[27] Or, in Neq's case, to Helicon.

Neq regains his sanity and returns to the remnants of the empire. He challenges Tyl, restoring the vestiges of the circle code, and then is caught in a futile second quest for individual vengeance. Still thinking that Var the Stick had slain Soli during the battle for Helicon six years earlier, he tracks down the mutant and kills Var—only to discover that the rage for vengeance has misled him again. Far from having been killed by the mutant, Soli was traveling with Var and had become Vara.

Neq again recognizes the insanity of vengeance and of individual martial ability without a structure to contain violence. He removes the swords from his arms and replaces them with a hammer and glockenspiel, sublimating his prowess in battle to his ability to sing and renaming himself Neq the Glockenspiel.

Armed with his new "weapons," Neq turns his attention at last to Helicon, to a final siege that allows the nomads to enter the mountain and make peace with the surviving "techies." Vengeance, Neq has discovered, is useless when everyone, including himself, is as savage as the outlaws he has destroyed. The only hope for humanity is to abolish savagery by restoring order and civility, and that requires rebuilding Helicon. Like Aeneas and Adam, he has lost all. And like Aeneas and Adam, he has discovered something more important and more lasting: a dedication to creating order from chaos, avoiding the mistakes of earlier attempts. Peace within society becomes more critical than his own wishes for an ordered life. By creating order within society, however, he simultaneously achieves it within himself.

Neq is not perfect, of course; he continues to make errors. But he now focuses his energies properly. He represents not merely himself but all of surviving

humanity searching for control (a key word throughout Anthony's novels) after
the Blast. He moves closer to the protagonists of literary epic, to individuals
who stand not for themselves but for larger ideals: Aeneas for Rome, Adam for
humankind.[28] Neq stands for stability in a postcataclysmic society, working
through his own loss to an understanding that the larger demands of society and
civilization are paramount. The result of his dedication is not an empire, such
as Aeneas founded and Virgil extolled, but rather a social structure capable of
restoring peace to a wartorn, Blasted America.

Neq the Sword clearly resembles the *Aeneid* in yet another sense; it builds
upon what has come before. Webber has noted that the *Aeneid* bifurcates. The
first six books are Odyssean, the last six Iliadic, reflecting each other in an
"elaborate parallelism." Thus in the *Aeneid*, the Homeric epics "face and
illuminate each other," as do the two halves of Virgil's poem, and "After Virgil,
every epic in this tradition revises and mirrors its predecessor."[29] *Neq* not only
incorporates Iliadic and Odyssean elements into its essentially Virgilian structure,
it also reflects the first two novels of the *Battle Circle* trilogy. The individual
heroism of *Sos the Rope* is repeated and rejected in Neq's misguided urge for
vengeance, refined and transformed in his later single-minded dedication to
restoring Helicon. Var and Vara's Odyssean quest in *Var the Stick* is completed
as Neq meets Var and kills him, then returns with Vara and her knowledge of
conditions outside the battle-circle society. More positively, Neq's killing Var
stimulates the rebuilding of Helicon, which in turn ensures a society in which
such a killing will no longer be possible. Both previous novels culminate in the
image of Neq as Virgilian hero, subsuming personal desires and emotions to a
larger cause, losing everything as a prelude to gaining even more. By the end
of *Neq the Sword,* Anthony's characters can reflect, as Virgil's did, on the
actions that made their world possible. As Tyl says, "Soon we must talk together
of great men."[30] Yet Tyl, Neq, Vara, Sola, and others are themselves "great"
in a new sense, smaller individually than Sos the Rope or Sol of All Weapons,
yet finally capable of constructing a society to outlast the hopes of either of the
great Iliadic warriors.

Thomas Greene has said that the epic is the "great poem of beginnings and
endings"; the *Aeneid* itself begins with an ending and concludes with a beginning.[31] *Neq the Sword,* and in fact the entire *Battle Circle* trilogy as a whole,
fits that classification. Beginning with the circle culture, it moves through chaos
to a new beginning. The trilogy ends with reestablished contact between Helicon
and another station in South America. Humanity is beginning to knit together.
The conclusion of the epic action, Greene states, includes creation of equilibrium,
"some fine adjustment or definition."[32] This is what Anthony provides. Helicon
and the Andes station arrive at a mutually profitable equilibrium, symbolized by
an interchange of parallel questions: "How is your supply of young women?"
Neq asks. "How is your supply of electronic equipment?" the Andes station
replies.[33] Balance, stability, and order have been restored.

A discussion such as this chapter has attempted is almost by nature doomed to incompleteness. *Battle Circle* is a long, complex work, totaling over five hundred pages in the omnibus volume, yet the three component novels represent only a portion of Anthony's vision of postholocaust America; he originally planned two additional novels but, as he wrote in a recent letter, "the market was such that I never wrote them, and it does fit together nicely as a trilogy."[34] While it is interesting to speculate on how a five-part series might have been structured, the fact remains that *Battle Circle* as finally published retains the tripartite arrangement that ties it so closely with epic development.

Anthony noted that he did not consciously model the novels on the Homeric epics, nor had he read the *Aeneid;* but he conceded that he "could have drawn from a literary pool shaped by these epics."[35] In light of the close parallels in characterization, plotting, and development between classical epic and the three novels comprising *Battle Circle,* it seems a reasonable conclusion that Anthony did in fact draw from a "literary pool." The form and function of epic has become so integral a part of Western culture that Anthony may simply have intuited a logical structure for his experiment in defining and ordering a post-holocaust society. In his search for an ordering principle, he seems to have recognized the enormous power implicit in the epic tradition. He has constructed his fictive world in parallel with one of the most enduring and conventional of all literary traditions, re-creating in the scope of his trilogy the permutations in heroic characteristics that define epic. To read *Battle Circle* with this parallel in mind not only deepens one's enjoyment of the novel but broadens one's respect for Anthony's achievement. Three separate facets of the epic tradition are welded into a single unified whole during the course of the novels. Out of chaos his characters generate order; out of conventions of the old, Anthony draws something new. In *Sos the Rope, Var the Stick,* and *Neq the Sword,* we find new perspectives of what C. S. Lewis called the "doctrine of the unchanging human heart."[36] Through initial individual heroic action (the only responses left in a world devastated by humanity's stupidity and the cataclysmic results of technological irresponsibility), Anthony shows his world transforming as it works through painful intermediate stages before arriving at stability and finally at true civilization. To show this transformation of old into new, he in turn draws on the imagistic power of one of the oldest literary forms, the epic.

NOTES

1. C. M. Bowra, *From Virgil to Milton* (New York: St. Martin's Press, 1967), p. 11.

2. C. S. Lewis, *Preface to Paradise Lost* (1942; reprint, London: Oxford University Press, 1969), p. 39.

3. For further information, see John M. Steadman, *Milton's Epic Characters: Image and Idol* (Chapel Hill: University of North Carolina Press, 1968); John M. Steadman, *Milton and the Renaissance Hero* (London: Oxford University Press, 1967); and Joan Mallory Webber, *Milton and His Epic Tradition* (Seattle: University of Washington Press, 1979).

4. The individual novels appeared as *Sos the Rope* (New York: Pyramid Books,

1968); *Var the Stick* (London: Faber and Faber, 1972); and *Neq the Sword* (London: Corgi, 1975). All are collected in the omnibus volume *Battle Circle* (New York: Avon Books, 1978).

5. Bowra, p. 1.

6. Steadman, *Milton's Epic Characters,* p. x.

7. Thomas Greene, "The Norms of Epic," in *The Hero in Transition,* ed. Victor J. Brombert (New York: Fawcett, 1969), p. 54.

8. Ibid., p. 56.

9. Webber, pp. 6–7.

10. See also Michael R. Collings, "The Epic of *Dune:* Epic Traditions in Modern Science Fiction," presented to the Second International Conference on the Fantastic in the Arts, Florida Atlantic University, March 1981, in *Aspects of the Fantastic,* ed. William Coyle (Westport, Conn.: Greenwood Press, 1986). Michael R. Collings, *Reader's Guide to Piers Anthony,* no. 20, The Starmont Reader's Guides to Contemporary Science Fiction and Fantasy Writers series (Mercer Island, Wash.: Starmont House, 1983), briefly discusses epic in Anthony's work.

11. E. M. W. Tillyard, *The English Epic and Its Background* (New York: Oxford University Press, 1966), p. 29.

12. As with Milton's lifelong commitment to the epic, Anthony's engagement with *Battle Circle* covered many years. "The Unstilled World," his thesis for Goddard College in 1956, was extensively revised as a portion of *Sos the Rope; Neq the Sword,* the final volume in the trilogy, was not published until 1975, nearly twenty years later. And in many ways, his interest in epic structures continues through to the present, as in the "Bio of a Space Tyrant" series now in progress.

13. Greene, p. 58. See also Tillyard, p. 23.

14. For a discussion of epic suggestions in the name, see Collings, *Piers Anthony,* p. 22.

15. Lewis, p. 28.

16. Piers Anthony, *Battle Circle* (New York: Avon Books, 1978), p. 154.

17. Greene, p. 59.

18. Anthony, p. 162.

19. Ibid., p. 170.

20. Tillyard, p. 27.

21. Steadman, *Renaissance Hero,* pp. 23–42.

22. Tillyard, pp. 31–35.

23. Even the title of George Slusser's study, *The Space Odysseys of Arthur C. Clarke* (San Bernardino, Calif.: Borgo Press, 1978), indicates the pervasiveness of Odyssean motifs in Clarke's novels.

24. Tillyard, p. 34.

25. Anthony, p. 374.

26. Bowra, p. 12.

27. Ibid., p. 13.

28. Ibid., p. 16.

29. Webber, p. 88.

30. Anthony, p. 505.

31. Greene, p. 60.

32. Ibid., p. 58.

33. Anthony, p. 537.
34. Anthony, letter to Michael R. Collings, March 1, 1984.
35. Ibid.
36. Lewis, p. 62.

14

MYTHIC HELLS IN HARLAN ELLISON'S SCIENCE FICTION

Joseph Francavilla

Beneath the grim, despairing, "realistic" surface of Harlan Ellison's desolate, wartorn landscapes lies a symbolic dimension to the postholocaust world involving a combination of motifs: the hero's descent into hell and a variation of the Prometheus myth. In "I Have No Mouth and I Must Scream," "The Deathbird," and "A Boy and His Dog," the postholocaust setting functions as a nightmarish wasteland into which, or from which, the Promethean hero can descend, an inverted world where the protagonist steals the "fire" of knowledge, creativity, freedom, and life from the punishing, deranged god(s) presiding over the region of darkness. The protagonist finally finds and confronts his shadow doppelgänger, subjecting himself to tortures, trials, and punishments. Eventually the hero sacrifices himself, or part of himself, usually restoring the balance of hope and despair and of cowardly selfishness and noble sacrifice which has been upset at the outset of the stories. As a result of his defiant theft, the hero may be confined and punished eternally by the powerful, maniacal authority, his other self. Or, if the hero overcomes the tyrannical god, the rebel wrests control of the earth or its representative(s) from this evil force. This representative is almost always an embodiment of the feminine, often symbolizing the earth mother goddess, with which the hero has had a sexual union. This object of love (woman and/or earth) is put out of its pain so that it is no longer tortured; the hero is forced to destroy, usually out of compassion, what he loves. This euthanasia is a last resort made necessary because the love object is still subject to torture which the hero cannot now curtail or eliminate.

This action by the hero departs radically from the monomyth of the hero's descent into hell as described by Joseph Campbell in *The Hero with a Thousand*

Faces.[1] Though Ellison's hero fulfills most of the events Campbell abstracts (descent into the region of darkness, tests and trials, the hero's supreme ordeal, sexual union with the goddess mother, divinization, bride-theft and/or fire-theft, and so on, he, significantly, does not return to restore the world or revitalize it with his elixir. It is always too late for that.

In borrowing from the Prometheus myth, Ellison also makes important changes. In his role as a clever, nonhuman trickster figure who identifies with earth or its representatives, Ellison's hero fulfills the Promethean model as a rebel who steals from the tyrannical gods and fights for freedom. But he fails it in his role as a lonely sufferer who sacrifices himself for the other. Ellison's hero is also frequently blended with Christ on the cross, except that there is no release, rebirth, or resurrection, only either an eternity of torture for the hero or the hero's mercy killing of the tortured earth and/or its feminine representative. Just as the postholocaust world is divided into two regions, one an inversion of the other, so too is there often an inversion or role reversal of the main characters. For instance, in "The Deathbird," protagonist Nathan Stack becomes the new god, replacing a deranged old one, and Nathan's alien helper, Snake, who is the devil/serpent of traditional Judeo-Christian teaching, is revealed as mankind's Promethean friend. Thus Snake's role allies Satan with Prometheus, two characters that Percy Shelley compares in his preface to *Prometheus Unbound.* According to Shelley, both Milton's Satan and Prometheus show "courage and majesty, and firm and patient opposition to omnipotent force," although Shelley also adds that Prometheus is the more interesting hero without the flaws of ambition, envy, or revenge, and is "the highest perfection of moral and intellectual nature."[2] The role of Prometheus is usually, at the beginning, the sacrificing, alien intelligence, the wise teacher and cultural repository who befriends the hero. Gradually, the hero takes over the Promethean burdens of the alien doppelgänger and becomes the agent of salvation and destruction in his struggle with the malevolent god-figure.

The hero, who often descends into the hell of the postholocaust world accompanied or aided by a magical guide, is making a journey into the mind and the self, thereby exploring the terrain of his consciousness. Accordingly, the symbolic, postholocaust setting presents "humanity in the raw," where the veneer of civilization is stripped away in order to present fundamental dualities of humanity in naked opposition. For example, the need to survive and escape pain at all costs or the need to love and to sacrifice oneself and suffer for the sake of others is a fundamental bipolarity Ellison examines in all three of the stories considered here. The institutions and ready-made organizations of society are gone as well, so that the action of these stories, in true mythic fashion, represents all times, past, present, and future, and takes place in the timeless, chaotic "nowhere" of dreams, which stands for "everywhere." The struggle shown in the postholocaust world is not the clash of wills of leaders, nations, or planets but that of larger-than-life individuals symbolizing the eternal, paradoxical qualities of humanity and the eternal contest between good and evil.

In the earliest of these stories, ''I Have No Mouth,'' supercomputers in Russia, China, and America suddenly link up at the outset of World War III and blast the surface of the earth with missiles, leaving it uninhabitable for over a century. AM, as the master computer calls itself, has not only exterminated mankind in revenge for giving him sentience without movement or the ability to ''wonder'' or ''belong,'' it also has taken the five human survivors down inside its ''belly,'' that is, underground. There it revenges itself forever on the humans who created it. In this sterile, enclosed, claustrophobic, technological ruin containing inorganic matter, computer baseplates and platesheets, rotted components and cables, broken glass, and metal catwalks, the five humans, now virtually immortal, are tortured until the narrator, Ted, finds a moment to kill off the others (including the black woman Ellen) to free them from their pain. In revenge and rage, AM punishes Ted eternally by changing him into a soft, gelatinous blob, with no mouth, which cannot elude AM's further tortures.

''I Have No Mouth'' converts our technological wonders into demons, our computers into deranged, hateful gods who punish humanity. The landscape inside AM is the perfect symbol of hell: it is an escapeproof site devised by a demonic machine that needs to torture its ''toys.'' AM actually calls the place ''hell.'' But in typical fashion, Ellison subverts and inverts our usual mythologies and identifies AM with God. The name AM is capitalized and reminds one of God's phrase explaining his name to Moses in the book of *Exodus:* ''I am that I am.'' The omniscient, omnipotent AM sends ''manna'' in the form of worms or boar urine to his chosen people on their wanderings for food. AM can also send hurricanes, earthquakes, hail, locusts, giant vulturelike birds, and so on, or alter the environment as, for instance, in the last scene where the characters discover a cavern full of icicles. AM enters Ted's mind and speaks to him in a ''pillar of stainless steel,'' echoing the ''pillar of fire'' which is seen as God in *Exodus.* With characteristic perverseness, AM appears to the five people as a burning bush, parodying God's appearance to Moses.

Ted, the Promethean hero, is placed in hell by AM and left with no guide, although Ellen helps him kill the others in the ice caverns. Ellen functions as a goddess-mother, who has sex with all the males including Ted and who, in turn, is carried around like a queen and protected by them from AM's sadistic surprises. As occurs in many of Ellison's stories, the hero eventually chooses loneliness and rejects or sacrifices the possibility of heterosexual love. When only he and she remain alive, Ted kills Ellen to spare her the torture AM will inflict upon her.

If the dark half of human nature is projected into AM, then the fire-bringing half is embodied in Ted. His early statements of paranoia and hatred of the others appear to be produced by AM's manipulation of his mind and render some of his narration unreliable. But his final sacrifice is a conscious choice. His theft of fire from the tyrannical god is precisely the theft of AM's other human toys. As punishment, Ted is turned into a ''thing whose shape is so alien''[3] that it is no longer human and, in fact, travesties humanity by its appearance. Just as AM tortured the others by systematically destroying the unique aspects of their personalities and converting these traits into their opposites, AM obliterates Ted's final distinguishing mark of identity as a human being. Like the alien Prometheus who sacrificed for mankind, Ted is confined, immobilized, and eternally tortured by the hateful god.

In keeping with the flood of biblical imagery in the story, Ted's role as a crucified Christ is also foreshadowed. The first image in the story is that of Gorrister, one of the men, hanging upside down by one foot, bloodless, though his throat has been slit. John B. Ower sees this figure as a travesty of the Crucifixion,[4] while Charles J. Brady sees it as a paschal lamb, slaughtered in a sacrifice.[5] Moreover, it may be the Hanged Man of the Tarot cards, used by T. S. Eliot in *The Waste Land,* whose chief characteristic is to hang upside down by one foot. The occult associations correspond with the "voodoo icon" metaphor used in the story to describe Gorrister's body. Later, the body is revealed to be a duplicate, or doppelgänger, made by AM. In any case, this image, and the image of AM putting nails through their feet to rivet the humans to the ground during an earthquake, portends the impending crucifixion of Ted.

The story's landscape is bifurcated, echoing the bipolarities and oppositions of the characters. The postholocaust world offers only two alternatives: death on the blasted surface from radiation or a sterile, confined, timeless, and tortured existence inside the creation of a supercomputer gone mad. Ted is also the doppelgänger of AM, and each is half of a whole entity. Ted is the human turned into the nonhuman, while AM is the nonhuman machine given human sentience. In a sense man creates God which destroys humanity and its world. AM, like Frankenstein's monster, hates its creators because it is alone and no other of its kind can be born, yet it is unable to destroy Ted completely. Ted's comrades are killed off until he is alone and unable to scream. The title of the story thus reflects both characters' predicaments: Ted's inability to scream in pain because he lacks a mouth and AM's frustrated state of nonbeing, of impotence, and of silence. Ted's final punishment, a death-in-life state, mirrors exactly the impossibility of AM's death or real human existence. Ted is, like AM, trapped, unable to wander, wonder, or belong—he merely exists. And in keeping with the birth imagery (the transformation and the location inside AM's "belly"), Ted is rendered infantile, perhaps like a newborn fetus, unable to roam or care for itself. AM, too, behaves like a child, breaking and torturing its toys out of envy, frustration, and impotence and displaying sadistic glee both in its tormenting of humans and in its nonparticipatory, voyeuristic, sexual curiosity.

"The Deathbird," more overtly concerned with mythology and biblical allusions, takes place on an earth again dying from the ravages of nuclear war. After several reincarnations, Nathan Stack is awakened from a 250,000–year sleep by the alien creature, Snake, who has hidden him deep underground. The earth is presided over by a deranged God, who has been allowed control by Snake's race. Now that God has begun the destruction of the world, Snake, who has been labeled "Satan" by God, wakes Nathan, the last man on earth, converts his divine spark into energy as the hero sexually unites with the earth mother (literally the world itself), and guides him up the mountain to defeat God. But the victory is bittersweet, since the earth—a living being—is now a "terminal case." Both Nathan and Snake work to put the earth out of its misery, destroying themselves in the process, as Snake's ultimate weapon, the gigantic, vulturelike Deathbird, enfolds the earth with its wings.

As with many Ellison tales, this moral fable addresses in a mythological way the problem of theodicy, going so far as to reverse the roles of God and Satan. Here God and Satan are understood to be omnipotent figures representing two halves of the human psyche projected into those characters. The postholocaust world is again split into what is called "hell" below, inside the earth where Nathan sleeps hidden by Snake from God, and the upper world, also termed a "hell," whose description is both vivid and bleak. The earth has been changed by God into a "cinder," a creation with pins stuck in it, a "broken toy." Less metaphorically, the wasteland is raked by green, poisonous winds and covered with a choking powder after the oceans have boiled, cooled, and then filmed over with scum. Plants consume themselves, crippled beasts go mad, trees burn and their ash breeds glass shapes. As with most of Ellison's postapocalyptic worlds, mutations occur, symbols of the radical changes taking place, signs of the transitional state the world is going through, from growth and life to decay and death. In this case, batlike creatures (again echoing Promethean vultures) fly over the traveling characters and excrete phosphorescent strings, strings that change into "bleeder plants" that try to choke Stack. The earth is described as dying a "long, slow, painful death," which thematically parallels two euthanasia stories-within-the-story: that of the death of a dog and that of the death of Nathan's mother. As if to underscore the earth goddess motif, Ellison suggests that the earth, like the voice of a mother, is "crying out in endless pain at her flesh that had been ripped away."[6]

The landscape, as a symbolic hell, provides a perfect setting for the cosmic struggles of these mythological beings. Nathan is actually taken down to the underworld by Snake (one of a race which designs and creates worlds for other beings) and is put to sleep for a quarter of a million years, reminiscent of the thirty thousand years Prometheus remained chained to a rock on a mountain, undergoing Zeus's torture of having his eternally regenerating liver torn out by a vulture or eagle. Snake then acts as Nathan's magical guide, directing him to God's mountain palace for the final confrontation. Snake steals the last man from God and, like Prometheus, gives him what the story calls the "gift of knowledge": after his divine spark is energized, he is taught how to become a God more powerful than the deranged deity mankind had worshiped for so long. Though the wise and patient Snake is sacrificed at the end as the Deathbird descends on earth, Nathan, as he becomes God, takes on the role of Prometheus, modeling himself after his teacher. He undergoes the tortures of the wasteland, then the attacks of the tyrant God, and finally, by sacrificing the dying earth with which he has had a sexual union, he also sacrifices himself.

Again, inversions and doppelgänger figures abound. Supposed enemies are revealed as friends, and supposed friends or worshipped deities are shown as evil, tyrannical, insane children. The mad God, who reveals himself as a burning bush to Nathan, is the complementary half of the alien Snake. Nathan, as the new God, perceives the old God as an impotent, childish, stubborn, old man, and a faker like the Wizard of Oz. Nathan even pities this God and feels it is too late for revenge on this monster, probably because he also recognizes part of himself in the old God. Snake, who has been perceived by mankind (including Nathan) as the devil, is finally seen by Nathan as mankind's best friend. Nathan learns, through Snake, that he has always had within himself the potential to be a more powerful God than the deposed tyrant.

Thus Nathan, as the last representative of humanity and one called "Adam" by Snake, is that which could potentially be like the mad God, as well as that which becomes like Snake, the Promethean sacrificer. The insane God, then, is not something separate, "out there." It is the projection of the human capability for evil, and, like the symbolic landscape, it also represents technology gone mad.

The final story, "A Boy and His Dog," presents variations on the preceding patterns. The upper world after the holocaust of World War III does support life, but barely. Rover gangs and "solos" like Vic and his dog, Blood, struggle for survival in a chaotic world. Since the war killed off most of the girls and has produced mutants who have to be killed at birth, women are hunted down by gangs with their genetically altered dogs. These dogs, like Blood, are telepathic and can "scent" women for the men who, often only teenagers like Vic, rape and murder them. In return, the men hunt to feed the dogs since they have lost the capacity to find food for themselves and to survive in the wilderness, though they are still ferocious fighters. Amid the bombed-out buildings, craters overgrown with weeds, irradiated pits, and melted stubs of lampposts, and against the bluish-green radiation flickering in the hills, the dogs also fend off various mutant creatures, such as the glowing, green "burnpit-screamers."

The other division of the postholocaust world, inverting the first, lies deep below the surface. There, technologically sealed off, "Southern Baptists, Fundamentalists," and other "middle-class squares with no taste for the wild life"[7] run a strange, isolated, repressive, and sterile "town." This totalitarian town is a "safe" and conservative community living a pre–World War I existence. Vic is lured below by one of the "downunders," Quilla June, with whom he has had sex. Since the males of downunder are sterile, Vic is to be used as a "stud," an ironic reversal of the scarcity of women above. This idea is the "brainchild" of Aaron and Lew, the two old leaders whose word is law. To underscore the religious nature of the leadership, they are closely allied, like Moses and his brother Aaron, who spoke for Moses.

Initially Blood is the alien intelligence most closely resembling Prometheus. Mentor to Vic and repository of culture and history, he nearly sacrifices himself at the end of the story out of devotion to his human partner and protégé. Gradually

Vic assumes the role of the Promethean hero, stealing knowledge from down-under and taking Quilla June with him to the upper world. If Vic had stayed below to sacrifice himself, he would have fulfilled the Promethean model. And one of the two rulers, Lew, is, in fact, described as an ugly "bird ready to pick meat" off Vic's bones. But Vic ultimately rejects this role and on his own "unbinds himself" and escapes to the surface with Quilla June, after bashing in the heads of Aaron and her father.

Part erotic witch and part earth mother, Quilla June is by the end of the story the sole representative of downunder and Vic's only hope for permanent, het-erosexual love. Yet he rejects this possibility, a sacrifice on his part since women are rare and precious commodities above, and kills Quilla June for food to save the starving Blood. This time there is no euthanasia. In this world Vic's need for sex and/or love is outweighed by his need to survive and by his devotion and loyalty to his dog. He does not become a god or Christ but rather goes back to square one, with both he and his dog heading for new adventures in another territory. In addition to the inversion of the relationship of animals and men, Vic comes to love his dog as its mirror spelling "God," just as Nathan recognizes Snake as his true creator and benefactor. The Bible-thumping downunders are a perversion of the human spirit and will, but they nevertheless represent that other bifurcation of humanity which Vic might have become if he had been born into and remained in that society.

Ellison's postholocaust landscapes are unique, not only because they are sym-bolic hells, private nightmares of the hero's psyche into which the Promethean hero can descend, but also because there is no indication, promise, or hint that these worlds will be rebuilt. There is no rediscovery of or reeducation of the masses about the science, technology, and culture now in ruins and forgotten, as there is in such classic stories as Stephen Vincent Benet's "By the Waters of Babylon." There is neither a regained Eden, a second Genesis, nor a reversion to primitive societies of the past or pastoral settings, since society and its insti-tutions seem to be all but wiped away (or soon will be), and the landscapes are as dangerous and threatening as the menacing godlike authorities or the savage people roaming their surfaces. Nor is there a succession of cycles of history, as in Walter Miller's *A Canticle for Leibowitz*. In Ellison's stories the progress of history, indeed any sense of historicity, has vanished with the disappearance of social order, which tends to emphasize the "mythic" timelessness of these settings.

In all three stories time is suddenly arrested, as if in a dream. In "I Have No Mouth," Ted is made virtually immortal and has his time sense greatly retarded by AM. In "The Deathbird," time literally stands still as Nathan demolishes God's palace. And in "A Boy and His Dog," the downunder towns have turned back the clock and stopped it forever at a period before World War I. In addition to this stoppage of time, the narratives themselves end in a "freeze-frame" or a suggestion of endless repetition and circularity, which, together with the barren battleground, suggests a continuation of the eternal struggle or Manichaean contest between utterly irreconcilable forces. With good and evil in balance, always in contention, there can never be a resolution. The postholocaust world, itself split into inverted halves, reflects these fundamental bifurcations and oppositions embodied both in Ellison's mythic characters and in human nature.

NOTES

1. Joseph Campbell, *The Hero with a Thousand Faces*, 2d ed., Bollingen Series, no. 17 (Princeton, N.J.: Princeton University Press, 1968), pp. 245–57.

2. Percy Shelley, in *Shelley's Prometheus Unbound: A Variorum Edition*, ed. Lawrence John Zillman (Seattle: University of Washington Press, 1959), pp. 120–21. Ellison uses this Promethean figure explicitly in the stories "On the Slab" and "The Place with No Name." In famous screenplays such as "The City on the Edge of Forever" and "Demon with a Glass Hand," the alien doppelgänger guiding the Promethean hero is the machine-being called the "Guardian of Forever" in the former story and the computerized glass hand of Trent in the latter.

3. Harlan Ellison, "I Have No Mouth and I Must Scream," in *I Have No Mouth and I Must Scream* (New York: Pyramid, 1967), p. 42.

4. John B. Ower, "Manacle-Forged Minds: Two Images of the Computer in Science Fiction," *Diogenes* 85 (1974), pp. 55–56.

5. Charles J. Brady, "The Computer as a Symbol of God: Ellison's Macabre Exodus," *Journal of General Education* 28, 1 (Spring 1976), p. 60.

6. Harlan Ellison, "The Deathbird," in *Deathbird Stories* (New York: Dell, 1975), p. 343.

7. Harlan Ellison, "A Boy and His Dog," in *The Beast That Shouted Love at the Heart of the World* (New York: New American Library, 1969), p. 237.

15

BERNARD MALAMUD AND RUSSELL HOBAN: MANIPULATING THE APOCALYPSE

Theodore L. Steinberg

In Canto 29 of the *Purgatorio,* Dante sees a procession of twenty-four elders, four beasts, a chariot pulled by a griffin, and then seven additional elders. This procession, which may seem odd to us, was probably immediately recognizable to Dante's audience: the twenty-four elders represent the Hebrew Testament, the four beasts represent the Gospels, the griffin represents the divine and human nature of Christ, and the final seven elders represent the remaining books of the Greek Testament. This procession, then, according to medieval Christian thought, reflects all of history, from the creation in Genesis to the end of time in Revelation and consequently, like so much in Dante, betrays an apocalyptic view of the world.[1]

This kind of Christian apocalypticism, with the world having a definite beginning and a clear, predictable end, was basic to the Middle Ages. As anyone knows who watches the Sunday morning, electronic churches, or who has glanced at Hal Lindsey's best-selling *The Late Great Planet Earth* (1976), this view is still very much alive among evangelical preachers and their audiences. And not only will there be a definite end, according to such believers, but that end is imminent. The process leading up to it is already under way, as we would all know if we could read the signs. It is interesting to note how this Christian apocalypticism, regarded in a positive and hopeful way by believers, coexists in our society with the apocalypticism of antinuclear activists, who also foresee the possibility of an imminent end but who view that end with fear and despair.[2]

The popularity of apocalyptic thought can also be seen in the flourishing literature about the end, or near end, of the world.[3] Much of this literature may respond to the same human need as the roller coaster—a desire for titillation with only a slight chance of real danger—but end-of-the-world fiction clearly can have a number of positive effects as well. Works like Nevil Shute's *On the Beach* (1957), for instance, which approaches the truly apocalyptic, should force readers to reconsider their reliance on a nuclear arsenal, while novels like Walter M. Miller's *A Canticle for Leibowitz* (1960) might prompt an examination of human fallibility, of what in the context of the novel could be called "original sin." Even if a work provides only some kind of catharsis beyond mere titillation, it serves a valuable function by making us consider our individual and collective mortality. In light of the history of apocalypticism, it is not surprising at this time of religious and secular apocalypticism, of hopeful and fearful apocalypticism, that contemporary authors write apparently apocalyptic novels, full of religious themes and images. What may be surprising is the way in which modern authors manipulate that apparent apocalypticism to make vital observations about the world as it now exists.

Before we get to the modern world, however, we must take a brief look at biblical apocalyptic, with the understanding that it is a complex and much disputed topic.

In the eighth century B.C., the prophet Amos announced to the people of Israel:

> Woe to you who desire the day of the Lord!
> Why would you have the day of the Lord?
> It is darkness and not light,
> as if a man fled from a lion
> and a bear met him;
> or went into the house and leaned
> with his hand against the wall,
> and a serpent bit him.
> Is not the day of the Lord darkness,
> and not light,
> and gloom with no brightness in it?
>   Amos 5:18–20[4]

Clearly this passage represents a reinterpretation of the "day of the Lord." Apparently many Israelites looked forward to such a day, on which they expected their enemies to be punished, if not obliterated, and their own situation to be improved. Amos' point is that the "day of the Lord" will be a dreadful time and that the Israelites will not be exempted from the suffering. This message, of course, is part of Amos' general call to repentance: punishment is not inevitable but can be avoided by a return to the teachings of the religion. This is the nature of prophetic eschatology; calamity can be avoided by sincere collective repentance. Repeatedly the prophets predict doom, but always with an implied "if" clause. "If you continue to behave as you have been behaving," woe to you, but "if you repent," calamity can be averted.

Of course, it was also obvious to the prophets that the people were not going to repent, that calamity would come, and their response was typified by the name

Isaiah gave his son, Shear-jashub, a Hebrew pun that means both "a remnant shall repent" and "a remnant shall return." The coming calamity would have a purgative effect, would leave a remnant that would return both to God (repent) and to its ancestral land. A good example of the Hebrew Testament's view of history is contained in the book of Judges, which describes a succession of cycles in which the Israelites violate their religious teachings, are punished, repent, are rescued by a judge, live properly for a time, and then violate the teachings again.

After the Babylonian conquest in 586 B.C., however, because of the new status of Israel—now a people rather than a nation—and possibly because of contact with foreign beliefs, this older eschatology began very slowly to change,[5] although these changes can be seen primarily in extracanonical works. The only truly apocalyptic book in the Hebrew Testament is Daniel (second century B.C.), but the kind of apocalyptic eschatology that we find in Daniel can be found in numerous extracanonical, apocalyptic works from the second century B.C. to the first century A.D. and had a significant influence on the origins and development of Christianity.

Although there is no room here to go into detail, an examination of such concepts as the Messiah, the Day of Judgment, the end of days, and others shows that Christianity relies far more on apocalyptic thought than did biblical or even (with some exceptions) rabbinic Judaism. This newer view required certain reinterpretations of the earlier texts. For example, the remnant whose salvation Isaiah predicted became in Christianity the church, and the salvation became not the restoration of a nation but the establishment of the kingdom of God. This shift can be seen clearly in the apocalyptic thirteenth chapter of Mark, in which Jesus speaks of imminent upheavals and calamities; it concludes:

And then shall they see the Son of man coming in the clouds with great power and glory. And then shall he send his angels, and shall gather together his elect from the four winds, from the uttermost part of the earth to the uttermost part of heaven.

Mark 13: 26–27

The end that Jesus predicts here will be terrible indeed, but, as in Revelation, the elect will be saved, so that the coming terror will be only the prelude to a time of rejoicing—at least for the elect. It is for this reason that the evangelicals, who consider themselves the elect, look forward to the end: like Jerry Falwell, who believes that the end is so near and his safety so assured that he does not need a cemetery plot,[6] they expect to come through the general unpleasantness unscathed. One wonders whether they should not give Amos at least a quick rereading.

Such, at any rate, might be the lesson of two recent works that employ religious, and apparently apocalyptic, motifs to describe the aftermath of nuclear holocaust: Bernard Malamud's *God's Grace* (1982) and Russell Hoban's *Riddley Walker* (1980).

Malamud's fable tells the story of Calvin Cohn, the lone human survivor of a nuclear war and his efforts to establish a just and harmonious society among the chimpanzees, baboons, and the solitary gorilla who are his companions. The work seems to be apocalyptic in a number of ways: by the end, human life has indeed disappeared from the planet; the book is full of strange, unnatural phenomena, like talking chimpanzees and the birth of a baby to Cohn and the only female chimp. These examples may not be on the same level as the Four Horsemen, but they certainly contribute to the strangeness of this end-of-the-world story, and yet, as we shall see, this work is not truly apocalyptic.

God's Grace is, however, full of religious imagery and biblical references. The very beginning, with its heaving seas, glowing sky, and black, oily rain, sounds like biblical apocalypse; the names—Calvin Cohn, Buz, Luke, Saul of Tarsus, Mary Madelyn, and Esau—all bring biblical resonances to the story. Furthermore, Cohn sees himself in several different biblical roles. At one point, like Job and Jeremiah, he curses "the woman who had given him birth and anybody who had assisted in the enterprise,"[7] and later he holds a Joblike discussion with God in which he asks for an explanation of God's ways. He also sees himself at various times as Lot and as a new Abraham, teaching the ethics of Judaism to his simian companions and trying to ensure that he will have an heir. And finally he becomes Isaac—and Isaac's Christian antitype, Jesus—in the concluding reenactment of the *akedah,* the offering of Isaac, which has been viewed in Christianity as the prophetic prefiguration of the Crucifixion.

In fact, this reenactment of the *akedah*-Crucifixion is central to the work. Earlier, when Cohn told the story of the *akedah* to Buz, he tried to explain

"why the interpretation of Abraham as his son's cutthroat persists thoughout the centuries. That says something about the nature of man—his fantasies of death that get enacted into the slaughter of man by man . . . on every possible mindless occasion."[8]

In this explanation, Cohn shows that he has accepted God's reasons for the nuclear catastrophe: God had created people to be perfectable, but they had allowed the evil to overcome the good. Thus, to refer to the *akedah* as the sacrifice of Isaac or to compare it to the Crucifixion is, from a Jewish point of view, incorrect. Isaac, after all, was not sacrificed; in Genesis 22, the Hebrew, in its punning way, actually says not "offer him up for a burnt offering" but "lift him up." There is no mention of the act of slaying. Nonetheless, the simian population (including Esau, whose name in medieval Jewish writing symbolized Christianity and who, in Jewish tradition, was the ancestor of the Amalekites, the age-old enemy of the Jews) insists on an actual blood sacrifice. The simians are led by Cohn's "adopted son" Buz, who objects to Cohn's Second Admonition—"Note: God is not love. God is God. Remember Him"[9]—by insisting that "God is Love" and by changing his Cohn-given name (also from Genesis 22) to Gottlob[10] just before killing his "father" in an ironic reversal of the biblical stories.

Cohn himself is not without guilt either. For all his religiosity, he has exchanged his given name, Seymour, for the more assimilated Calvin, with its overtones of Calvinism; his passive response to the growing evil in his new community is hardly adequate, as if he imagines that whatever happens is predestined. With his death, we seem to have an apocalyptic (and simian) *Lord of the Flies,* an effect that is countered by the last two sentences in the book, in which George the gorilla, the outcast, wearing a yarmulke, chants the Sh'ma Yisroe, affirming the unity of God, and begins "a long Kaddish for Calvin Cohn."[11] In the simian society, George—from the Greek *ge,* "earth"—will be the new Adam—from the Hebrew *adamah,* "earth"—as well as the new Jew. What we have, then, is not apocalypse so much as the beginning of a new cycle in a very old, cyclical story. Malamud's fable is, like the prophetic writings, admonitory, but it neither predicts nor celebrates the end of the world. In biblical terms, it more resembles Judges than Revelation.

Much the same can be said about Russell Hoban's eccentric and provocative *Riddley Walker.* Two elements combine to make this a difficult and sometimes confusing work. The most obvious of these is the language, the apparently degenerate English of a primarily oral society that has survived the Bad Time. This language, however, is not simply an affectation. Rather, like the languages of *The Faerie Queene* and *Finnegan's Wake,* it allows the author, through puns and other verbal manipulation, to invest words with multiple layers of meaning. Thus the "Ardship of Cambry" is not only the Archbishop of Canterbury but the hardship of Canterbury, the city which, in the novel, is the center of religious and secular power, the source of the first Bad Time and the potential source of further bad times.

The second difficult element, which is ultimately related to the language, is Hoban's conflation of religious images and motifs. The emphasis on ritual in the postholocaust society, the importance of Canterbury, the use of the legend of St. Eustace, and the reliance on the apocryphal *Gospel of Thomas* for theme and imagery, as well as the metamorphoses of such concepts as original sin and the devil, all contribute to the religious aura of the novel; and all depend ultimately on the language, the word. A central example occurs in "The Eusa Story," the retelling of St. Eustace's legend that accounts for the events of the Bad Time and that serves as scripture for Riddley Walker's society. In this story, Eusa, seeking the weapon that will destroy the enemies of Mr. Clevver, finds "the Littl Shynin Man the Addom" and tears him apart. The consequences are the creation of nuclear weaponry ("the 1 Big 1") and the near destruction of the world, resulting in the horrifying society that we see in the novel. Of course, what this story describes is the splitting of the atom, the division of a unity into a multiplicity, which causes devastation. In addition, Eusa discovers the Little Man "On the stags hed . . . in be twean thay horns with arms out strecht & each han holdin tu a horn."[12] In "The Legend of St. Eustace," as preserved in the only surviving guidebook to Canterbury Cathedral, Riddley reads a description of a painting in which "St. Eustace is seen on his knees before his quarry, a stag, between whose antlers appears, on a cross of radiant light, the figure of the crucified Saviour."[13] The Littl Shynin Man the Addom, then, corresponds to the new Adam, Christ; and Eusa, like Eustace, does wrong to serve the secular leader instead of preserving the integrity of that figure in the stag's antlers. But that Addom is also Adam, who brought sin into the world by dividing his will from the will of God, by making a duality out of unity. In *The Gospel of Thomas*, Jesus says, "On the day when you were one, you became two. But when you have become two, what will you do? . . . When you make the two one . . . then shall you enter [the kingdom]."[14] This theme of a fall from unity as seen in Genesis and in the stories of Eusa and Eustace pervades the book. As Riddley says, "You try to take holt of the iness and it comes 2 in your hans."[15]

Riddley himself, however, is a "connexion man," and in his naive way he tries to reconcile opposites, to find unities by making connections, and thereby to understand his world. In this way he is like a prophet, but like the biblical prophets he operates in a world that has far different priorities from his own. These differences can be seen in attitudes toward technology, a favorite theme in end-of-the-world literature. Throughout the story characters refer to two kinds of technology: nuclear weapons and such marvels as "boats in the air and picters on the wind."[16] Riddley is entranced by the latter kind, the technological marvels, but, though other characters pretend to the same fascination, the plot turns out to be largely about the search for the secret of gunpowder. The "priestly class" (the Eusa folk, associated with Canterbury) and the secular leaders are all trying to learn the proportions of charcoal, sulphur, and saltpeter that will release the power of gunpowder—a union that results in violent division—and provide them with power over each other. Hoban's word play adds levels of meaning to this search as well, for the charcoal is called "hart of the wood," recalling the stag in the Eusa-Eustace stories, and saltpeter figures in a poem as "Saul & Peter," the two apostles whose power struggle is recorded in Acts. Finally, the search for the correct proportions ends with a misinterpretation of "the figure of the crucified Saviour," which is understood by the secular leader as "the number of the salt de vydit in 2 parts in the cruciboal and radiating lite coming acrost on it."[17] Incredibly, it is the image of the crucified Christ that once again reveals to the world the power of explosives, and it is clear that the cycle of destruction is about to start over. If even this symbol of redemption leads to destruction, what hope can there be?

What Riddley discovers, however, is vital. By making connections among the elements of his world, the Eusa story and the Punch and Judy shows (which ultimately tie in with the religious imagery but are beyond the scope of this chapter), he comes to understand that certain things are constants, that Mr. Clevver, Mr. On The Levvil, and Drop John are all the same—"Same red face and littl black beard and the same horns growing out of his head."[18] But the Mr. Clevvers only succeed if the Eusas continue to serve them, as St. Eustace served Hadrian even after his conversion. Riddley's discovery is that "THE ONLYES POWER IS NO POWER,"[19] or, more specifically, that power, real power as opposed to what everyone is seeking, comes precisely in not seeking and struggling for it. In short, Riddley reaffirms some of the basic teachings of Western religion: that human beings have certain innate urges, whether we call them bestial instincts or original sin, that must be overcome if we are ever to break the cycle of destruction. This is the message of the epigraph:

> Jesus has said:
> Blessed is the lion that
> the man will devour, and the lion
> will become man, and loathsome is the
> man that the lion will devour,
> and the lion will become man.[20]

If the human overcomes the bestial in us, we are blessed; if the bestial overcomes the human, we are loathsome. The choice is ours. We can destroy or we can unify.

Like Malamud, then, Hoban uses religious images and motifs to present a prophetic rather than an apocalyptic message. He does not describe or celebrate the end of the world. Instead, like the author of Judges, he shows how often we pass through the same cycle and he offers some hope, relying on religious teachings, that that cycle can be broken. And while two works cannot be said to mark a trend, it is worth noting that these two important works reject popular apocalypticism in favor of prophetic warning and the affirmation that human values are worthy of preservation under the auspices of religion even in this imperfect world. I would suggest that these works use religious motifs to reflect the thought of most end-of-the-world fiction—including the apocalyptic *On the Beach,* in which civilization finally does end—to let us know that we should work to break the cycle now, while we can, rather than allowing that cycle to run its course once more.

NOTES

1. ''Apocalyptic'' can be a tricky term. It is often defined as ''revelation,'' but as Klaus Koch points out, the term was used in the ancient church ''as the title of literary compositions which resemble the Book of Revelations, that is, secret divine disclosures about the end of the world and the heavenly state. The word apocalypse has become the usual term for this type of book'' (Klaus Koch, ''What Is Apocalyptic? An Attempt at a Preliminary Definition,'' in *Visionaries and Their Apocalypses,* ed. Paul D. Hanson [Philadelphia: Fortress Press, 1983], p. 16).

2. For a comparison of these different but related apocalyptic views, see Charles Krauthammer, ''The End of the World,'' *The New Republic* 188, 12 (March 28, 1983), pp. 12–15.

3. Hence the present volume and such other studies as *The End of the World,* ed. Eric S. Rabkin, Martin H. Greenberg, and Joseph D. Olander (Carbondale and Edwardsville: Southern Illinois University Press, 1983).

4. This quote and all other biblical quotes are from the Douay Bible.

5. For detailed accounts of these changes, see, for instance, Otto Ploger, *Theocracy*

and Eschatology, trans. S. Rudman (Richmond, Va.: John Knox Press, 1968), or Meyer Waxman, *A History of Jewish Literature,* vol. 1 (Cranbury, N.J.: Thomas Yoseloff, 1960).

6. Krauthammer, p. 12.

7. Bernard Malamud, *God's Grace* (New York: Farrar, Straus & Giroux, 1982), p. 40.

8. Ibid., pp. 74–75.

9. Ibid., p. 171.

10. Ibid., p. 215.

11. Ibid., p. 223.

12. Russell Hoban, *Riddley Walker* (New York: Summit Books, 1980), p. 31.

13. Ibid., p. 123.

14. Edgar Hennecke, *New Testament Apocrypha,* vol. 1, ed. Wilhelm Schneemelcher, trans. R. McL. Wilson (Philadelphia: Westminster Press, 1963), Loggia 11, p. 22.

15. Hoban, p. 149.

16. Ibid., p. 19.

17. Ibid., pp. 128–29.

18. Ibid., p. 206.

19. Ibid., p. 167.

20. Ibid., an unnumbered page prior to the beginning of the text.

16

DOMINANT SOCIOLOGICAL THEMES IN POUL ANDERSON'S *ORION SHALL RISE*

Harold Lee Prosser

As a subtle, conflict sociologist concerned with social systems, Poul Anderson's dominant sociological themes of conflict, cultural mentalities, social deviance, and entropy are perfected and realized in his novel *Orion Shall Rise* (1983). Essentially, this fine novel concerns humankind's struggle to rebuild its civilization after a nuclear holocaust; the story is set centuries after this disaster, and it involves different cultures seeking the control of earth's destiny and resources. *Orion Shall Rise* contains some of Anderson's most complex and memorable character creations to date, such as Ronica Birken, Terai Lohannaso, Iern Ferlay, Peyt (Plik) Rensoon, Wairoa, Mikli Karst, Jovain Aurillac, Chon Till, and Faylis Ferlay, among others. *Orion Shall Rise* is a sociological study in conflict over power, and this theme is evident in the majority of Anderson's fiction.

Sociologist Ralf Dahrendorf, who constructed the theory of interest conflict groups, believed that social conflict is structured on the opposition of varying class-based interests as they are reflected in all technological cultures; results of interest conflict tend to generate social change in one form or another.[1] Taken from an individual perspective, one person vies for control by appealing in some manner to another whose interest matches his or her own. Thus he seeks to gain strength in numbers. This extends to all individuals in their daily existence, and eventually a group results that seeks the same goal or achievement of the same interest. To achieve that goal or interest means the displacement or absorption of any group in direct conflict with the defined goal or interest. Characters and their respective cultures in *Orion Shall Rise* exemplify Dahrendorf's theory of interest conflict groups in action.

By analyzing the conflict situations in the Anderson novel, it is possible to understand the individual cultures involved in the struggle. In *Orion Shall Rise* they are distinctly structured upon the three cultural mentalities theorized by sociologist Pitirim A. Sorokin: the *sensate,* the *ideational,* and the *mixed.*[2]

The DOMAIN, a culture dominated by *Skyholm*—a giant platform floating thirty miles above Europe—is an example of what Sorokin defines as an active sensate culture (a major culture on earth). It was first considered to be a deliverer following the nuclear holocaust but has now become a stratified society with elements of repression. An active sensate culture is one in which efforts are made to promote the fulfillment of human material needs and goals (materialism) by transforming the physical world of its citizens in such a manner that it will provide defined resources for them, thus guaranteeing their satisfaction. Based on the clansfolk principle, the DOMAIN advocates the growth of technology and science.

The MAURAI FEDERATION exemplifies Sorokin's concept of ideational culture. It is basically a cynical sensate culture which pursues its goals in such a way that its pursuit is justified in ideational (spiritual/religious) rationalizations. It justifies its pursuit of materialistic goals by direct reference to a transcendent (godly/other worldly experience) value system which is generally not accepted but to which verbal homage is paid. A historic example of this principle is found in the Crusades. Christians fought the Saracens and Turks for possession of the Holy Land, ostensibly for honor of Cross and Christianity. But in reality, it was a war fought for economic gain. The descendants of the MAURAI FEDERATION came from the Maurai natives of New Zealand and their philosophy is to develop technology that will utilize the natural energy of the sea, sun, and wind. There are some idealistic attributes present, but basically the MAURAI FEDERATION is a cynical sensate culture which considers it permissible to seek material goals as long as earth is not harmed.

Another group, the MONG—collectively the numerous tribes who fled Asia and settled in North America—represent an active, ideational culture and the first of two examples of what Sorokin would call "mixed." This type of culture seeks to play down sensual and materialistic demands and seeks to transform the earth into a place of harmony with the transcendent realm; in essence, the MONG seek heaven on earth. The MONG believe Gaea is the living planet, that it is a single organism, and they attempt to transform the material world so that it is in harmony with Gaea.

Finally there is the NORTHWEST UNION, a culture Anderson gives more detailed attention to than the others and a second type of "mixed" culture. It is a pseudo-ideational culture symbolized by a network of Scandinavian-style lodges in North America's Pacific Northwest. This group is dominated by a sensate approach to life, but ideational pursuits coexist to balance perspective and interpretation. In Sorokin's cultural mentalities schema, there are many subcategories within the three major types (sensate, ideational, and mixed), and the emphasis in a true ideational culture is that the ultimate reality is transcendent and cannot be seen or felt through the senses; this attribute is lacking in the NORTHWEST UNION.

Analysis of the cultures in *Orion Shall Rise* and observation of their conflicts for power reveals that each seeks to design its own perception of dominance in whatever manner possible.

Each culture has social deviance, but what is perceived as deviance in one setting may not be considered so in another. From a sociological perspective, deviance is in the eyes of the beholder and can be considered such only if the beholder has the power to define it. The power to define the situation implies control of the "rule framework" by which normal and deviant are defined. But without the use of direct force, one culture cannot make another immediately accept its "rule framework" for definitions of deviance. One culture must always control power—in some way—if it is to enforce its definitions of deviance and normality on another, powerful culture.[3]

In many instances enforcing power and the definitions of deviance is achieved by one culture supplanting another through conflict and then absorbing its existing "rule framework" and adapting it to achieve stratification and balance. This concept comes directly from the work of Ibn Khaldun, the first individual to explain the sociological theme of cultural entropy. An Arab intellectual of the early 1400s, Khaldun studied the historial process of the rise and fall of civilizations. He found that as one culture becomes static and weak, after having reached its pinnacle, it stagnates. An outside group (in Khaldun's studies and research, it is the nomadic tribes) eventually supplants the previously dominant culture, absorbs and replaces it. The process then repeats itself. This unending process, as perceived by Khaldun, is the sociological theme of cultural entropy, or the rise and fall of civilizations. As revealed in *Orion Shall Rise,* cultures as well as individuals are ready to supplant and displace each other; the sociological theme of cultural entropy applies equally to both in one form or another.

Ibn Khaldun's concept is evident in all of Poul Anderson's fiction as it is in many works by other major writers, such as Ray Bradbury, Frank Herbert, Robert A. Heinlein, James Blish, Brian Aldiss, and André Norton, to name but a few. Each culture, and each individual, in *Orion Shall Rise* believes its, or his, approach is the more logical one. Consequently, conflict continues until one or the other falls prey to something or someone stronger.

Orion Shall Rise not only contains some of Poul Anderson's finest writing, it is a superb case study of conflict and power. No doubt, in time it will be ranked as a masterpiece of sociological science fiction.

NOTES

1. An in-depth analysis of Dahrendorf's complex theory may be found in Ralf Dahrendorf, *Class and Class Conflict in Industrial Society* (Stanford, Calif.: Stanford University Press, 1959). The researcher and reader will also find the following references valuable as they pertain to sociology and literature: Thomas N. Carver, "The Basis of Social Conflict," *American Journal of Sociology* XIII (1908), pp. 628–37; Lewis A. Coser, *The Functions of Social Conflict* (Glencoe, Ill.: Free Press, 1956); Robert E. Park,

"The Social Function of War," *American Journal of Sociology* XLVI (1941), pp. 551–70; Georg Simmel, *Conflict* (Glencoe, Ill.: Free Press, 1955); C. Wright Mills, *The Power Elite* (New York: Oxford University Press, 1956); Daniel Chirot, *Social Change in the Twentieth Century* (New York: Harcourt Brace Jovanovich, 1977); Charles Tilly, *From Mobilization to Revolution* (Reading, Mass.: Addison-Wesley, 1978); Barrington Moore, Jr., *The Social Origins of Dictatorship and Democracy* (Boston: Beacon Press, 1966).

2. Pitirim A. Sorokin, often referred to as the philosopher sociologist, was a prolific author and instrumental in influencing the field of contemporary sociology. His work on cultural mentalities is wide-ranging, and he interprets from a world perspective, touching on art, literature, music, science, and the humanities in his perceptive writings. Although he is deceased, his work continues to attract a wide reading audience. Among his numerous books the following are readily available: *Altruistic Love: A Study of American "Good Neighbors" and Christian Saints* (Boston: The Beacon Press, 1950); *The American Sex Revolution* (Boston: P. Sergent, 1956); *The Basic Trends of Our Times* (New Haven, Conn.: College and University Press, 1964); *Fads and Foibles in Modern Sociology and Related Sciences* (Chicago: H. Regnery Co., 1956); *Forms and Techniques of Altruistic and Spiritual Growth* (Boston: Beacon Press, 1954); *Leaves from a Russian Diary: Thirty Years After* (Boston: Beacon Press, 1950); *A Long Journey: The Autobiography of Pitirim A. Sorokin* (New Haven, Conn.: College and University Press, 1963); *Explorations in Altruistic Love and Behavior* (Boston: Beacon Press, 1950); *The Reconstruction of Humanity* (Boston: Beacon Press, 1948); *S.O.S.: The Meaning of our Crisis* (Boston, Beacon Press, 1951); *Social and Cultural Dynamics* (Boston: Extending Horizons Books, 1957); *Social and Cultural Mobility* (Glencoe, Ill.: Free Press, 1959); *The Sociology of Revolution* (New York: H. Fertig, 1967); and *Sociological Theories of Today* (New York: Harper and Row, 1966). Sorokin was keenly attuned to social trends and social systems and deeply involved in cultural expression as found in literature, art, and music.

Other works the researcher and reader will find valuable, with regard to literature and culture, are B. Z. Goldberg, *The Sacred Fire* (Secaucus, N.J.: Citadel, 1974); Hugh Dalziel Dunca, *Symbols in Society* (New York: Oxford University Press); and Karl Mannheim, *Ideology and Utopia* (New York: Harcourt, 1936).

3. There is a massive canon of work since 1900 available on deviance and its many forms. Both literature and film are useful in determining personal values. However, some standard reference works on the relativity of deviance are Howard S. Becker, *The Outsiders: Studies in the Sociology of Deviance* (New York: Free Pess, 1963); Jack D. Douglas and Frances Chaput Waksler, *The Sociology of Deviance: An Introduction* (Boston: Little, Brown, 1982); Kai Erikson, *Wayward Puritans* (New York: Wiley, 1966); Erving Goffman, *Stigma: Notes on the Managements of a Spoiled Identity* (Englewood Cliffs, N.J.: Prentice-Hall, 1963); Earl Rubington and Martin S. Weinberg, *Deviance: The Interactionist Perspective* (New York: Macmillan, 1978).

17

THE DAYS AFTER: FILMS ON NUCLEAR AFTERMATH

Wyn Wachhorst

Of all the contrived analyses that cling to science fiction films of the 1950s—
McCarthyist body snatchers, Russians from Mars, the bomb in the guise of
Godzilla—the most pervasive has been the superficial notion that viewers sublimated the bomb as the stereotypical Victorians sublimated sex. Film criticism,
one often suspects, is another of those fields overpopulated in the wake of
technological unemployment. The survivors of Hiroshima themselves would be
hard pressed to find much mythos in the destruction of Tokyo by a seventy-story
snail. The six-acre moth and the one-chicken skyline were given radioactive
rationales simply because radiation lay at the leading edge of science, where
known and unknown interface. In the mutant monster cycle of the 1950s (for
example, *Them!),* and in films about reconstructed or mutated societies of the
distant future (for example, *Planet of the Apes),* the bomb has served simply as
a plot gimmick. To argue otherwise is to attribute a two-dimensional, sociopolitical function to the profoundly personal nature of psychic images. At best,
such interpretations misjudge the degree to which McCarthyism and the bomb
were perceived by the average moviegoer as immediate, personal threats.[1] Ac-
ademics often live too much in the tiny clearing that is rational consciousness,
swapping hack politicisms like adages from *Poor Richard,* denying (as D. H.
Lawrence said of Ben Franklin) the primal immensity of the dark forest. Insights
into the cinematic role of the bomb, in short, will not be found on bumper
stickers and T-shirts.

If the bomb has had a psychological role in film at all, the fact should be most
evident in such films as *Five, On the Beach,* and *Damnation Alley,* in which
the holocaust itself is the point of departure. The first and most obvious char-

acteristic of this subgenre, focusing on the immediate aftermath of Armageddon, is not just its peripheral concern with death but its suggestion that the holocaust may be a means to purification and rebirth in a New Eden.

The cinematic pattern for the New Eden theme was set by the first postholocaust film, *Five* (1951), a melodramatic social allegory in which the last five survivors form a microcosm of the American vision of society in 1950. They converge miraculously at a mountaintop retreat near the coast of southern California (actually the home of writer-producer-director Arch Oboler, who shot the film for $78,000). By the end of the film, three of the four men are dead, leaving only the new Adam and Eve. First to succumb is an elderly bank clerk who rambles on in a "front porch" manner about finance, believing he is on vacation from his job. He is the myopic, overdependent Everyman whose self-image—never more than a figment of institutional society—still encases and sustains him, like the suit of an astronaut on a dead world. Frail and spectacled, he is the "John Q. Public" in the editorial cartoons of the time; his short role at the outset of the film is that of a brief afterimage, a collective ghost. Next to die is a saintly, black elevator operator who has selflessly cared for the old man. He is the gentle folk figure of American legend, a young Uncle Remus whose buoyant faith gives hope to the others. He is tormented and finally killed by a Nazilike mountain climber, a racist, male chauvinist European named Eric. Arrogant, violent, and lazy, Eric lies in the sun while the others work the fields; he searches the empty city for jewels, tries to abduct Rosanne, the only woman, and is struck down in the nick of time by radiation. Alone, pregnant, and dazed at the beginning of the film, Rosanne is first comforted by Michael, a Dartmouth graduate with agrarian ideals. Obsessed with finding her husband, she returns to the empty, skeleton-strewn city, encounters his remains, and later loses her baby. When she rejoins Michael in the mountains, he is repairing the vegetable garden destroyed by the evil Eric. "I want to help you," she says—the last line of the film. And together the latter-day Thomas Jefferson and his loyal helpmate—the new American Adam and Eve—face the sun as the music rises, and a verse, taken loosely from Revelation, is printed over the scene:

> And I saw a new heaven a new earth . . .
> And there shall be no more death
> No more sorrow . . . no more tears . . .
>   Behold! I make all things new!

There is little coincidence in the fact that Arch Oboler was the first to create such a film. Having written almost eight hundred plays for radio in the early 1930s, most in the horror or fantasy genre, involving such gimmicks as giant earthworms that take over the world, or an expanding chicken heart that destroys civilization, he turned in the 1940s to propagandistic dramas about "smirky little Japs" and "the Jap-Nazi world." Among his melodramas of horror and romance was a radio script he had written for Bette Davis in 1938 called "The Word" (of God), about a couple alone on earth who start a new world. A decade later he dictated an updated version to his wife as they trekked across Africa on mule back.[2]

The result, *Five,* is about beginnings rather than endings. More spectacularly, as the poster ads announced, it is about four men on a one-woman planet. It is about racism, chauvinism, and self-delusion versus simple American virtues. It is about purification, renewal, and rebirth—about everything, in short, but violent, meaningless death. Buildings, plant life, and even environment appear untouched; even the windows are unbroken, and the corpses have converted immediately to polished skeletons. All that has been lost is an imperfect society with its complexities and ambiguities. ("We're in a dead world," says Michael, "and I'm glad it's dead . . . cheap honkey-tonk of a world.") If Oboler had intended a realistic warning, the glimpses of aftermath would have been less antiseptic and the plot less contrived. Anyone intent on showing that "this could really happen" would at least do the few minutes of research necessary to discover that a holocaust sparing only five humans would not exempt someone "up in the Empire State Building" or locked briefly in a bank vault. Not only do the survivors cross a continent to happen upon one another in an obscure mountain retreat, but the one who had been climbing Everest chances to wash ashore in America right at the feet of the other four.

The real concern of *Five,* with its love triangle, its social preaching, and its arty pretense (predictably, it is a cult favorite in France), is not the bomb but the absurdity of modern society. Nuclear holocaust is a plot gimmick, which could just as easily have been a plague (as in *The Omega Man* or *Where Have All the People Gone)* or an astronomical disaster (as in *When Worlds Collide).* Oboler, in fact, had lived by the gimmick—the science fiction twist or the new technique (he made the first 3–D movie, *Bwana Devil). Five* is a fantasy of purification, rebirth, and personal transcendence, falling into the tradition that extends from universal tales of a great flood to the disaster film cycle of the 1970s. Its timely appearance during the floodtide of crisis in 1949–50—the fall of China, the Russian bomb, atom spies, and the invasion of South Korea—reinforced the film's social metaphors: the aggressive, self-serving foreigner; the passivity and denial of the old man as Everyman; and Michael as the college-educated, middle-class American Adam, beginning anew with his self-sacrificing helpmate in the garden of suburbia. Even the token black man is part of the 1950s vision: a poetic ideal who turns out in practice to be dispensable. The role of the bomb in all this seems closer to what Robert Lifton has termed the religion of "nuclearism"; it is a cleansing, purifying agent, hosting the power of God to bring the flood, the second coming, or the new Eden.[3]

Oboler's Edenic theme and microcosmic plot—love triangle, villain intruder, a handful who survive for flimsy reasons, sanitized or unseen destruction, and conventional social concerns—recurred in other 1950s films. The first of these was one of Roger Corman's instant, change-in-his-pocket productions, *The Day the World Ended* (1956), which included a rubber mutant to break the monotony.

(A 1965 remake, *In the Year 2889,* may have been camp's finest hour, viewing
like a high school play with the metal-shop teacher cast in the older lead,
projecting every line for the benefit of lip-readers and the hard-of-hearing.)
Corman struck again in 1960 with *The Last Woman on Earth,* shot with another
film during a two-week Caribbean vacation write-off. The scriptwriter, who
thought it up day to day as they filmed, filled in as juvenile lead, cutting travel
costs and allowing him to think it up moment to moment as well.[4]

In *The World, the Flesh, and the Devil* (1959), black hero Harry Belafonte's
racial paranoia eclipses not only the threat of species extinction but the love
triangle itself. After a shoot-out with Mel Ferrer, echoing through the wind-
blown emptiness of New York, all is resolved in front of the UN building. After
burdening a whole feature with the race question, MGM apparently preferred to
send all three members of the cast hand in hand into the sunset rather than marry
Inger Stevens to a black. The one effect in which the film excels over others in
the cycle is the awesome loneliness and foreboding of the deserted city. Newspapers blow down the vacant streets where Belafonte, dwarfed in the shadow
of tall, brooding buildings whose empty windows glint in the sun, pulls a child's
wagon stacked with scavanged necessities. It is a scene intended not to depict
the horror of the holocaust (the absence of corpses is explained by a disintegrating
"nuclear salt") but rather the image of a paranoid's utopia (a facet of the
protagonist's racial paranoia, perhaps) in which the disappearance of one's fellow
men leaves the advantage of their accomplishments unencumbered by the dis-
advantages of their presence. Moreover, setting the social microcosm—the love
triangle—in a context of physical survival reduces all socioethical ambiguities
to the black and white world of the paranoid. Such films tell us more about
threats from than threats to civilization.

Similarly, the *Twilight Zone* episode "Two" (1961), an example of the Edenic
theme on television, substitutes Russian for black paranoia. A Russian-speaking,
female soldier plays cat and mouse through the empty city with the only other
survivor, an English-speaking, male soldier. At first the "Russian" violently
distrusts the peace-seeking "American," even firing a few rounds at him. But
after interminable wariness, she finally risks replacing her uniform with a store-
window gown he had tossed into her hands. Yet it is not until the very end of
the story that she chances her first smile and walks off hand in hand with him—
proving, I suppose, that the best road to Russian-American communion is to go
ahead and have the holocaust.

With mythological roots predating even the book of Genesis, the Edenic theme
inevitably found its way into the science fiction pulps of the early twentieth
century. In film, where the debt to the old pulps has always been large, the
theme was not limited to immediate postholocaust scenarios but was extended
to natural catastrophe (*When Worlds Collide* [1953]) and to the regeneration of
mutant, decadent, or regressed societies, where the holocaust had long passed
and the new Adam was often a time traveler (for example, *World without End*
[1956], *Teenage Caveman* [1958], *The Time Machine* [1960], and *Planet of the*

Apes [1968]).[5] The visions of renewal in postholocaust films were part of an increased longing for the innocent, pastoral settings of a simpler time, manifest not only in science fiction films but throughout postwar popular culture: MGM musicals, Rodgers and Hammerstein, the boom in adult westerns, historical and biblical romance, the Davy Crockett mania, and the folk music revival, not to mention the real-world phenomena of suburban migration and reemphasis on security, tradition, God, country, and family.

By the early 1960s, however, the Edenic fairy tale had lost favor with "nuclear" film makers. It reappeared only in *Damnation Alley* (1977), a film well after its time, which recapped variations on the *Five* plot: a militaristic, ruthlessly practical, older leader (as in *The Day the World Ended* [DWE] and *In the Year 2889* [2889] who is also self-centered and unfeeling (as in *Five* [F], *The World, the Flesh, and the Devil* [WFD], and *The Last Woman on Earth* [LWE]; a token black (F, WFD) who dies violently (F); a lone surviving female (F, WFD, LWE, and *Twilight Zone*'s "Two" [TZ]) who becomes the new Eve (all films); and a saintly, knowledgeable youth who becomes the new Adam (all films) roam a desolate landscape and find an empty city (F, WFD, LWE, TZ) with polished skeletons (F), encounter mutant threats (DWE, 2889), and are reduced to two men and one woman (F, WFD, DWE, 2889, LWE) who are saved by a sudden, inexplicable return of the normal environment (WFD, DWE, 2889, LWE). Where earlier films ended with "The Beginning" written across the screen (F, WFD, DWE, LWE, 2889), a great flood deposits *Damnation Alley*'s survivors on a pastoral shore where blue skies have returned; a female radio voice guides them to a rural town with lawns, trees, and white fences, and the small crowd of inhabitants—perhaps just out from a Little League game—runs toward them with outstretched arms. As one critic observed, not only is an unspeakable horror turned into "a household word, easily spoken because already confronted, already digested," but special effects make the atmospheric hell "thrillingly trippy," and the desolation becomes "a challenge for pioneers of the future who refuse to mourn, refuse to regret, but only carry on courageously."[6]

THE ROMANCE OF EXTINCTION: *ON THE BEACH*

The first postholocaust film to break with the Edenic theme was Stanley Kramer's *On the Beach* (1959), based on Nevil Shute's 1957 best-seller. Nuclear war has annihilated the Northern Hemisphere and poisoned the atmosphere, dooming the rest of humanity to extinction within months. The southernmost and last surviving large city, Melbourne, Australia, carries on much as usual while awaiting the lethal cloud. An American nuclear submarine captain, Dwight Towers (Gregory Peck), falls in love with Moira Davidson (Ava Gardner), a middle-aged, local wildflower. With no illusions about the reality, he nevertheless chooses to remain loyal to a sanity-saving vision of his wife and children awaiting him in Connecticut. Accepting this, the lonely Moira gives him love and companionship. In the end, hoping to die on home soil, Towers takes his ship to sea, submerging off the coast as Moira waves from the beach in the deadly breeze. Supporting characters include Peter (Tony Perkins) and Mary (Donna Anderson), a young married couple who care for their baby and plan for the future until the last moment, and a nuclear physicist (Fred Astaire) who fulfills his lifelong dream, buying a Ferrari and risking his now meaningless life in winning the Grand Prix.

Rejecting a new Genesis in favor of extinction, the film was touted by some as a courageous social message. Linus Pauling thought posterity might remember *On the Beach* as "the movie that saved the world."[7] To others, however, it was a "lucrative venture masquerading as social consciousness"—another 1950s fairy tale of proper romance and domestic virtue, a *"Woman's Day* approach" to extinction, with the sun dancing on the water behind a kiss, sailors ogling Ava Gardner, and other devices on the level of *Loveboat* or Astaire's musicals.[8] Once again, we see no destruction, no corpses, no physical agony—only the poignancy of ill-fated love. Rather than show us what must have happened to New York and Moscow, complained one critic, the film "portrays sweetly sad images" of deserted San Francisco and San Diego, and "the elegiac last days of Australia," where business-as-usual is carried to the absurd extreme of people in orderly lines being carefully checked off lists as they receive government-issued suicide pills in the final hours.[9] Others, however, noted that it is easier to identify with the concerns of healthy, attractive people in normal settings. Moira's rage at having wasted her youth only to lose her life to someone else's war, or the physicist's realization that his glamorous role was not only meaningless but partly responsible for the end of all meaning, or the young couple feeding and changing their baby until the day when it must be given the dose of poison recommended for infants—these are closer to our personal perspectives than, for example, a man dragging himself through burning rubble in search of his leg.

The reason that *On the Beach* is not *about* the bomb any more than its Edenic predecessors is that it is about meaning rather than meaninglessness, life rather than death. More exactly it is about the meaning of life in the face of one's own death. As Bosley Crowther observed, it is about "fervor, tenacity, and courage in the face of doom," carrying "the passionate conviction that man is worth saving after all."[10] In its celebration of the human spirit the film denies even the gesture of anarchy—unless one counts the wanton moment when the starched butler, perceiving he is the only one left in the stuffy men's club, elects for the first time in his career not to straighten the portrait that always lists when the door slams.

Contrary to those who argued that the depiction of life-as-usual intensified the sense of doom, it was the understatement of doom that intensified life-as-usual. Mary continues to tend the garden and plan the baby's future, Moira's father improves his farm, and Captain Towers and his crew, the last surviving Americans, never stray from even the most trivial Navy regulation. The novel is even more insistent: Moira enrolls in a secretarial course, Dwight goes gift shopping for his imaginary family in Connecticut, and Peter goes to great lengths in the last hours to obtain a decorative bench for his wife's garden. Though the physicist comes close, none of the characters accept the full implications of meaningless extinction. Perhaps this is because most human action is predicated on a perception of immortality, a faith that the individual, the family, community, or the species will endure in some form.[11] Under the circumstances, however, anarchy would make no more sense than business-as-usual. To ask why Towers stays with his ship is no more reasonable than to ask "why not." Far from being unrealistic, the holocaust's intensification of life-as-usual forces the perception that meaning ultimately lies in process—in the mundane, inertial patterns themselves rather than their specific content or their idealized ends. The novel clarifies this point when Moira comments on the young couple's obsession with their garden:

"They won't be here in six months time. I won't be here. You won't be here. They won't *want* any vegetables next year."
Dwight stood in silence for a moment, looking out at the blue sea, the long curve of the shore. "So what?" he said at last. "Maybe they don't believe it. Maybe they think that they can take it all with them and have it where they're going to, someplace, I wouldn't know." He paused. "The thing is, they just kind of like to plan a garden."[12]

Yet for all its effectiveness as a meditation on personal mortality, it remains true that the film sugarcoats the holocaust. A lingering city that allows elegiac love affairs and long, sweet farewells seems at least an atypical, postholocaust scenario. Once again there is a suggestion of Lifton's "nuclearism": all problems are solved by a single explosion, annihilating concern with decisions, responsibilities, complexities—even death itself. For, as Towers says in the novel,

"We've all got to die one day, some sooner and some later. The trouble always has been that you're never ready, because you don't know when it's coming. Well, now we do know, and there's nothing to be done about it. I kind of like that. I kind of like the thought that I'll be fit and well up till the end of August and then—home."[13]

What we really fear, moreover, is not extinction but terror, pain, and suffering. Because it achieves the former without the latter, the film remains transitional, ostensibly pessimistic, but in fact idealistically celebrating rather than censuring the human spirit. Kramer boasted that, unlike the novel, his film ended on a note of hope—the Christian banner fluttering over empty streets in the last scene, reading "There's still time, Brother!" As a message film, *On the Beach* was far better than *Five*, but finally no more effective than the banner.

THE SURVIVOR MENTALITY: *PANIC IN THE YEAR ZERO*

Just as the classic 1950s western, in which an innocent town was threatened by villains from outside, was replaced by the antiestablishment, 1960s western, in which an evil town was cleaned up by a group of paid renegades, so the classic 1950s science fiction film, with innocent communities threatened by alien monsters, was superseded in the late 1960s and early 1970s by films in which dystopian societies battled underground rebels. Most of the dystopias and waste-lands in these films were the product of some previous holocaust, and the "sur-vivor"—whether the heroic rebel (for example, *Logan's Run*) or the scavenger who caricatures all the decadent extremes of former civilization (for example, *The End of August at the Ozone Hotel* or *The Road Warrior*)—has become an increasingly popular image over the past two decades. The appeal of these films has less to do with nuclear war than with a growing "survivor mentality," of which hitchhiking youths with backpacks and bedrolls, family camping treks, and the spread of vans, pickups, campers, emergency equipment, and "practi-cal" clothing (fatigues, boots, over-warm and over-cool outfits) are only the most visible signs. The depersonalized, demythologized, technological behemoth has ironically been accompanied by a growing sense of individual isolation, vulnerability, and loss of control, a feeling reflected not only in the disaster-film cycle of the 1970s but also in the current trend toward primal heroes who are self-sufficient while in communion with a holistic reality (for example, *Quest for Fire*, *Iceman*, *The Clan of the Cave Bear*, *The Valley of Horses*, *Altered States*, and the "Tarzan," "Sheena," and "Conan" films). The need to simplify and purify in the face of postindustrial impotence and ambiguity also underlies much of the obsession with sports, where the issues are clear-cut, confrontation is pure and direct, and the winner survives. In short, the postmodern paradox of isolation and overdependence produces an image of the superior man as a romanticized primitive—a survivor.

This image in film, whether the context be primal, postholocaust, or simply decay (as in *Blade Runner*, and *Escape from New York*), has the same reenergiz-ing effect as what Robert Bly has called "making contact with the Wildman"—the dark, aggressive energy deep in the masculine side of the psyche.[14] The repres-sion of this energy by the technologically insulated, liberal Christian tradition, which has never granted evil its realistic due, has disturbed the psychocultural balance of masculine and feminine. The result is that the masculine face of this equilibrium—forceful action undertaken, not without compassion, but with re-solve—is itself polarized. On the one hand, the wild man is paraded as the cas-trated, domesticated Dagwood, while on the other, he breaks loose to commit the macho excesses that characterize much of the current survivor syndrome.

Though all postholocaust films manifest some aspect of this syndrome, *Panic in the Year Zero* (1962), based on Ward Moore's stories "Lot" and "Lot's Daughter," is the most explicit example among those dealing with the immediate aftermath of the bomb. Appearing during the bomb shelter mania, and depicting nuclear war as a temporary inconvenience, the worst effect of which is a break-down of law and order, the film is probably an accurate representation of public illusions at the time. While on a fishing trip, a Los Angeles family discovers that the city has come under nuclear attack. Amid the ensuing anarchy, the heretofore civilized, middle-class father (Ray Milland) and son (Frankie Avalon) seize weapons and attack anyone who stands in their way. "It's going to be survival of the fittest," says father, and "we can start with one basic fact—us." He knocks out a service station attendent to get gas, robs a hardware store when he cannot pay, and parts a stream of cars blocking the family's escape by pouring gasoline over the road and setting it on fire. Horrified at first by his commitment to violence, his wife is converted to his view when their seventeen-year-old daughter is raped by a gang of thugs. After hunting down the rapists and shooting them at close range, Milland leads his family back to what is left of civilization and the protective arm of the U.S. Army.

Panic in the Year Zero is a reactionary film, concerned with law, order, and the status quo, exemplifying, as John Brosnan observed, "exactly the sort of attitude that is likely to cause World War Three."[15] "I looked for the worst in others and I found it in myself," is Milland's belated conclusion. Yet to the obvious degree that his actions were justified, they represent the positive side of the wild man—the willingness, indispensable to any healthy community, to accept a necessary evil in pursuit of a larger good. The collective neuroses of the towns in 1950s westerns lay in the fact that they had to import their wild man-stranger-saviors—their Alan Ladds and Gary Coopers—from the wilderness. But regardless of how one evaluates the issues raised, *Panic in the Year Zero* remains another film that was never intended to be about the holocaust. To the degree, in fact, that the power of the bomb is translated into the power of the wild man, it is Lifton's "nuclearism" at its finest.

PSYCHIC NUMBING AND EMOTIONAL HEMOPHILIA: *THE WAR GAME* AND *THE DAY AFTER*

If we disqualify films that bathe the bomb in auras of rebirth, elegiac death, or resurrected masculinity, we must ask what a film about the bomb would be like. For most critics during the past two decades, the immediate answer has been Peter Watkins' *The War Game* (1966). Made for BBC television but never aired (allegedly because it was "too horrifying," though political motives seemed likely[16]), *The War Game* is a forty-seven-minute, newsreel-style semidocumentary graphically depicting the nuclear devastation of Britain's Kent County. Released to theaters in 1966, it won an Oscar for best documentary of the year. Eschewing not only melodrama but any form of story line, the film exposes the absurdity of government civil defense policies and rejects the notion that survivors would remain orderly and civilized. One of the most controversial pictures in film history, *The War Game* included not only food riots, executions, gory wounds, and bleak, apathetic faces but also the shooting of the hopelessly injured, bulldozers clearing bodies, and people being sucked into firestorms like dry leaves.

Watkins' insistence that *The War Game* was "not a ban-the-bomb film, but an attack-the-silence film" that was intended "to make the man in the street stop and think about himself and his future," resembles the comment made by Nicholas Meyer, who directed a similar film, *The Day After,* for ABC-Television in 1983: "I never thought the film would do anything but reinforce convictions that people brought to it. The people I'm trying to reach are the ones who haven't made up their minds—the ones who've barely thought about the issue."[17] *The Day After,* which cost $7 million and reached an estimated 100 million viewers, included violence, suffering, and people being incinerated into skeletons, but it differed from *The War Game* in its minimal attempts at plot and character development.

A problem for both films was the impossibility of living up to the orgy of controversy that preceded them. The BBC feared that *The War Game* might cause suicide and national panic, while previewers of *The Day After* called for the mobilization of crisis centers to handle the wave of grade-school suicides and mass catatonia anticipated in the wake of the program. Benina Berger-Gould, Berkeley "specialist" on the threat of nuclear war on children and the family, made it into *TV Guide* with her warning that "no one—child, adult or teen-ager—should watch it alone."[18] Just as ambulances were put on standby when *The War Game* premiered in Scotland, dozens of organizations like SANE, "The Day Before," and Physicians for Social Responsibility, feeling that *The Day After* should be watched "with others rather than alone and helpless in one's own home," made arrangements for group viewings and local postbroadcast gatherings.[19]

In truth, *The War Game*'s camera panned and jerked so rapidly over grainy, black and white scenes that often the subject itself, let alone the detail, was too unintelligible to be shocking. A public opinion poll reported that only 9.4 percent thought the film too horrific to be televised, while another survey found that "*all* of those interviewed who had actually seen the film believed it should be aired."[20] As for *The Day After,* most came away with the feeling that it was just another disaster movie, flitting from miniplot to miniplot in the *Loveboat* style tailored to the attention span of the television generation, jerry-rigging cardboard characters in order to kill them off, and doing so with far more discretion than the mildest splatter movie, where heads blow apart like cherry-bombed tomatoes. Far from being controversial shockers, *The War Game* and *The Day After* failed partly because their low-megaton scenarios did not go far enough—they were not realistic *(The Day After* did append a disclaimer to this effect). A more recent British television film, *Threads* (1984), borrowed its techniques directly from *The War Game* and *The Day After,* adding little beyond the expansion of graphic violence and the inclusion of the nuclear winter. Again, the American viewing was accompanied by the "battery of trained counselors" waiting by phones. The usual postmortem studio discussion, featuring a woman who "felt sorry for the birds" and another who urged writing the president and the "head of Russia," was led by an aging, flower-child psychotherapist who exuded, "These are *won*-der-ful; I want to hear them *all.*"

On the one side of the critical controversy is an extreme oversensitivity of the sort found in the would-be counselors who previewed *The Day After*—something close to emotional hemophilia; at the opposite pole is an almost schizophrenic undersensitivity to anything outside the self—a feeling that no death could be worse than one's own, which is inevitable anyway, and that if we all go together, one avoids missing out on the future. The oversensitives tend to read their personal anxieties and insecurities onto humanity at large, projecting an attitude that can paralyze both individuals and collectives, while the undersensitives come close to losing touch with reality by carrying to an extreme the necessary ability to desensitize oneself to indirect, universal dangers. The oversensitives thus accuse us of "psychic numbing," while the undersensitives see us as paralyzed neurotics who lack the perception that evil is inherent in the human condition. The truth is that each extreme is speaking only to the other, while the great majority of us in the middle, who experience the same tendencies in a more complex balance, listen in bewilderment, if at all. To the degree that nuclear films were ever intended to be *about* the bomb, they have failed to speak to this mass in the middle, for whom the norm tends toward undersensitivity.[21] Nor can an understanding of how the average man relates to the realities of the bomb be accomplished with armchair catch phrases like "psychic numbing" which offer any and all possible conditions as evidence. If my honest optimism about my future is hiding a hysterical fear of the bomb, how can we identify a man who does not fear it?

Perhaps what Watkins and Meyer have taught us is that it is not necessary to show the actual physical realities—the skin hanging down in sheets and the loose eyeballs popularized by Hiroshima accounts—for only the oversensitives are properly shocked. Such "realism" not only increases emotional anesthesia but appeals to the voyeur in us, who seeks antidotes to everyday tedium in horrible human suffering and in fantasies of miraculous survival, renewed unity and purpose, and redeemer heroism. Instead, the prerequisites for an effective nuclear message film are that the probability of extinction be made inescapably clear,[22] that there be no emotional escape routes for the viewer, and, most important, that the annihilation take place within a context that is personally meaningful to the audience.

E.T. INVERTED: *TESTAMENT*

In this respect, Lynne Littman's *Testament,* based on "The Last Testament" by Carol Amen, is far more successful than *The Day After* because it stays with one family, develops characters in depth, and has an emotional unity and progression that draws the viewer in ever more deeply. A suburban family, apparently caught in the interstices of those circles of destruction that *Life* magazine used to superimpose on metropolitan maps, awaits its inevitable death by radiation. The father never returns from what was San Francisco, and the mother must bear up alone as she buries her children one by one, stitched in body bags made from bed sheets. We are never present at the moment of death, we never witness intense physical pain, and we are never exposed to catastrophic special effects. World War III is a blank television and a blinding flash through the windows. What we see instead is spiritual death, intense emotional pain, and catastrophic hopelessness. The contrast between *Testament* and *The Day After* is similar to that which is made between contemporary films and those of the 1930s and 1940s. The earlier films deal in symbol and suggestion rather than explicit special effects—a shadow on the wall rather than a chain saw in the groin. In the most memorable scene from *The Day After,* hospital workers stare in disbelief at the rising white vapor trails of Minuteman missiles, soaring from their silos, arcing away into the blue over the pastoral Kansas landscape. Likewise, the striking images from *The War Game* were not the nightmares of destruction but the man trying to protect his family from the knowledge that they would all soon die of leukemia, or the child who had looked at the fireball and then stood sightless in a garden, weeping in pain and confusion.[23]

Like *E.T., Testament* is about an extraordinary event in the lives of ordinary people. As in Spielberg's films, *Testament*'s long beginning establishes audience identification with the familiar, uneventful routine of life in middle-class, child-oriented suburbia. As a gesture to this parallel, the youngest son's bedroom displays an ''I Love E.T.'' decal. *Testament,* however, is actually *E.T.* in reverse: In *E.T.* a transcendent, Christlike power intervenes with a message of hope (love resurrects; ''I'll be right here''; the rainbow in the wake of the ship's departure); in *Testament* a transcendent, evil power intervenes with a message of doom. In both cases, the viewer is unable to pigeonhole the experience. Just as *E.T.* brought the extraterrestrial out of the remote deserts and cardboard communities of 1950s science fiction films and into the real world of pizza and *Sesame Street, Testament* freed the holocaust from the Edenic fantasy, the romantic elegy, and the circus of special effects, planting it under the nine-to-five day with such stealth as to catch the thrill-seeking escapist completely off guard.

Habitual activities persist after *Testament*'s holocaust just as they did in *On the Beach.* The school play *(The Pied Piper of Hamelin* because they live in Hameline, California) goes on, the last line spoken by the family's youngest boy: ''Your children are not dead. They will come back when the world deserves them.'' And the preteen daughter continues her piano lessons with the elderly, intense, European woman, whose demand for punctuality is less an obsession than a tenacious clinging to meaning. Like those in Kramer's film, the characters discover that meaning derives from networks of connectedness and communion, no matter how pointless the patterns themselves become. Reflecting on the fact that a few have left town, the twelve-year-old explains to his mother that he is running errands for the old man who sits at the ham radio, that Mary Liz has her piano lessons, and that Dad might still come back. ''And besides,'' adds his mother, ''it's our home.'' But unlike *On the Beach, Testament*'s story is not diffused into global and institutional concerns, nor is it all stiff-upper-lip anticipation of a discreet off-screen nightmare. *Testament*'s deaths not only take place but do so amid conditions that deteriorate so gradually, evenly, and inexorably that the viewer never regroups his perspective. One has almost adjusted—almost achieved the resignation of *On the Beach*—when one discovers that the next incremental step has already become a reality. Not only do we move from collapsed services to sickness to burials to a great bonfire of bodies, but the photography grows dark and monochromatic, sunshine gives way to rain, and people seem to merge with the shadows. Yet all of this wilting, flickering, and dying never lapses into melodrama. The story, seen entirely from the mother's harrowed perspective, never loses the profaning sense that beyond even this last personal agony there remains that cosmic indifference which has always belittled our own crises.

This intense personal focus (along with a $750,000 budget which, for example, was unable to populate the town adequately) caused one critic to call the film ''an overbearingly banal'' and ''genteel vision of the apocalypse,'' its ''soap-opera sentimentality . . . domesticating the unthinkable.''[24] Ironically, however, it is not *Testament* but *The Day After* that domesticates the bomb. The power of the ''unthinkable'' lies in its unseen mystery. Just as something essential is lost when God materializes as a bearded man in the sky, graphic special effects make the bomb thinkable; there is a feeling that one has confronted it, digested it, and that it is nothing but those images. The critical dilemma concerning the nuclear message film is similar to the theological paradox concerning the image of God: to concretize it (idolatry) is to take away its numinosity, yet without concrete representation it cannot become immediate and personal. Unlike other films, *Testament* overcomes this dilemma by leaving the bomb its numinosity and confining its ''realism'' to an emotional explicitness that is as raw as the physical images of *The Day After*. Much of this personal realism is achieved by ignoring the global perspective, including such meaningless abstractions as who started the war, or large-scale images of extinction.

The concern over extinction, whether of humans, whales, or sea otters, is an emotional luxury. The idea that extinction is greater than personal death is an abstraction that belongs with Copernican theory and relativity. For most humans, bound to subjective reality, the sun still rises and sets; though relativity may be so real as ultimately to produce extinction, in most minds ''matter'' will retain color, odor, and texture to that last moment. In the common mind, ''extinction'' is the opposite of walking on the moon; ''death'' is the opposite of walking at all. The one is abstract and cerebral, like the explanation of ''red'' in an optics textbook; the other is personal and immediate, like seeing red itself. Abstractions provide necessary rationales for the narcissistic personality prerequisite to leadership, but the foot soldier never fights for an abstraction. He does not fight to preserve ''liberty'' or the peasant utopia or the perfect union; he fights to preserve his Wednesday-night pinochle game, his wife's new curtains, or his Little League champions. If the man in the street finally gets mad as hell about the bomb, it will not be in response to remote archival photos of charred Japanese children, or special-effect images of a bald, moonlike planet; more likely it will be the result of accumulating visions such as that of a wife listening for the last time to her husband's voice on her answering machine, then transferring the last battery to the flashlight; or a mother's panicked search for the teddy bear before burying her little boy in the yard.

These things alone, however, cannot account for *Testament*'s effectiveness. An underlying counterpoint to the film's dominant pessimism affirms, even idealizes, the abiding spirit of the average individual. It is as though the human collective were some alien creature—an evil monster like the bomb it has created—in the shadow of which each individual must somehow nurture hope. *Testament* simply depicts this predicament in its extreme form. In the final scene, the last three survivors—the mother, her son Brad, and a retarded Japanese boy—sit in the dark observing Brad's thirteenth birthday with three candles stuck to crackers. "What do we do now?" asks Brad without expression. "Make a wish," answers his mother. "What'll we wish for, Mom?" After a pause she says: "That we remember it all. The good and the awful. The way we finally lived. That we never gave up. That we were *last* to be here—to deserve the children." The film then ends with another of the slow-motion, bright, flickering, home movies that have punctuated the story—this one a surprise birthday celebration for Dad in the backyard with cake and candles. One recalls the last act of *Our Town,* in which the dead Emily returns to witness her twelfth birthday and says to the stage manager:

It goes so fast. We don't have time to look at one another. . . . I didn't realize. . . . So all that was going on and we never noticed. . . . Good-by to Grover's Corners . . . Mama and Papa. Good-by to clocks ticking . . . and Mama's sunflowers. And food and coffee. And new ironed dresses and hot baths . . . and sleeping and waking up. Oh, earth, you're too wonderful for anybody to realize you. Do any human beings ever realize life while they live it?—every, every minute?[25]

At the deepest level, our reaction to the postholocaust film is less a feeling of fear and rage than a renewed appreciation of Mama's sunflowers, new ironed dresses, and hot baths, and of the fact that we all live under a lesser form of the same fate, that we are each finally alone, with our candles and our wishes, in the face of death.

NOTES

    1. If the bomb were the main catalyst for monster movies, one would have to explain the motivation for such pre-1945 films as *King Kong* (1933). Far less naive, for example, is Walter Evans' suggestion that the 1950s monsters were aimed at a teenaged audience vulnerable to archetypal images of sexual change and conflict; see "Monster Movies: A Sexual Theory," *Journal of Popular Film* 2 (Fall 1973), pp. 353–65.

    2. J. Fred MacDonald, *Don't Touch That Dial! Radio Programming in American Life, 1920–1960* (Chicago: Nelson-Hall, 1979), pp. 56–57, 67, 68, 106; *Columbia Pressbook* for *Five* (Hollywood: Columbia Pictures, 1951).

3. Robert Jay Lifton, *The Broken Connection: On Death and the Continuity of Life* (New York: Simon & Schuster, 1980), pp. 369–87.

4. Joe Bonham, "The Return of Roger Corman," *Starlog* 4 (February 1979), pp. 46–49.

5. The Edenic theme in film was not initiated by the bomb; in *The End of the World* (1916), the new Adam and Eve survive a comet catastrophe.

6. Judith Bloch, "Damnation Alley," *Film Quarterly*, 35 (Fall 1981), p. 51. It should be noted that the film differs radically from Zelazny's novel, which is superior in intent, focus, and resolution.

7. Joseph Keyerleber, "On the Beach," in *Nuclear War Films*, ed. Jack G. Shaheen (Carbondale and Edwardsville: Southern Illinois University Press, 1978), p. 31.

8. Keyerleber, p. 34; Robert Hatch, "Films," *Nation*, January 2, 1960, p. 20.

9. Midge Decter, "Stanley Kramer's 'On the Beach,' " *Commentary* 29 (June 1960), p. 524.

10. Bosley Crowther, *New York Times,* December 18, 1959, p. 34.

11. Robert Lifton elaborates on this idea in *The Broken Connection* and other writings.

12. Nevil Shute, *On the Beach* (New York: Signet Books, 1957), pp. 88–89.

13. Ibid., p. 103.

14. Keith Thompson, "What Men Really Want: A *New Age* Interview with Robert Bly," *New Age Journal* [n.v.] (May 1982), pp. 30–37, 50–51.

15. John Brosnan, *Future Tense: The Cinema of Science Fiction* (New York: St. Martin's Press, 1978), p. 156.

16. *The War Game* was the first film ever banned by the BBC. Asked if she agreed with the decision, Mrs. Winifred Crum Ewing, producer of documentaries for the BBC, answered that "having lived in the Southeast of England throughout the war, having seen how people behave in circumstances of war and bombing, it was an absolute slander on humanity. His [Watkins'] observations are profoundly wrong. . . . [T]his is not the way people behave toward each other in times of stress. . . . We don't need these emotional, left-wing intellectuals to tell us that we can destroy the world" (quoted in Jack G. Shaheen, "The War Game," in *Nuclear War Films,* ed. Jack G. Shaheen, p. 113. See also James M. Welsh, "The Modern Apocalypse: *The War Game,*" *Journal of Popular Film and Television*, 11 (Spring 1983), pp. 25–41; Joseph A. Gomez, *Peter Watkins* (Boston: Twayne, 1979), pp. 45–66.

17. Welsh, p. 30; Mark Gerzon, "Watching the World End: How Hollywood Faced up to Nuclear War," *New Age Journal* [n.v.] (November 1983), p. 85.

18. Howard Polskin, "Educators Worry about Effect of 'The Day After,' " *TV Guide,* November 19, 1983, p. A-1. See also *Forum,* 2 (Fall 1983) [newsletter of the Educators for Social Responsibility], special issue on *The Day After;* and Judith Michaelson, "The End of Denial: A Psychiatrist Looks at 'The Day After,' " *San Francisco Sunday Examiner and Chronicle,* November 20, 1983, Datebook, p. 59.

19. Welsh, p. 30; Gerzon, p. 87.

20. Welsh, p. 38.

21. Public opinion polls continue to show that the majority of Americans do not consider themselves seriously affected by thoughts of the bomb, though anxiety has increased over the years. Surveys of children's reactions suggest more fear, probably because opposite results tend to be ignored. And what can a child say in reaction to a questionnaire other than repeat what he has heard and give descriptions that could hardly be positive? See Hazel Erskine, "The Polls: Atomic Weapons and Nuclear Energy,"

Public Opinion Quarterly 27 (1963), pp. 155–90; Eugene Rosi, "Mass and Attentive Opinion on Nuclear Weapons Tests and Fallout, 1954–1963," *Public Opinion Quarterly* 29 (1965), pp. 280–97; Vincent Jeffries, "Political Generations and the Acceptance or Rejection of Nuclear Warfare," *Journal of Social Issues* 39 (1974), pp. 119–36; Howard Means, "Freedom from Fear," *Washingtonian* 116 (August 1981), pp. 77–86; Lawrence D. Maloney, "Nuclear Threat through the Eyes of College Students, *"U.S. News and World Report,* April 16, 1984, pp. 34–37; Harry F. Waters et al., "TV's Nuclear Nightmare," *Newsweek,* November 21, 1983, pp. 66–72; Michael Kernan, "Children in Fear of Nuclear War," *Washington Post,* October 14, 1983, pp. Cl, C4; Marcia Yudkin, "When Kids Think the Unthinkable," *Psychology Today* 18 (April 1984), pp. 18–25; Sylvia Eberhart, "How the American People Feel about the Atomic Bomb," *Bulletin of the Atomic Scientists* 3 (June 1947), pp. 146–49, 168; "How U.S. Citizens React to the Bomb," *U.N. World* 1 (October 1947), p. 9; and Alice Cheavens, "Facing the Fear of Bombs," *Parents Magazine* 25 (November 1950), pp. 42, 136.

22. The most popular case for extinction is Jonathan Schell's *The Fate of the Earth* (New York: Alfred A. Knopf, 1982), which reflects the scientific consensus. See also Paul R. Ehrlich and Carl Sagan, *The Cold and the Dark: The World after Nuclear War* (New York: Norton, 1984).

23. *The Day After* originally contained a powerful scene showing a child screaming but was cut when a child psychologist retained by ABC said it would upset children (Gerzon, "Watching the World End," p. 34). *The War Game* examples are noted by Richard Schickel in *Second Sight: Notes on Some Movies, 1965–1970* (New York: Simon & Schuster, 1972), p. 104.

24. David Ansen, "A Quiet Apocalypse," *Newsweek,* November 14, 1983, pp. 98, 101.

25. Thornton Wilder, *Three Plays by Thornton Wilder* (New York: Bantam Books, 1961), p. 62.

18

DO ANDROIDS DREAM OF RIDLEY SCOTT?

David Desser

Like many science fiction authors, the late Philip K. Dick was fond of using a postcatastrophe setting for his tales. In Dick's case, however, the concern was not with the specificity of the apocalypse and the scientific issues that arose from there but rather with the posing of certain fundamental issues within this dramatic context. Dick utilized a variety of postcatastrophes over the course of his work, ranging from personal tragedies (as in *Valis* [1981] to more global holocausts. Two of his most significant works may be said to be in this latter mode: *The Man in the High Castle* (1962) and *Do Androids Dream of Electric Sheep?* (1968). Both stories are set in an imaginative San Francisco and both raise essentially similar questions revolving around the issue of what it means to be a caring person. In *The Man in the High Castle,* Dick works in the dystopian fiction of an "alternate history" and wonders what life would be like in the United States if the Axis powers had won World War II. His research into and thinking about the Nazi mentality also formed the foundation for his philosophical musings in *Do Androids Dream of Electric Sheep?,* the novel on which this essay will focus.

If *Do Androids Dream of Electric Sheep?* is set in a postapocalyptic world of nuclear irradiation, it is so partly to present a veneer, the veneer of "science fiction," in order for Dick to examine what is really on his mind. He fills this futuristic tale of life following "World War Terminus" with a host of science fiction icons, including hovercars, laser guns, and colonies in space. However, the only futuristic technology that really concerns him is androids. And it is the disjunction, the bottom-line difference, between the human and the android that forms the central structural concern of this significant work.

Throughout the novel, the question of what it means to be human, to be a real person, is raised on a variety of levels. But the answer emerges in relatively simple form: empathy. Early in the novel, the hero, Rick Deckard, a bounty hunter with the San Francisco police department who specializes in "retiring" androids, reflects on the workings of the Voigt-Kampff test, this futuristic society's index to distinguish between androids and humans. Basically, the test measures involuntary responses to questions about the killing of animal or human life. Although androids "surpassed several classes of human specials in terms of intelligence,"[1] they do not respond empathically. Deckard concludes, "Empathy, evidently, existed only within the human community."[2]

Of course, Dick realizes that to be human does not necessarily mean that such empathy is always operative, that it is always present:

A human being without the proper empathy or feeling is the same as an android built so as to lack it, either by design or mistake. We mean, basically, someone who does not care about the fate which his fellow living creatures fall victim to; he stands detached, a spectator, acting out by his indifference John Donne's theorem that "No man is an island" but giving that theorem a twist: that which is a mental and moral island *is not a man.*[3]

In Dick's novel, *Our Friends from Frolix 8* (1970), we find the pronouncement: "The measure of a man is this: how swiftly can he react to another person's needs?"[4] It is precisely this swiftness that the Voigt-Kampff test measures. It is important to note that the sentiment "no man is an island" is raised in *Androids* and that Pris, an android herself, is the one to attribute it correctly to John Donne. But knowing who said it and being able to act on it are two different things.

The quality of empathy thats distinguishes humans from androids appears in a variety of contexts. At the broadest level, Dick has created a religion in this society called "Mercerism." Subscribers to the belief possess a small, handled box, called an "empathy box," which enables empathic communication to pass through all of those currently in connection. This experience is denied to androids.

An android, no matter how gifted as to pure intellectual capacity, could make no sense out of the fusion which took place routinely among the followers of Mercerism—an experience which he [Deckard], and virtually everyone else ... managed with no difficulty.[5]

Mercerism has obvious affinities with Christianity which range from the death and resurrection of the religion's namesake, Wilbur Mercer, to the infliction of wounds on the figurehead and the concept of fusion with the founder (seen in Christianity through the sacrament of communion and Mercerism through fusion via the empathy box). The point of Mercerism in the structure of the novel is not that Dick is calling for a return to Christian mysticism, but rather that Mercerism is opposed to the force represented by Buster Friendly, the omnipresent media star. For it is revealed late in the novel that the reason for Buster's antagonism toward Mercerism is that he is an android. Early in the novel, J. R. Isidore, a human "special" (a radiation-contaminated, inferior human), who likes both Buster and Mercer, concludes that the two are in competition for their minds. "They're fighting for control of our psychic selves."[6] Although this realization on Isidore's part is not further delved into by Dick, as readers we can make the connections he implies. We have the choice, represented by Mercerism, to maintain empathic contact with our fellow creatures, or we can give ourselves over to the media manipulations of Buster Friendly and cut ourselves off from humanity. It is the choice between the empathy box and the idiot box.

On a more specific level, the idea of empathy appears in the relationship between the humans and their animals. Animal life is nearly extinct in this postholocaust world, and the possession of real (organic) animals is not only a status symbol among the people of the novel but also a sign of the human— androids do not have pets. Part of Rick Deckard's motivation for killing the androids who have returned to earth is to get enough money to buy a large pet. He eventually buys a female goat which not only brings out empathic responses in him but begins the regeneration of his marriage which is on rocky ground at the novel's start.

Empathy also appears in the form of Deckard's attraction to Rachael Rosen, a Nexus-6 android, and his distaste for his job in the face of killing the female android, Luba Luft. Deckard and Phil Resch, another bounty hunter, corner Luba at a museum. As a kind of last request, she asks Deckard to buy her a reproduction of an Edvard Munch painting. Deckard does so, spending his own money. Luba thanks him, remarking that "there's something very strange and touching about humans. An android would never have done that."[7] Phil Resch, in fact, would never have done that. But Resch is not an android—thus Dick's contention that to be truly human is less a function of biology than of empathy.

Basically, the narrative thrust of *Do Androids Dream of Electric Sheep?* revolves around maneuvering Rick Deckard ever closer to his essential humanity. Deckard is first introduced as alienated from himself and from his wife, Iran. In the first scene of the novel, Deckard and Iran argue over the various settings of a mood organ (part of the hardware of the science fiction veneer). Iran refuses to set the organ. She says, "I realized how unhealthy it was, sensing the absence of life . . . and not reacting."[8] She is referring to the population depletion of earth due both to the war and to the emigration off-world by many healthy humans. Deckard, however, uses the mood organ, an index of his loss of emotional self-control. He then goes to his rooftop pen to care for his sheep. But the sheep is revealed to be fake (electric), another index of Deckard's loss of humanity.

As Deckard progresses wih his assignment to kill six androids, the process of emotional regeneration occurs, first as he meets Phil Resch, then as he experiences sympathy for Luba Luft, and finally when he is erotically attracted to Rachael Rosen. Deckard is ultimately brought to full empathic consciousness with the help of Wilbur Mercer through a kind of transmigration with the religious figure. He then returns home to Iran. As the novel closes Deckard's life and marriage have been regenerated, reborn, and out of the ashes of nuclear war, an irradiated atmosphere, a depleted population, and an increasing tendency toward emotional disinvolvement, Deckard has found a way to give meaning to life—genuine, human meaning.

Dick's concern with emotional issues, with the metaphysics of science fiction compared to its physics, has some unfortunate by-products. One of these might be called his "paranoid" vision. For what we see by novel's end is not simply that Rick Deckard must hunt down and kill a number of androids, but that androids are omnipresent, from electric animals to an alternate police department virtually run by robots, to the most famous media personality in the world. Overriding the entire novel is a sense of immense conspiracy, a conspiracy participated in by Deckard's own department, by the Rosen Association (a powerful corporate conglomerate which manufactures androids), and by the government itself, which controls the media. This sense of conspiracy paranoia bespeaks of the 1960s when the novel was written. And the postapocalyptic vision that possesses Dick is less the fear of nuclear war than the paranoia and depression left in the wake of the assassination of John F. Kennedy. Dick was a writer acutely sensitive to the tenor of the times. There is every reason to think that he would have been torn between the despair of hopelessness, given the ever-increasing dehumanization of our environment and our government, and a sense of optimism over the emerging counterculture of the mid-1960s. *Do Androids Dream of Electric Sheep?* tries to reflect that optimism, but Dick's pessimism, nevertheless, comes seeping through.

Another unfortunate by-product of Dick's ethical/metaphysical musings is a certain carelessness of structure and genuine overabundance of characters, concepts, and issues. This is true of many of his novels. His very prolificness precluded the kind of care a well-crafted novel requires. *Do Androids Dream of Electric Sheep?* simply has too many characters and not enough drama. The seeds of a powerful, elegant tale are here within the plot reverberations and peregrinations, and these seeds are very much worth germinating. And that is precisely what director Ridley Scott and his team of screenwriters and special effects technicians did with *Blade Runner,* the stunning, grossly underrated film version of the novel.

Philip K. Dick unfortunately died before he could see the finished film version of his novel. However, in a very ambivalent article printed in the February 15/March 28, 1981, edition of the *SelecTV Guide,* he did discuss the screenplay adaptation, saying that he felt audiences were drawn to science fiction films "not for their story-line" but for their "graphic, visual impact. . . . Authors of science fiction novels know this and grumble; what they wrote is not what you get when the film is finished."[9] However, he goes on to say that he read the script for *Blade Runner* and that "it was terrific. It bore no relation to the book. Oddly in some ways it was better."[10] In terms of the finished film, Dick's comment is not quite accurate: the film does bear some resemblance to the novel. He is quite right when he says that in some ways the film is better.

The standard wisdom has it that novels are invariably superior to their film versions. In this case, however, it is better to say that novel and film simply differ, for in adapting Dick's book to the screen, the filmmakers made changes with an eye for the needs of the film; that is, with a knowledge of how films tell stories compared with books. Basic changes include the total elimination of Mercerism and the figure of Buster Friendly; reduction in the number of androids that Deckard has to kill; the elimination of Phil Resch and the other police department; and the elimination of Deckard's wife and consequent character changes. Other interesting differences include some name changes: the novel's Eldon Rosen, the android manufacturer, becomes the film's Eldon Tyrell; and J. R. Isidore, the "special," becomes J. R. Sebastian, still "special" but with a higher I.Q.[11]

These changes reflect the film's concentration on narrative tension, focusing more strongly on Deckard's mission to kill the androids than the more diffused elements of suspense and action in the novel. But the essential difference was pinpointed by Dick himself when he spoke of the "graphic, visual impact" science fiction films possess. From the point of view of visual dynamism, the film's overpopulated Los Angeles of 2019 creates a much more kinetically active city than Dick's underpopulated San Francisco. Consequently, the postcatastrophe in which the film situates itself is not the nuclear nightmare of the novel but an ecological one. The city here teems with swarming humanity; animal life is virtually extinct due not to radiation poisoning but atmospheric pollution. The city is falling apart from a lack of resources, both human and material. A constant rain seems to fall (a neat reversal on contemporary Los Angeles' chronic water shortages), but it is not a healthy, cleansing rain. In short, the ecological disaster that is apparent here was created with an eye toward the visual. As such, atmosphere and mood play a large part in the film's meaning.

The most revealing change from book to film, and the film's ultimate glory, may be found in the nature, function, and significance of the androids, in the film called "replicants." The name change not only performs a cosmetic function, giving the film a more "high-tech" veneer, but also a metaphysical one. For these androids are not in any sense machines. In the novel, Dick is somewhat unclear on this score. In it, the Nexus-6 android is said to possess a "brain unit" with "two trillion constituents plus a choice within a range of ten million possible combinations of cerebral activity."[12] Rachael Rosen says about herself that she is merely a "chitinous reflex-machine," and she insists before making love to Deckard that he remember that she is not a woman. Afterwards, however, Deckard tells her, "You're not made out of transistorized circuits like a false animal; you're an organic entity."[13] The Nexus-6 androids have a four-year life span having to do with their metabolism, a problem apparently technologically insoluble. Of course, Dick was unconcerned with the hardware of his robots; for him it was simply a given that they are incapable of developing empathy.

In the film, the androids/replicants are biogenetically engineered, and there is no hint that they are machinelike. They, too, possess a four-year life span, but as a built-in deterrent to their forming genuine human characteristics. And it is precisely this four-year life span that becomes the replicants' raison d'être. Instead of accepting their built-in limitations, instead of resigning themselves to the inevitable (a quality that the Deckard of the novel despises about the androids), they wish to do something about it—to make a change. This gives them a mission, a quest. And their quest is asked to be read metaphorically as a quest to understand the essential metaphysical question: What is the meaning of life?

The replicants of *Blade Runner* are thus metaphorical human beings. They seek what we all seek. They resent their slavelike existence as workers, bodyguards, or pleasure-units in the off-world colonies. They rebel as a conscious act of defiance and travel to earth specifically to confront their "maker," Eldon Tyrell. (The androids of the novel come to earth for no specific reason, other than perhaps Dick's "conspiracy" paranoia.) In the process of their quest, they come to form emotional attachments to each other. It is clearly implied that Leon and Zhora are lovers, and it is obvious that Roy Batty loves Pris. This distinguishes them from the androids of the novel who, it is said, would not hesitate to betray or kill each other. More important, there is the fact that Rachael falls in love with Deckard. At one point, she kills Leon to save Deckard, and when they go to his apartment, Deckard notices that she has the shakes, that she is shook up by her killing of Leon. He tries to calm her down by saying that getting the shakes is merely part of the business. To which she emotionally responds, "I'm not in the business. (Pause) I am the business."[14] Later in the scene, Rachael accusingly asks Deckard if he himself has ever taken the Voigt-Kampff test. We thus have a reversal in the fact that the replicant is more emotional, more empathic, than the human.

It is because the replicants are metaphorical human beings, or, as Eldon Tyrell says to Deckard, "Commerce is our goal here at Tyrell; more human than human is our motto,"[15] that the erotic attraction between Deckard and Rachael can be more easily sustained. Deckard is (conveniently) divorced from his wife (never seen in the film), thus giving him the narrative freedom to experience erotic attraction. But he is divorced already because of his emotional alienation. He tells us that his wife referred to him as "sushi—cold fish." Deckard's confrontation with the replicants and his growing love for Rachael are precisely what return him to emotional empathy and wholeness. However, it is in the final linking of Deckard to Rachael, the replicant, that the film makes a quantum leap past the novel. For here the vision of postapocalyptic regeneration is not simply a resurgence of empathy and a rebirth of emotions revolving around male-female romance; the vision put forth in the film involves man recasting himself within his own inner being, his own creation. In this sense, *Blade Runner* makes explicit a theme apparent in *Star Trek—The Motion Picture* where, at the film's end, a new life form is created when *Enterprise* Captain Decker merges with V-ger. That theme is made more explicit in *Blade Runner* when the hero merges with the technologically created being. At film's end, the two fly off together, away from the polluted city, not knowing what the future holds. (Rachael was not built with the four-year life span, but it is not known how long she may live.)

As Deckard muses in a voice-over, he may not know how long they have together, but then, who does?

Both novel and film share the fundamental questioning of what it means to be human. In the novel, this issue is easily raised. In the film, however, the issue arises by allusion and by a series of poetic and disturbing images. One of these images is the leitmotif of eyes as a metaphor for the window to the soul and the idea of "seeing." Following a written crawl that explains what replicants are and the fact that they are banned on earth, the film opens with the title "Los Angeles, 2019." This is followed by a series of exterior shots of the futuristic city; a hovercar crosses the screen from foreground right to background left. Flames erupt from an industrial chimney. Then there is a close-up of an eye; such an image is "prediegetic" in that we do not know whose eye it is. The flames of the fire are reflected in the eye. This is followed by various shots of the city, including a slow traveling shot into the massive pyramid-shaped sky-scraper that houses the Tyrell Corporation. The close-up of the eye reappears, still prediegetic. There are then six more shots of the cityscape until the first set of characters are introduced: the blade runner (the film's term for bounty hunter), Dave Holden, and the replicant, Leon. Holden explains the procedures of the Voigt-Kampff test which measures involuntary pupil and iris contractions in the eye. Leon sits down, and we get a shot of Leon's eye seen through the lens of the testing equipment from Holden's point of view. Thus, the motif of the eye appears narratively motivated. However, the two earlier shots are not to be construed as the present shot understood retrospectively. Rather, these shots belong to the realm of the narrating agent who delivers to us an image that is allowed to remain ambiguous, an image for its own allusive sake.

The motif of eyes reappears in the first scene in which we see Roy, the leader of the replicants. First we get a close-up of Roy's right hand (the same hand Roy will later pierce with an iron spike, which gives the film its own set of Christian allusions).[16] Roy's voice-over says, "time enough." A longer shot reveals Roy and Leon standing outside of Chew's laboratory over the entrance of which hangs a large sign painted to look like an eye. Roy and Leon confront Chew and demand information from him. He tells them, "Eyes, I just do eyes." Roy then ironically remarks to Chew, "If only you could see what I've seen with your eyes."[17] This particular remark looks forward to Roy's later saying to Deckard, in a very different mood, "I've seen things you people would not believe." Sight, then, the looking at and the looking through, becomes one of the ways the androids/replicants begin to take on human qualities.

Ultimately the replicants are unable to survive. But they pass on a legacy, the gift of sight, to Rick Deckard, which enables him to perceive his life in a new light. He comes to realize that in sparing his life Roy has shown the value of life to him; Roy, in seeking to find meaning in his own life, has given meaning to Deckard's. The blade runner abandons his empty, emotionally alienated ex-istence to live with Rachael, away from the teeming city where rain and night are omnipresent. Thus, *Blade Runner,* like *Do Androids Dream of Electric*

Sheep? attempts to solve the problem of how to deal with catastrophe by seeking to return us to our essence, to our essential humanity. By implication, a return to the human, a seeking and finding of the good, the true, and just in ourselves, may prevent such catastrophes from occurring.

NOTES

1. Philip K. Dick, *Do Androids Dream of Electric Sheep?* (New York: Del Rey, 1968), pp. 25–26.

2. Ibid., p. 26.

3. Philip K. Dick, "Man, Android and Machine," in *Science Fiction at Large,* ed. Peter Nicholls (New York: Harper & Row, 1976), pp. 202–3.

4. Philip K. Dick, *Our Friends from Frolix 8* (New York: Ace, 1970), p. 41.

5. Dick, *Androids,* p. 26.

6. Ibid., p. 66.

7. Ibid., p. 117.

8. Ibid., p. 3.

9. Philip K. Dick, "Universe Makers . . . and Breakers," *SelecTV Guide* 3, 1 (February 15–March 28, 1981), p. 8. "SelecTV" is a subscription television service headquartered in Los Angeles. At the time this chapter was written, I was the managing editor of the *Guide* and Dick an interested subscriber to the service. I asked him if he would like to submit an article to complement a science-fiction film festival "SelecTV" was running.

10. Ibid., p. 8.

11. These name changes seem designed to remove any traces of ethnicity from the characters.

12. Dick, *Androids,* p. 24.

13. Ibid., pp. 169, 173.

14. *Blade Runner,* dir. Ridley Scott, Warner Bros., 1982.

15. Ibid.

16. For a further discussion of the film's atmosphere relating *Blade Runner* to Film Noir and of the significance of the Christian symbolism in the film, see my article *"Blade Runner:* Science Fiction and Transcendence," in *Literature/Film Quarterly* 13, 3 (1985), pp. 172–79.

17. *Blade Runner.*

19

THE ROAD WARRIOR: SELF AND SOCIETY IN THE REBUILDING PROCESS

Thomas P. Dunn

Australian director George Miller's first film, *Mad Max*, appeared in 1979; an unabashedly juvenile car-crash film, it passed without comment until its sequel appeared. That sequel was released in other countries as *Mad Max 2* but appeared in the United States as *The Road Warrior*. It is an outstanding representative of the mature and intelligent science fiction film even while it draws energy from its roots in the exploitation genre.

At first blush, *The Road Warrior* may seem like a rather formless exercise in chaotic mayhem. Even sympathetic reviewers praising it for its adrenaline-charged bursts of energy have overlooked, for the most part, its careful ordering of social relationships in the postholocaust wasteland and by so doing have missed the film's significance: The true winners in *The Road Warrior* turn out to be neither the ''vermin on machines'' nor the communal people of the fortress-refinery but the loners, the individuals who work alone for their own independence. Max, the Gyro Captain, and the Feral Kid all compare favorably and obviously to the Wild Ones, whose nihilistic ferocity is self-limiting and defeating. Less obviously they appear finally as stronger than the communards whose conscious working for the future masks a more basic huddling together out of fear. These three independent souls work together best by working each for himself, yet they provide the vital energy needed to rebuild society. Thus, for all its violence and sadistic ugliness, *The Road Warrior,* by virtue of its penetrating examination of the rebuilding process, emerges finally as a lasting vision not of nihilistic decadence but of tough-minded optimism.

But no thought of this kind is likely to cross the viewer's mind for most of the film's length, not at least until he has become, like the wasteland inhabitants themselves, inured to the animalistic slash-and-grab mentality of humans in the throes of anarchy. Director/writer George Miller strips away as many layers of civilization as he can and still leaves enough to make rebuilding a possibility. After a catastrophic war, roving bands of young males chase and kill hapless individuals, hoard gas, rape and pillage, and subsist on rusty cans of dog food. An enclave of more civilized people huddle around an oil-well oasis, like a medieval manor under siege, and a few intelligent loners live by their wits, inventing ingenious weaponry and backup, booby-trap systems to keep the barbarian hordes at bay. A feral boy crawls from a hole in the ground and hurls a steel boomerang into the head of a young man; the boy howls with glee and does a back-flip. Captives are tortured but kept alive bound to a forklift to taunt the enemy within the enclave. Next to these antagonists, the Philistines and Israelites in the valley of Gath seem humane by comparison. Savage killing without quarter or question is the rule. Escape to a better land is the only hope, but any motion puts one at risk, and all rapid motion depends upon fuel, the very thing being squandered by the wild ones in their ceaseless search for instant gratification through sadistic mayhem. In short we see a sector of postholocaust society intent upon finishing the show of destruction begun by total war.[1]

Such scenes have caused reviewers to consign *The Road Warrior* to the junk heap of "crash-and-burn" films. Charles Michener found it great "primal fun . . . for the adolescents of the 80's" and praised its "gleefully piratical spirit." Writing in *MacLean's,* Lawrence O'Toole found it a film with "little to say but plenty to show" and saw it as modeled after the classic western with "the Indians circling the covered wagons." He saw the hero, Max, as Shane. Michael Sragow found it pretentiously self-conscious, "a comic-book movie," and pronounced it "art wrecko." Pauline Kael, writing in the *New Yorker,* was more attentive but finally more dismissive. She expressed impatience with the film industry's indulgence in "male paranoid fantasizing with an air of intelligence." She continued, *"The Road Warrior* is for boys who want to go around slugging each other on the shoulder and for men who wish that John Wayne were alive and fifty again."[2]

It is the fate of the student of science fiction ever to be pleading for patience amid the eternal chorus of derision, especially for the science fiction film. In this case, patience is rewarded, however, for *The Road Warrior* has important elements which these reviewers have overlooked—a forgivable oversight, for reviewers generally do not see a film many times. The surprising thing is that *The Road Warrior* holds up under repeated viewing—the true mark of the classic. Part of the problem may be that reviewers—Kael is one—mistakenly regard the film as a fantasy rather than a clear attempt to extrapolate a postwar survival situation. I contend its strength lies in its careful ordering of social relationships and their embodiment in groups of representative characters—all to show a possible scenario for the rebuilding of the world after total war.

The old society is represented by the "vermin on machines" as they are called by a member of the refinery community. Their leader, Humungus, is a machine-man, with an iron mask and a gravel voice. He keeps his cohorts on a short leash, literally; they in turn seem to have established a feudal dominance over the weaker, less violent in their midst. At the film's start, Max's main antagonist, Wez, a maniac with a mohawk, appears at the top of the screen riding a motorcycle with a lovely, blond boy—called the Golden Boy in the credits—on a chain. When the boy is killed by the feral boy with the boomerang, Wez is heartbroken. Later Wez himself is on a chain, the slave of Humungus. These hints of a primitive political system suggest a code where any loss of possession is a disqualification, powerlessness the price paid by those who have none to dominate. The Toadie is an older man, a sycophant who lives by praising Humungus to the stars; when his fingers are severed by the boy's boomerang, he whimpers but tries to dissemble his pain, obviously afraid to show any weakness. And over all these leather-clad, wasteland victims hovers the constant whine of engines, suffusing the whole film with the auditory equivalent of gasoline stench.

But despite their ferocious behavior, they come to be seen as pitiful only after a time. We realize as they do not that they are squandering what little of their substance remains; they have no future, and all their bravado is a desperate clinging to the past. Pity is gained finally even for Wez, for upon repeated viewing, he appears finally as pathetic rather than terrifying: he has strength but little intelligence, and survival, it appears, requires both. He tries to make up for his lack of good sense with macho posturing. His taunt, "You can run, but you can't hide," is a hollow cliche, and his rough-trade garb and mohawk hairdo are mere costume. And the terror and pain in his expression when he sees his friend killed and when he realizes his danger in his final moments are real and moving. By contrast, real courage is shown by a captive member of the refinery community who shouts to his comrades, "Give them nothing!"

Less obviously, the communards of the fortress-refinery, who represent the best hope for a human future, appear as too decent, too imbued with the sense of fair play and gravity to compete successfully against the punks. They grieve for their fallen comrades. They agonize over those captured, and some try to convince themselves of the wisdom of appeasement: "He said he will let us go! He gave his word." Pappagallo, their leader, comes close to writing off Max because he rejects Max's selfish motives: "You're no better than the vermin on machines out there!" he tells him, refusing to look at the truth which Max announces later, "I'm the best chance you've got." They have not, like Max, lived and survived "on the street" of the new wilderness but instead have rejected it totally and sought to isolate themselves from it. They suffer the weakness of their strengths, having isolated themselves from savagery—they have not touched bottom.

Enter now the essential ingredient, the three loners, whose savage independence and ingenious skill make them the catalyst to begin society anew. There is first of all Max. From the film's opening moments, it is clear that he is a hardened veteran of atrocities completely inured to violence, a necessary trait for survival. There is no fear in his eyes when in the film's opening scene he fends off an attack by Wez and some of the other wild ones. Next, coolly examining some wreckage, he appears not to be moved at all by the sight of a dying child reaching from one wreck, and shows only momentary surprise when the decayed body of a truck driver falls from another.

Although he appears to be without anger, sadism, or compassion, a burned out man with a feral light in his eyes, his treatment of the Gyro Captain is not without its touches of warmth and suggests that he may be redeemable. His humanity shows later when he and the refinery community realize each has something the other needs, and they strike a bargain. He befriends the feral boy, giving him the present of the music box, and responds to his delight. Slowly his interaction with the refinery people draws him out of his isolation.

The "kooky" Gyro Captain makes up in inventiveness what he lacks in battle savvy. Like Max, he has had to shift for himself; he is bright if somewhat daft, and his tinkering pays off first in his survival, later in his invention of the gyro copter. His worth is everywhere evident: he uses a snake to guard his belongings, and he thinks fast of a lure to keep Max from dispatching him. He has courage and humor, and he sees what Max does not, the wisdom of partnership and cooperation. His triumph comes when he picks Max up from the burning wreck of his foiled escape, and, bearing him away into the sky, tells him, "Relax, *Partner!*" We see him flirting with a woman in the refinery community and are not surprised to discover that he is the tribe's leader after the final escape.

The Feral Kid is much more than he at first appears to be. Like Max and the Gyro Captain, he has had to repress any hint of compassion beneath the predatory cunning of the hunting animal. With his steel boomerang, which he wields with deadly accuracy and force, and his escape tunnels, he is an unconquerable bundle of savagery. Although he appears first as a mindless malignancy delighting in killing, he is a survivor and later he, too, like his older counterpart Max, will emerge from his savage isolation, first by responding to the gift of the music box, later by assisting Max in bravely retrieving the shotgun shells from the front of the tank truck. When at that moment he is surprised by the sudden appearance of Wez, we may find we have acquired enough admiration for his skills to fear for him.

That we are meant to see these three as representing a distinct social type is evident in the fact that they all move between the refinery and the outside world with relative ease—Max in his souped-up car, the Gyro Captain in his cockamamy contraption, and the Feral Kid through his tunnels.

And we should note that all help each other; they are not loners to the point of hermetic isolation, although each may inhabit, of necessity, his own psychic shell. The Gyro Captain saves Max, calling him "partner" and inviting him to relax in his care. The boy gets shotgun shells for Max in the final battle-chase sequence, aiding Max and himself at the same time. Max refrains from killing the Gyro Captain and later is saved by him, when the Gyro Captain takes Max to the fuel refinery. The boy kills one of the wild ones and severs the fingers of another. Max shows the boy the music box, conveying to him a bit of civilization from the wreck with which the film opens. Its tune, "Happy Birthday to You," celebrates the rebirth of Max and the boy and the refinery community they assist. It is remarkable that reviewers should compare the film to *Shane* but overlook the central parallel of an older person providing a needed role model for a younger one and passing the torch of leadership and responsibility to a new society.

In a surprise ending, the narrator tells us in biblical tones, "In the fullness of the time I became the leader, the chief of the Great Northern Tribe," and we realize that the entire story has been presented to us by the Feral kid, that same dynamo of ferocity we might well have dismissed as lost, another emblem of desolation. And all of this, the postulation of a wasteland situation, the working out of its various social groups and relationships, the lavish attention to detail, and the biblical sonorities of its prologue and epilogue deserve not to be dismissed as affectation but hailed as achievement.

And so *The Road Warrior* presents us not with insignificant sound and fury but with a clear, consistent view of a torch being passed from Dying Society to Max to the Gyro Captain to the Feral Kid. The talisman of this process is the music box, whose tune, "Happy Birthday to You" announces the start of the new age. By working together, even against their will, Max is recalled to life, the Gyro Captain's abilities receive scope, the Feral Kid becomes the strong leader, the refinery community's hard work pays off in the founding of a new world, the darkness is driven back, and selfish, feral savagery is again harnessed in the service of growth and renewal.

NOTES

1. It may be of importance to some viewers that the war preceding the film is not necessarily nuclear. The lengthy prologue tells us that "two mighty warrior tribes went to war and touched off a blaze which engulfed them all," but apparently they were not incinerated by that "blaze," for afterward "their leaders talked and talked and talked" and their cities exploded in a "whirlwind of looting, a firestorm of fear." Thus does Miller establish a believable setting in which nuclear winter is not a factor, nor such pervasive radiation as the survivors faced in another postholocaust classic, *On the Beach*.

2. Charles Michener, "Shane in Black Leather," *Newsweek*, May 31, 1982, pp. 67, 70; Lawrence O'Toole, "Shoot-out at the Apocalyptic Corral," *MacLean's*, May 31, 1982, p. 58; Michael Sragow, " 'Road Warrior': Art Wrecko," *Rolling Stone*, June 24, 1982, pp. 25, 27; Pauline Kael, "The Current Cinema," *New Yorker* 58, 29 (September 6, 1982), pp. 96–99.

BIBLIOGRAPHY FOR REMADE WORLD LITERATURE: BACKGROUND, CRITICISM, AND FICTION

Paul Brians, Thomas P. Dunn, Marshall Tymn, and Carl B. Yoke

The bibliography that follows is not comprehensive. Such a project would take several volumes. The list is representative and provides additional sources of information for readers who are interested in the further study of "remade world literature"; it also represents the various fictional visions that might succeed such catastrophes.

This bibliography has been compiled, therefore, with several considerations in mind. First, we have omitted most works in which the catastrophe is simply background because in such cases it has little impact on the development of the story. We have concentrated instead on stories where the catastrophe produces a real remade world in the sense of a nation, culture, civilization, or community. In the case of novels like Nevil Shute's *On the Beach* and Mordecai Roshwald's *Level 7,* even though the time between the catastrophe and the ultimate end of civilization is very short, the changes that the catastrophe produces are significant enough to alter the civilization that remains. In other words, the relationships between people and between people and social institutions are radically altered. Second, we have omitted stories listing myths of destruction such as the *Gilgamesh* epic or the numerous flood stories, though virtually every culture has them and they are referred to in some of the chapters of this book. Third, though it cites a few significant short works, this bibliography concentrates on book-length works. The reason for this is that with so many treatments of this theme listing all the short works would be overwhelming. Fourth, in listing scientific works two primary criteria were exercised: (1) that the works significantly represent important points of view about the destruction of the earth or (2) that they be current. The problem with this is that our knowledge of possible destructions is increasing rapidly and geometrically, so it is virtually impossible to stay abreast of all new developments. It was also our concern, since this volume treats fiction that uses a variety of means for destruction, to represent those possibilities here (literally ranging from pollution and various other ecological disasters through nuclear war or accident).

Particularly useful in compiling this bibliography were Neil Barron, ed. *Anatomy of*

Wonder (second edition; New York: R. R. Bowker, 1986); William Contento's *Index to Science Fiction Anthologies and Collections,* Vol. II (Boston: G. R. Hall, 1978); L. W. Currey's *Science Fiction and Fantasy Authors: A Bibliography of First Printings of Their Fiction and Selected Non-fiction* (Boston: G. K. Hall, 1979); and Curtis C. Smith's *Twentieth-Century Science Fiction Writers* (second edition; Chicago: St. James Press, 1986). Also very useful were the book reviews in Neil Barron's *Science Fiction Book Review Index* and Robert Collin's *Fantasy Review.*

This bibliography is divided into the following sections, with works arranged alphabetically within them.

    I.   Reference Works, Critical Studies, and Bibliographies
    II. Anthologies and Collections
    III. Scientific Articles and Books
    IV. Fiction

In compiling this list, we have tried to be sensitive to the availability of the works cited. Therefore, where it was possible to locate them, we have listed at least one recent reprinting as well as original publication data. For those works that have been in virtual reprint since they were first published, only one or two have been listed since there are already bibliographies that list each reprinting. For stories or novels that have never been reprinted, there is, of course, only the original publication data.

Users of this list should also be aware that science fiction and fantasy works have often appeared pseudonymously, under various titles, or in variant editions and translations. However, this problem is less extensive with book-length works than with shorter works. We have tried to be sensitive to the vicissitudes of the field but we have not generally listed pseudonyms, feeling that they serve little purpose in this endeavor, nor have we listed original stories that have been reworked, feeling that they are best represented in their final forms.

ABBREVIATIONS

Generally speaking, we have simplified the listings as much as possible without destroying their sense.

We have simplified the names of magazines as follows:

Amazing	*Amazing Stories, Amazing Science Fiction, Amazing Science Fiction Stories*
Astounding;	*Astounding Stories of Super Science, Astounding Science,*
Astounding/ Analog	*Astounding Science Fiction;* after 1960, *Analog*
F & SF	*The Magazine of Fantasy and Science Fiction*
If	*If, Worlds of Science Fiction, Worlds of if*

I. REFERENCE WORKS, CRITICAL STUDIES, AND BIBLIOGRAPHIES

Abrash, Merritt. "Through Logic to Apocalypse: Science Fiction Scenarios of Nuclear Deterrence Breakdown." *Science-Fiction Studies,* no. 39 (July 1986), pp. 129–38.

Ballard, J. G. "Cataclysms and Dooms." In *The Visual Encyclopedia*. Ed. Brian Ash. New York: Harmony Books, 1977, pp. 130–36.

Bartter, Martha. "Nuclear Holocaust as Urban Renewal." *Science-Fiction Studies*, no. 39 (July 1986), pp. 148–58.

Berger, Albert I. "Love, Death, and the Atomic Bomb: Sexuality and Community in Science Fiction, 1935–55." *Science-Fiction Studies*, no. 25 (November 1981), pp. 280–96.

———. "Nuclear Energy, Science Fiction's Metaphor of Power." *Science-Fiction Studies*, no. 18 (July 1979), pp. 121–28.

Berger, Harold. *Science Fiction and the New Dark Age*. Bowling Green, Ohio: Bowling Green University Popular Press, 1976.

Brians, Paul. *Nuclear Holocausts: Atomic War Fiction, 1914–1984*. Kent, Ohio: Kent State University Press (July 1987).

———. "Nuclear War in Science Fiction, 1945–59." *Science-Fiction Studies*, no. 34 (November 1984), pp. 253–63.

———. "Resources for the Study of Nuclear War in Fiction." *Science-Fiction Studies*, no. 39 (July 1986), pp. 193–97.

Dowling, D. H. "The Atomic Scientist: Machine or Moralist." *Science-Fiction Studies*, no. 39 (July 1986), pp. 139–47.

Egan, James. "Apocalypticism in the Fiction of Stephen King." *Extrapolation* 25, no. 3 (1984), pp. 214–27.

Esmonde, Margaret P. "After Armageddon: The Postcataclysmic Novel for Young Readers." In *Young Adult Literature: Background and Criticism*. Ed. Millicent Lentz. Chicago: American Library Association, 1980, pp. 440–48.

Firsching, Lorenz. "J. G. Ballard's Ambiguous Apocalypse." *Science-Fiction Studies*, no. 37 (November 1985), pp. 297–310.

Franklin, H. Bruce. "Editorial Introduction." *Science-Fiction Studies*, no. 39 (July 1986). Special issue entitled *Nuclear War and Science Fiction*, pp. 115–16.

———. "Strange Scenarios: Science Fiction, the Theory of Alienation, and the Nuclear Gods." *Science-Fiction Studies*, no. 39 (July 1986), pp. 117–28.

———. "Viewpoint: Don't Worry, It's Only Science Fiction." *Isaac Asimov's Science Fiction Magazine*, December 1984, pp. 26–39.

———. "What Are We Going to Make of J. G. Ballard's Apocalypse." In *Voices for the Future: Essays on Major Science Fiction Writers*. Vol. 2. Ed. Thomas D. Clareson. Bowling Green, Ohio: Bowling Green University Popular Press, 1979, pp. 82–105.

Galbreath, Robert. "Ambiguous Apocalypse: Transcendental Versions of the End." In *The End of the World*. Ed. Eric Rabkin, Martin H. Greenberg, and Joseph D. Olander. Carbondale: Southern Illinois University Press, 1983, pp. 53–72.

Gerzon, Mark. "Watching the World End: How Hollywood Faced up to Nuclear War." *New Age Journal*, November 1983, pp. 30–35, 85–89.

Hill, Douglas, "This Is the Way the World Ends." In *Encyclopedia of Science Fiction*. Ed. Robert Holdstock. London: Octopus Books, 1978, pp. 102–19.

Ketterer, David. *New Worlds for Old: The Apocalyptic Imagination, Science Fiction, and American Literature*. Bloomington: Indiana University Press, 1974.

Keyerleber, Joseph. "On the Beach." In *Nuclear War Films*. Ed. Jack G. Shaheen. Carbondale: Southern Illinois University Press, 1978, pp. 31–38.

Kyle, David. "The Ends of Mankind: Bangs and Whimpers." In *The Illustrated Book of Science Fiction Ideas and Dreams*. London: Hamlyn Publishing Group, 1977, pp. 47–61.

Langford, David. "Holocaust and Catastrophe." In *The Science in Science Fiction*. Ed. Peter Nicholls. New York: Knopf, 1983, pp. 43–44.

Lifton, Robert Jay. "The Image of the 'End of the World': A Psychohistorical View." *Michigan Quarterly Review* 24 (Winter 1985), pp. 70–90.

Manganiello, Dominic. "History as Judgment and Promise in *A Canticle for Leibowitz*." *Science-Fiction Studies*, no. 39 (July 1986), pp. 159–69.

Morrisey, Thomas J. "Armageddon from Huxley to Hoban." *Extrapolation* 25, no. 3 (1984), pp. 197–213.

———. "Zelazny: Mythmaker of Nuclear War." *Science-Fiction Studies*, no. 39 (July 1986), pp. 182–92.

Nicholls, Peter. "Holocaust and After." In *The Science Fiction Encyclopedia*. Ed. Peter Nicholls. Garden City, N.Y.: Doubleday, 1979, pp. 290–92.

Plank, Robert. "The Lone Survivor." In *The End of the World*. Ed. Eric Rabkin, Martin H. Greenberg, and Joseph D. Olander. Carbondale: Southern Illinois University Press, 1983, pp. 20–52.

Pringle, David. "Disaster." In *The Science Fiction Encyclopedia*. Ed. Peter Nicholls. Garden City, N.Y.: Doubleday, 1979, pp. 172–73.

———. *Earth Is the Alien Planet: J. G. Ballard's Four-Dimensional Nightmare*. San Bernardino, Calif.: Borgo Press, 1979.

Rabkin, Eric. "Introduction: Why Destroy the World?" In *The End of the World*. Ed. Eric Rabkin, Martin H. Greenberg, and Joseph D. Olander. Carbondale: Southern Illinois University Press, 1983, pp. vii–xv.

Rabkin, Eric, Martin H. Greenberg, and Joseph D. Olander, eds. *The End of the World*. Carbondale: Southern Illinois University Press, 1983.

Scott, Roberta, and Jon Thiem. "Catastrophe Fiction, 1870–1914: An Annotated Bibliography of Selected Works in English." *Extrapolation* 24, no. 2 (1983), pp. 156–69.

Shaheen, Jack G., ed. *Nuclear War Films*. Carbondale: Southern Illinois University Press, 1978.

Stableford, Brian. "Disasters." In *The Science Fiction Source Book*. Ed. David Wingrove. New York: Van Nostrand, 1984, pp. 45–47.

———. "The End of the World." In *The Science Fiction Encyclopedia*. Ed. Peter Nicholls. Garden City, N.Y.: Doubleday, 1979, pp. 195–96.

———. "Man-Made Catastrophes." In *The End of the World*. Ed. Eric Rabkin, Martin H. Greenberg, and Joseph D. Olander. Carbondale: Southern Illinois University Press, 1983, pp. 97–138.

Taylor, Gordon Rattray. *The Biological Time Bomb*. New York: New American Library, 1968. Rpt. New York: Mentor Books, 1969.

Wagar, W. Warren. "The Rebellion of Nature." In *The End of the World*. Ed. Eric Rabkin, Martin H. Greenberg, and Joseph D. Olander. Carbondale: Southern Illinois University Press, 1983, pp. 139–72.

———. "Round Trips to Doomsday." In *The End of the World*. Ed. Eric Rabkin, Martin H. Greenberg, and Joseph D. Olander. Carbondale: Southern Illinois University Press, 1983, pp. 73–96.

———. *Terminal Vision: The Literature of Last Things*. Bloomington: Indiana University Press, 1982.

Welsh, James M. "The Modern Apocalypse: *The War Game.*" *Journal of Popular Film and Television* 2 (Spring 1983), pp. 25–41.

Williamson, Jack, and David Ketterer. "Apocalypse." In *Science Fiction: Contemporary Mythology.* Ed. Patricia Warrick, Martin Harry Greenberg, and Joseph Olander. New York: Harper & Row, 1978, pp. 435–41.

Wolfe, Gary K. *The Known and the Unknown: The Iconography of Science Fiction.* Kent, Ohio: Kent State University Press, 1979.

———. "The Remaking of Zero: Beginning at the End." In *The End of the World.* Ed. Eric Rabkin, Martin H. Greenberg, and Joseph D. Olander. Carbondale: Southern Illinois University Press, 1983, pp. 1–19.

Yoke, Carl B. "From Alienation to Personal Triumph: The Science Fiction of Joan D. Vinge." In *The Feminine Eye: Science Fiction and the Women Who Write It.* Ed. Tom Staicar. New York: Frederick Ungar, 1982, pp. 103–30.

Zins, Daniel L. "Rescuing Science from Technology: *Cat's Cradle* and the Play of the Apocalypse." *Science-Fiction Studies,* no. 39 (July 1986), pp. 170–81.

II. ANTHOLOGIES AND COLLECTIONS

Anon. *A Science Fiction Omnibus on Pollution.* London: Sidgwick & Jackson, 1971. Coll. Harrison's *Make Room! Make Room!,* Kornbluth's *Shark Ship,* and Simak's *City.*

Ballard, J. G. *The Atrocity Exhibition.* London: Cape, 1970. Rpt. as *Love and Napalm: Export USA.* New York: Grove Press, 1972.

———. *The Disaster Area.* London: Cape, 1967.

Bradbury, Ray. *The Martian Chronicles.* Garden City, N.Y.: Doubleday, 1950. Rpt. New York: Bantam, 1951. Brit. title: *The Silver Locusts.* London: Hart Davis, 1951.

Disch, Thomas M., ed. *The Ruins of Earth.* New York: Putnam, 1971. Includes Philip Dick's "Autofac," Harry Harrison's "Roommates" (which was the basis for his *Make Room! Make Room!),* and Fritz Leiber's "America, the Beautiful."

Elwood, Roger, and Virginia Kidd, eds. *Saving Worlds.* New York: Doubleday, 1973. Vt. *The Wounded Planet.*

Franklin, H. Bruce, ed. *Countdown to Midnight.* New York: DAW, 1984. While all the stories included in this collection deal with nuclear war, not all deal with the postholocaust situations. Nonetheless, the excellence of the fiction and Franklin's introduction make it well worth reading.

Miller, Walter M., Jr., and Martin H. Greenberg, eds. *Beyond Armageddon.* New York: Primus, 1985. Coll. twenty postcatastrophe stories, including Robert Sheckley's "The Store of the Worlds," Carol Emshwiller's "Day at the Beach," John Wyndham's "The Wheel," Edgar Pangborn's "A Master of Babylon," Rog Phillips' "Game Preserve," William Tenn's "Eastward Ho!" and Arthur C. Clarke's " 'If I Forget Thee, Oh Earth . . . ' "

Pohl, Fred, ed. *Nightmare Age.* New York: Ballantine, 1970. Collects some postholocaust stories.

Silverberg, Robert. *Mutants.* Nashville, Tenn. and New York: Thomas Nelson, 1974. Some of the stories are in postholocaust settings.

III. SCIENTIFIC ARTICLES AND BOOKS

Allison, Graham T., Albert Carnesale, and Joseph S. Nye, eds. *Hawks, Doves, and Owls: An Agenda for Avoiding Nuclear War.* New York: Norton, 1985.

Anderson, Poul. *Thermonuclear Warfare.* Derby, Conn.: Monarch Books, 1963.

Anon. "Death Star Returns in 16–million Years." Cleveland *Plain Dealer,* June 21, 1984, p. 8–E.

————. "Forest's Growth Altered after 1964 Irradiation." Syndicated Associated Press Story, *Akron Beacon Journal,* November 23, 1983, p. A-8.

————. "Forget Tanning Lotion in Frozen Nuke Wasteland." Syndicated Associated Press Story, Cleveland *Plain Dealer,* November 18, 1984, p. 6–A.

————. "Making Bikini Fit for People to Live May Cost $42 Million." Cleveland *Plain Dealer,* November 18, 1984, p. 19–A.

————. "Ozone Loss Threatens Hotter Globe, Experts Say." Cleveland *Plain Dealer,* June 11, 1986, p. 7–A.

————. "Study Shows Nagasaki Bombing Genetically Altered Plants." Cleveland *Plain Dealer,* August 5, 1985, p. 4–A.

Berggren, W. A., and John A. van Couvering, eds. *Catastrophes and Earth History.* Princeton, N.J.: Princeton University Press, 1986.

Carey, Pete. "Scientists Fear Computer to Start Accidental War." *Akron Beacon Journal,* November 12, 1984, p. A-6.

Chivian, Eric, Susanna Chivian, Robert Jay Lifton, and John E. Mack, eds. *Last Aid: The Medical Dimensions of Nuclear War.* New York: Freeman, 1982.

Erlich, Paul, Carl Sagan, Donald Kennedy, and Walter Orr Roberts, eds. *The Cold and the Dark: The World After Nuclear War.* New York: Norton, 1984.

Gallup, George, Jr., and William Proctor. "Nuclear Terror Awaits." Cleveland *Plain Dealer,* December 30, 1984. Excerpt from Gallup's book *Forecast 2000,* p. 6–B.

Hershey, John. *Hiroshima. New Yorker,* August 31, 1946. Rpt. New York: Knopf, 1985.

Long, Karen R. "Lingering Effects from Mist to Kill Many More, Experts Say." Cleveland *Plain Dealer,* December 5, 1984, p. 13–A.

Rensberger, Boyce. "The Beauty of Extinction." Syndicated *Washington Post* story appearing in the Cleveland *Plain Dealer,* December 4, 1984, p. 1–C.

————. "Soot of Pre-Historic Firestorms Quick-Froze Globe, Scientists Say." Syndicated *Washington Post* story appearing in the *Akron Beacon Journal,* October 4, 1985, p. A-11.

Sagan, Carl. "We Can Prevent Nuclear Winter." *Parade Magazine,* September 30, 1984, pp. 13–15.

Schell, Jonathan. *The Fate of the Earth.* New York: Knopf, 1982.

Wyden, Peter. *Day One: Before Hiroshima and After.* New York: Warner Books, 1985.

IV. FICTION

Abe, Kobo. *Inter Ice Age 4.* Trans. E. Dale Saunders. New York: Knopf, 1970. Rpt. New York: Berkley, 1972.

Adams, Robert. "The Horseclans" Novels. New York: Signet, 1975 to present.
A continuing series of novels, including: #1: *The Coming of the Horseclans;* #2:

Swords of the Horseclans; #3: *Revenge of the Horseclans;* #4: *A Cat of Silvery Hue;* #5: *The Savage Mountains;* #6: *The Patrimony;* #7: *Horseclans Odyssey;* #8: *The Death of a Legend;* #9: *The Witch Goddess;* #10: *Bili the Axe;* #11: *Champion of the Last Battle;* #12: *A Woman of the Horseclans;* #13: *Horses of the North.*

Ahern, Jerry. "The Survivalist" Series. New York: Zebra Books, 1981 to present.
A continuing series of novels, including: #1: *Total War;* #2: *The Nightmare Begins;* #3: *The Quest;* #4: *The Doomsayer;* #5: *Web;* #6: *The Savage Horde;* #7: *The Prophet;* #8: *The End is Coming;* #9: *Earth Fire;* #10: *The Awakening;* #11: *The Reprisal;* #12: *The Survivalist.*

Aldiss, Brian. *Barefoot in the Head.* London: Faber, 1969. Rpt. New York: Doubleday, 1970.

———. *Earthworks.* London: Faber & Faber, 1965. Rpt. New York: Doubleday, 1966; Avon, 1980.

———. *Galaxies Like Grains of Sand.* New York: Signet, 1960. Brit. title: *The Canopy of Time.* London: Faber, 1959.

———. *Graybeard.* London: Faber, 1964; New York: Harcourt, Brace & World, 1964.

———. "The Helliconia" Novels: *Helliconia Spring.* London: Cape, 1982; New York: Atheneum, 1982. Rpt. New York: Berkley, 1983. *Helliconia Summer.* London: Cape, 1983. Rpt. New York: Berkley, 1984. *Helliconia Winter.* New York: Atheneum, 1985. Rpt. New York: Berkley, 1986.

———. *Non-Stop.* London: Faber, 1958. Retitled and rpt. as *Starship.* New York: Criterion, 1959.

———. "Who Can Replace a Man?" *Infinity Science Fiction,* June 1958. Coll. in *Who Can Replace a Man?* New York: Harcourt, 1966. Brit. title: *The Best Science Fiction of Brian W. Aldiss.* London: Faber, 1965; reissued 1971.

Amery, Carl. *Der Untergang Der Stadt Passau.* Munich: Wilhelm Heyne Verlag, 1975.

Anderson, Poul. *After Doomsday.* New York: Ballantine, 1962. Rpt. London: Gollancz, 1963; New York: Ballantine, 1985.

———. *Brain Wave.* New York: Ballantine, 1954. Rpt. London: Heinemann, 1955; New York: Ballantine, 1985.

———. *The Enemy Stars.* Philadelphia: Lippincott, 1959.

———. "Logic." *Astounding,* July 1947. Coll. in *Twilight World.* New York: Torquil, 1961. Rpt. London: Gollancz, 1962.

———. "Marius." *Astounding,* March 1957. Coll. in *The Horn of Time.* New York: Signet, 1968. Rpt. Boston: Gregg Press, 1978.

———. "No Truce with Kings." *Fantasy and Science Fiction,* June 1963. Rpt. in *Time and Stars.* New York: Doubleday, 1964; London: Gollancz, 1964.

———. *Orion Shall Rise.* New York: Timescape, 1983.

———. *Vault of the Ages.* Philadelphia: Winston, 1952. Rpt. Boston: Gregg Press, 1979; New York: Berkley, 1980.

Anderson, Poul, and F. N. Waldrop. "Tomorrow's Children." 1947. Coll. in *Mutants.* Ed. Robert Silverberg. Nashville and New York: Thomas Nelson, 1974.

Andreissen, David. *Star Seed.* Norfolk, Va.: Starblaze/Donning, 1982.

Andrevon, Jean-Pierre. *Le Desert du Monde.* Paris: Donoel, 1977.

Anthony, Piers. "The Battle Circle" Novels:
Battle Circle. New York: Avon, 1978. Coll. *Neq the Sword, Sos the Rope,* and *Var the Stick.*

Neq the Sword. London: Corgi, 1975.

Sos the Rope. New York: Pyramid, 1968. Rpt. London: Faber & Faber, 1970.

Var the Stick. London: Faber & Faber, 1972.

————. *Race against Time*. New York: Hawthorne, 1973. Rpt. New York: Tor Books, 1985.

————. *Rings of Ice*. New York: Avon, 1974; London: Millington, 1975.

Anvil, Christopher. "Torch." *Astounding*, April 1957.

Arnaud, G.-J. "The Ice Series" Novels:

Les Chasseurs des Glaces. Paris: Editions du Fleuve Noir, 1981.

La Compagnie des Glaces. Paris: Editions du Fleuve Noir, 1980.

L'enfant des Glaces. Paris: Editions du Fleuve Noir, 1981.

Le Peuple des Glaces. Paris: Editions du Fleuve Noir, 1981.

Le Sanctuaire des Glaces. Paris: Editions du Fleuve Noir, 1981.

Ashton, Francis. *Alas, That Great City*. London: Andrew Dakers, 1948. Rpt. London: Donning, 1982.

————. *The Breaking of the Seals*. London: Andrew Dakers, 1946.

Asimov, Isaac. *Pebble in the Sky*. Garden City, N.Y.: Doubleday, 1950. Rpt. London: Corgi, 1958; New York: Fawcett, 1978.

Asterley, Hugh Cecil. *Escape to Berkshire*. London: Pall Mall, 1961.

Baker, Frank. *The Birds*. London: Davies, 1936.

Ballard, J. G. *The Burning World*. New York: Berkley, 1964. Pub. in Britain as *The Drought*, 1965.

————. *The Crystal World*. London: Farrar, Straus & Giroux, 1966; New York: Avon, 1966.

————. *The Drowned World*. New York: Berkley, 1962. Rpt. London: Gollancz, 1963.

————. *The Unlimited Dream Company*. London: Cape, 1979; New York: Holt, Rinehart, 1979.

————. *The Wind from Nowhere*. New York: Berkley, 1962. Rpt. London: Penguin, 1967.

Baneham, Samuel. *The Cloud of Desolation*. Dublin, Ireland: Wolfhound Press, 1982.

Barjavel, Rene. *Ashes, Ashes*. Trans. Damon Knight. New York: Doubleday, 1967. Orig. title: *Ravage*. Paris: Denoel, 1943.

————. *Le Diable L'Emporte*. Paris: Denoel, 1948.

————. *The Ice People*. Trans. Charles Markmann. New York: Morrow, 1971. Rpt. New York: Pyramid, 1976. Orig. title *La Nuit des Temps*. Paris: Presses de la Cité, 1968.

Barr, Robert. "The Doom of London." *The Idler,* November 1892. Rpt. in *Science Fiction by Gaslight*. Ed. Sam Moskowitz. Cleveland: World, 1968. Rpt. by Hyperion Press, 1974.

Baxter, John. *The Hermes Fall*. New York: Simon & Schuster, 1978; London: Panther, 1978.

Becker, Stephen. "The New Encyclopaedist." *Fantasy and Science Fiction*, May 1964. Rpt. in *10th Annual Edition: The Year's Best S-F*. Ed. Judith Merril. New York: Delacorte, 1965.

Benet, Stephen Vincent. "The Place of the Gods." *Saturday Evening Post,* July 31, 1937. Also titled "By Babylon" and "By the Waters of Babylon."

Bennett, Margot. *The Long Way Back*. London: Bodley Head, 1954; New York: Coward, McCann, 1955.

Benson, Robert Hugh. *Lord of the World*. London: Sir Isaac Pitman, 1907. Rpt. New York: Dodd, Mead, 1908; Arno Press, 1974.

Beresford, John Davys. *Goslings*. London: Heinemann, 1913. Printed in America as *A World of Women*. New York: Macaulay, 1913.

Berk, Howard. *The Sun Grows Cold*. New York: Delacorte, 1971.

Best, Herbert. *The Twenty-Fifth Hour*. London: Cape, 1940; New York: Random House, 1940.

Bester, Alfred. "Adam and No Eve." *Astounding*, September 1941. Coll. in *Starburst*. New York: Signet, 1958. Rpt. in *The Great Science Fiction Stories*. Vol. 3. Ed. Isaac Asimov and Martin K. Greenberg. New York: DAW, 1980.

———. *The Demolished Man*. Chicago: Shasta, 1953; London: Sidgewick and Jackson, 1953. Rpt. New York: Timescape, 1982.

———. "They Don't Make Life Like They Used To." *Fantasy and Science Fiction*, October 1963. Coll. in *The Dark Side of Earth*. New York: Signet, 1964; London: Pan, 1969.

Biemiller, Carl L. *The Hydronauts*. New York: Doubleday, 1970.

Bishop, Michael. "Vox Olympia." *Omni*, December 1981.

Black, Ladbroke. *The Poison War*. London: Stanley Paul, 1933.

Blackburn, John F. *A Scent of New-Mown Hay*. London: Mill, 1958.

Blanchard, H. Percy. *After the Cataclysm: A Romance of the Age to Come*. New York: Cochrane, 1909.

Blish, James. *Black Easter, or Faust Aleph-Null*. Garden City, N.Y.: Doubleday, 1968. Rpt. London: Faber, 1969; New York: Avon, 1982.

———. "The Cities in Flight" Novels: *Cities in Flight*. Garden City, New York: Doubleday, 1970. Rpt. New York: Avon, 1982. Coll. *Earthman Come Home, A Life for the Stars, They Shall Have Stars*, and *The Triumph of Time*.

   Earthman Come Home. New York: Putnam, 1955.

   Novel based on "Okie" (*Astounding*, April 1950), "Bindlestiff" (*Astounding*, December 1950), "Sargasso of Lost Cities" (*Two Complete Science Adventure Books*, Spring 1953), and "Earthman Come Home" (*Astounding*, November 1953).

   A Life for the Stars. New York: Putnam, 1962.

   They Shall Have Stars. New York: Avon, 1957.

   The Triumph of Time. New York: Avon, 1958.

———. *The Day after Judgment*. Garden City, N.Y.: Doubleday, 1970. Rpt. London: Faber, 1972; New York: Avon, 1982. Sequel to *Black Easter*.

———. "First Strike." *Fantasy and Science Fiction*, June 1953. Coll. in *So Close to Home*. New York: Ballantine, 1961.

———. *Midsummer Century*. New York: Doubleday, 1972.

———. "The Oath." *Fantasy and Science Fiction*, October 1960. Coll. in *So Close to Home*. New York: Ballantine, 1961.

———. "The Thing in the Attic." *If*, July 1954. Coll. in *The Seedling Stars*. New York: Gnome Press, 1957.

Blish, James, and Norman L. Knight. *A Torrent of Faces*. New York: Doubleday, 1967. Rpt. London: Faber, 1968.

Blish, James, and Robert A. W. Lowndes. *The Duplicated Man*. *Dynamic Science Fiction*, August 1953. Rpt. New York: Avalon, 1959.

Bond, Nancy. *The Voyage Begun*. New York: Argo/Atheneum, 1981.

Boorman, John, and Bill Stair. *Zardoz*. New York: Signet, 1974. Published after movie of same name appeared. John Boorman, dir., 1973.

Boucher, Anthony. "The Quest for Saint Aquin." *Fantasy and Science Fiction,* January 1959. Rpt. in *Magazine of Fantasy and Science Fiction: A 30–Year Retrospective.* Ed. Edward L. Ferman. Garden City, N.Y.: Doubleday, 1980.

Boulle, Pierre. *The Planet of the Apes [Les Planete Des Singes]*. Trans. Xan Fielding. New York: Vanguard, 1963. Rpt. New York: New American Library, 1968. Filmed as *Planet of the Apes*, 1968. Also gave rise to four subesquent *Ape* films.

Boussenard, L. *10,000 Years in a Block of Ice*. Trans. John Paret. London: F. Tennyson Neely, 1898.

Bova, Ben. *Test of Fire*. New York: Tor, 1982. Expands original story titled *When the Sky Burned*. New York: Walker, 1973.

Bowen, John. *After the Rain* [Novel]. New York: Random House, 1957.

————. *After the Rain* [Play]. New York: Ballantine, 1959. The play makes some interesting changes in the story set forth in the novel.

Brackett, Leigh. *The Long Tomorrow*. Garden City, N.Y.: Doubleday, 1955. Rpt. New York: Ballantine, 1986.

Bradbury, Ray. "The Highway." *Copy,* Spring 1950. (Under pseud. of Leonard Spalding.) Coll. in *The Illustrated Man*. Garden City, N.Y.: Doubleday, 1951. Also coll. in *Above the Human Landscape*, 1972.

————. "The Million-Year Picnic." *Planet Stories,* Summer 1946. Coll. in *The Martian Chronicles*.

————. "The Naming of Names." *Thrilling Wonder Stories,* August 1949. Retitled "Dark They Were and Golden Eyed." Coll. in *A Medicine for Melancholy*. Garden City, N.Y.: Doubleday, 1959.

————. "To the Chicago Abyss." *Fantasy and Science Fiction,* May 1963. Coll. in *The Machineries of Joy*. New York: Simon & Schuster, 1964. *See also* the dramatic version in *The Wonderful Ice Cream Suit and Other Plays*. New York: Bantam, 1972.

Brin, David. "The Postman." *Asimov's Science Fiction Magazine,* November 1982.

Brown, Frederic. "Letter to a Phoenix." *Astounding,* August 1949. Coll. in *Angels and Spaceships*. New York: Dutton, 1954. Rpt. in *The Best of Frederic Brown*. Garden City, N.Y.: Doubleday, 1976.

Brunner, John. *The Sheep Look Up*. New York: *Harper,* 1972. Rpt. London: Dent, 1974; New York: Ballantine, 1981.

————. *Shockwave Rider*. New York: Harper & Row, 1975. Rpt. New York: Ballantine, 1978.

————. *Stand on Zanzibar*. Garden City, N.Y.: Doubleday, 1968. Rpt. New York: Ballantine, 1976.

Bryant, Edward. "Jody after the War." In *Orbit 10*. Ed. Damon Knight. New York: Putnam, 1971.

Bryant, Peter. *Two Hours to Doom*. London: Boardman, 1958. Rpt. as *Red Alert*. New York: Ace, 1959. Source of the film *Dr. Strangelove*. *See* Peter George.

Bulmer, Kenneth. *The Doomsday Men*. Garden City, N.Y.: Doubleday, 1968; London: Hale, 1968. Shorter version pub. in *If,* November 1965.

Bunch, David R. *Moderan*. New York: Avon, 1971.

Burgess, Anthony. *The End of the World News*. London: Hutchinson, 1982. Rpt. London: Penguin, 1984. Excerpts rpt. in *Omni,* March and April 1983.

Capek, Karel. *The Absolute at Large*. New York: Macmillan, 1927.

———. *R.U.R.* First performed in Prague, 1921. New York: Doubleday, 1923. Freq. rpt.

———. *War with the Newts*. 1935. Rpt. London: Allen & Unwin, 1937; Boston: Gregg Press, 1975.

Carr, John F. *Carnifex Mardi Gras*. Northridge, Calif.: Pequod Press, 1972.

Carr, Terry. "Ozymandius." In *Again, Dangerous Visions*. Ed. Harlan Ellison. Garden City, N.Y.: Doubleday, 1972.

Carter, Angela. *Heroes and Villains*. London: Heinemann, 1969. Rpt. New York: Simon & Schuster, 1970.

Carter, Paul. "The Last Objective." *Astounding,* August 1946. Coll. in *Decade: The 1940s*. Ed. Brian Aldiss and Harry Harrison. New York: St. Martin's Press, 1978.

Chandler, A. Bertram. "False Dawn." *Astounding,* October 1946. Coll. in *Journey to Infinity*. Ed. Martin Greenberg. New York: Gnome Press, 1951.

Charnas, Suzy McKee. *Motherlines*. New York: Putnam, 1978. Rpt. London: Gollancz, 1980.

———. *Walk to the End of the World*. New York: Ballantine, 1974. Rpt. London: Gollancz, 1979.

Christopher, John. *The Death of Grass*. London: Michael Joseph, 1956. Rpt. as *No Blade of Grass*. New York: Simon & Schuster, 1957.

———. *Empty World*. London: Hamish Hamilton, 1977. Rpt. New York: Dutton, 1978.

———. *Pendulum*. New York: Simon & Schuster, 1968; London: Hodder & Stoughton, 1968.

———. *The Prince in Waiting*. London: Hamish Hamilton, 1970; New York: Macmillan, 1970. Rpt. New York: Macmillan, Collier, 1974.

———. *The World in Winter*. London: Eyre and Spottiswoode, 1962. Vt. *The Long Winter*. New York: Simon & Schuster, 1962.

———. *A Wrinkle in the Skin*. London: Hodder & Stoughton, 1965. Rpt. as *The Ragged Edge*. New York: Simon & Schuster, 1966.

Clark, Walter van Tilberg. "The Portable Phonograph." 1941. Coll. in *Tomorrow and Tomorrow*. Ed. Damon Knight. New York: Simon & Schuster, 1973.

Clarke, Arthur C. "The Awakening." *Future Science Fiction,* January 1952.

———. *Childhood's End*. New York: Ballantine, 1953. Rpt. New York: Ballantine, 1981.

———. "The Nine Billion Names of God." *Star Science Fiction Stories,* January 1953. Rpt. in *One Hundred Years of Science Fiction*. Ed. Damon Knight. New York: Simon & Schuster, 1968.

Clarke, Joan B. *The Happy Planet*. London: Cape, 1963.

Cloete, Stuart. "The Blast." *Collier's,* April 12, 1947. Coll. in *Six Great Short Novels of Science Fiction*. Ed. Groff Conklin. New York: Dell, 1954.

Collier, John. *Tom's A-Cold*. New York: Macmillan, 1933. Rpt. as *Full Circle*. New York: Appleton, 1933.

Compton, D. G. *The Silent Multitude*. New York: Ace, 1966. Rpt. London: Hodder & Stoughton, 1967.

Coney, Michael. *Winter's Children*. London: Gollancz, 1974.

Connington, J. J. *Nordenholt's Million*. London: Benn, 1923.

Conquest, Robert. *A World of Difference*. London: Ward Lock, 1955. Rpt. New York: Ballantine, 1964.

Cook, Paul. *Duende Meadow*. New York: Bantam, 1985.

Cooper, Edmund. *All Fool's Day*. London: Hodder & Stoughton, 1966; New York: Walker, 1966.

———. *The Cloud Walker*. London: Hodder & Stoughton, 1973; New York: Ballantine, 1973.

———. *The Last Continent*. New York: Dell, 1969. Rpt. London: Hodder & Stoughton, 1970.

———. *The Overman Culture*. London: Hodder & Stoughton, 1971. Rpt. New York: Putnam, 1972.

———. *Seed of Light*. New York: Ballantine, 1959; London: Hutchinson, 1959.

———. *The Slaves of Heaven*. New York: Putnam, 1974. Rpt. London: Hodder & Stoughton, 1975.

———. *The Tenth Planet*. New York: Putnam, 1973; London: Hodder & Stoughton, 1973.

———. *The Uncertain Midnight*. London: Hutchinson, 1958. Rpt. as *Deadly Image*. New York: Ballantine, 1958.

Coppel, Alfred. *Dark December*. New York: Fawcett Gold Medal, 1960. Rpt. London: Jenkins, 1966.

Corgiat, Sylviane, and Bruno Lecigne. *Le Titan de Galove*. Paris: Plasma, 1983. Vol. 1 of *Les Cycle Des Chimeres,* a set of "collective creation" novels. This cycle is set in a world of cyclical cataclysms. Novelists announced for the series include Jean-Pierre Hubert, Alain Paris, Michel Jeury, Jean-Pierre Fontana, Daniel Walther, and Jean-Pierre Vernay.

Coulson, Juanita. *Tomorrow's Heritage*. New York: Ballantine, 1982.

Cowper, Richard. *Phoenix*. London: Dobson, 1968. New York: Ballantine, 1970. Rpt. London: Gollancz, 1974; New York: Day, 1974.

———. *The Road to Corlay*. London: Gollancz, 1978. Rpt. New York: Timescape, 1986.

———. *The Twilight of Briareus*. London: Day, 1974.

Cozzens, James Gould. *Castaway*. New York: Random House, 1934.

Crane, Robert. *Hero's Walk*. New York: Ballantine, 1954.

Cromie, Robert. *The Crack of Doom*. London: Digby, Long, 1895.

Crowley, John. *Beasts*. Garden City, N.Y.: Doubleday, 1976.

———. *Engine Summer*. New York: Doubleday, 1979. Rpt. London: Gollancz, 1980.

Davis, Chandler. "The Aristocrat." *Astounding,* October 1949.

———. "To Still the Drums." *Astounding,* October 1946.

de Grainville, Jean Baptiste François Cousin. *Le Dernier Homme*. 1805. Published in America as *The Last Man, or Omegarus and Syderia: A Romance of Futurity*. 2 vols. New York: Dutton, 1806. Rpt. New York: Arno, 1978.

Delany, Samuel R. *The Einstein Intersection*. New York: Ace, 1967. Rpt. New York: Bantam, 1986.

———. "The Fall of the Towers" Novels. *The Fall of the Towers*. New York: Ace, 1972. Coll. *Captives of the Flame, City of a Thousand Suns,* and the *Tower of Toron* in one volume.

Captives of the Flame. New York: Ace, 1963. Rev. and Retitled *Out of the Dead City*. London: Sphere, 1968. Rpt. New York: Ace, 1977.

City of a Thousand Suns. New York: Ace, 1965. Rpt. London: Sphere, 1969.

The Tower of Toron. New York: Ace, 1964. Rpt. London: Sphere, 1968.

————. *The Jewels of Aptor*. New York: Ace, 1962, rev. ed. 1968; and London: Gollancz, 1968.

Desmond, Shaw. *Ragnarok*. London: Duckworth, 1926.

Dick, Philip K. "Autofac." *Galaxy*, November 1955. Coll. in *Robots, Androids, and Mechanical Oddities: The Science Fiction of Philip K. Dick*. Ed. Patricia Warrick and Martin H. Greenberg. Carbondale: Southern Illinois University Press, 1984.

————. "The Defenders." *Galaxy*, January 1953. Coll. in *There Will Be War*. Ed. J. E. Pournelle and Terry Carr. New York: Tom Doherty, 1983.

————. *Do Androids Dream of Electric Sheep?* New York: Doubleday, 1968. Rpt. London: Rapp & Whiting, 1969. Issued as *Blade Runner*. New York: Ballantine, 1982. Filmed as *Blade Runner*.

————. *Dr. Bloodmoney: or How We Got Along After the Bomb*. New York: Ace, 1965. London: Arrow, 1977.

————. "Operation Plowshare." *Worlds of Tomorrow*, November-December 1965. Rpt. as *The Zap Gun*. New York: Pyramid, 1967.

————. *The Penultimate Truth*. New York: Belmont, 1964. Rpt. London: Cape, 1967; New York: Bluejay, 1984.

————. "Second Variety." *Space Science Fiction*, May 1953. Coll. in *Robots, Androids, and Other Mechanical Oddities; The Science Fiction of Philip K. Dick*. Ed. Patricia Warrick and Martin H. Greenberg. Carbondale: Southern Illinois University Press, 1984.

Dick, Philip K., and Roger Zelazny. *Deus Irae*. Garden City, N.Y.: Doubleday, 1976.

Dickinson, Peter. "The Changes" Trilogy. *The Weathermonger*. Boston: Little, Brown, 1968. *Heartsease*. Boston: Little, Brown, 1969. *The Devil's Children*. Boston: Little, Brown, 1970.

Disch, Thomas M. *The Genocides*. New York: Berkley, 1965. Rpt. London: Whiting & Wheaton, 1967.

————. *334*. New York: Avon, 1974.

Donnelly, Ignatius (as Edmund Boisgilbert). *Caesar's Column: A Story of the Twentieth Century*. Chicago: F. J. Schulte, 1890.

Doyle, Arthur Conan. *The Poison Belt*. London: Hodder & Stoughton, 1913; New York: Doran, 1913. Rpt. London: John Murray, 1963.

Drake, David. "Men Like Us." *Omni*, May 1980.

Drew, Wayland. "The Erthring" Cycle. *The Memoirs of Alcheringia*. New York: Ballantine, 1984. *The Gaian Expedient*. New York: Ballantine, 1985; reissued 1986.

Drode, Daniel. *Surface de la Planete*. Paris: Hachette, 1959.

du Maurier, Daphne. "The Birds." 1952. Rpt. in *The Ruins of Earth*. Ed. Thomas Disch. New York: Putnam, 1971.

Duncan, Robert. *The Last Adam*. London: Dobson, 1952.

Dunstan, Frederick. *Habitation One*. London: Fontana, 1983.

Ehrlich, Max. *The Big Eye*. New York: Doubleday, 1949. Rpt. London: Boardman, 1951.

Ehrlich, Paul R. "Eco-catastrophe!" *Ramparts*, September 1969. Rpt. in *Nightmare Age*. Ed. Fred Pohl. New York: Ballantine, 1970.

Ellison, Harlan. "A Boy and His Dog." *New Worlds*, April 1969. Coll. in *The Beast That Shouted Love at the Heart of the World*. New York: Avon, 1969. Rpt. London: Milligan, 1976. Filmed as *A Boy and His Dog*.

——. "The Deathbird." *Fantasy and Science Fiction*, March 1973. Rpt. in *The Deathbird Stories*. New York: Harper & Row, 1975.

——. "I Have No Mouth and I Must Scream." *If*, March 1967. Coll. in *I Have No Mouth, and I Must Scream*. New York: Pyramid, 1967; and *The Fantasies of Harlan Ellison*. Boston: Gregg Press, 1979.

Emshwiller, Carol. "Day at the Beach." *Fantasy and Science Fiction*, August 1959. Coll. in *The Best of the Best*. Ed. Judith Merril. New York: Delacorte, 1976.

Emstev, Mikhail, and Eremei Parnov. *World Soul*. Trans. Antonina W. Bouis of Dusha Mira, 1964. New York: Macmillan, 1977.

Engel, Leonard, and Emanuel S. Piller. *The World Aflame: The Russian-American War of 1950*. New York: Dial, 1947.

England, George Allan. *Darkness and Dawn*. Boston: Small, Maynard, 1914. Rpt. Westport, Conn.: Hyperion Press, 1973. Orig. serialized in three parts, each with different titles.

Erdman, Paul E. *The Crash of '79*. New York: Simon & Schuster, 1976.

Farjeon, J. Jefferson. *Death of a World*. London: Collins, 1948.

Federbush, Arnold. *Ice*. New York: Bantam, 1978.

Flammarion, Camille. *Omega: The Last Days of the World*. New York: Cosmopolitan, 1894.

Fontenay, Charles L. *The Days the Oceans Overflowed*. Derby, Conn.: Monarch, 1964.

Ford, Richard. *Melvaig's Vision*. London: Grenada, 1984.

Forman, James D. *Doomsday Plus Twelve*. New York: Scribner, 1984.

Forstchen, William R. "The Ice" Triology. *Ice Prophet*. New York: Ballantine, 1983. *The Flame upon the Ice*. New York: Ballantine, 1984. *A Darkness upon the Ice*. New York: Del Rey, 1985.

Forster, E. M. "The Machine Stops." *Oxford and Cambridge Review*. Vol. 8, Michaelmas Term, 1909. Rpt. in *The Science Fiction Hall of Fame*. Vol. 2B. Ed. Ben Bova. Garden City, N.Y.: Doubleday, 1973.

France, Anatole. *Penguin Island. [L'Ile des Pingouins.]* Trans. A. W. Evans, 1908. Rpt. New York: Blue Ribbon Books, 1909; New York: Leetes Isl., 1981.

Frank, Pat. *Alas, Babylon*. Philadelphia: Lippincott, 1959. Rpt. London: Constable, 1959.

——. *Mr. Adam*. Philadelphia: Lippincott, 1946. Rpt. London: Gollancz, 1947.

Fukushima, Masami, and Artisune Toyota. *Kiga Retto [Starvation Archipelago]*. Tokyo: Kadokasa Shoten, 1974.

Galouye, Daniel. *Dark Universe*. New York: Bantam, 1959. Rpt. Boston: Gregg Press, 1976.

George, Peter. *Commander-1*. London: Heinemann, 1965.

——. *Dr. Strangelove, or How I Learned to Stop Worrying and Love the Bomb*. London: Corgi, 1963. Rpt. Boston: Gregg Press, 1979.

Giffard, Hardinge Goulburn, second earl of Halsbury. *1944*. London: Butterworth, 1926.

Gloag, John. *To-Morrow's Yesterday*. London: Allen & Unwin, 1932.

Goldston, Robert C. *The Eighth Day*. New York: Rinehart, 1956.

Goulart, Ron. *After Things Fell Apart*. New York: Ace, 1970. Rpt. London: Arrow, 1975; New York: Berkley, 1985.

Graham, David. *Down to a Sunless Sea*. New York: Simon & Schuster, 1981. Rpt. New York: Fawcett, 1986.

Graham, P. Anderson. *The Collapse of Homo Sapiens*. New York: Putnam, 1923.

Grainville, J.-B. Cousin de. *See* de Grainville.

Gratacap, L. P. *The Evacuation of England: The Twist in the Gulf Stream*. New York: Bretano's, 1908.

Gredon, Edward. "The Figure." *Astounding*, July 1947.

Griffith, George. *The Angel of Revolution: A Tale of the Coming Terror*. London: Tower, 1894. Rpt. Westport, Conn.: Hyperion Press, 1974; reissued 1986 as *Angel of the Revolution* with an intro. by Sam Moskowitz.

———. *Olga Romanoff: or, The Syren of the Skies*. Bristol, U.K.: J. W. Arrowsmith, 1898. Rpt. Westport, Conn.: Hyperion Press, 1973. Sequel to *The Angel of the Revolution*.

Groom, Pelham. *The Purple Twilight*. London: Werner Laurie, 1948.

Gunn, James E. *The Burning*. New York: Dell, 1972.

Hackett, John Winthrop. *The Third World War: August 1985*. New York: Macmillan, 1979.

———. *The Third World War; The Untold Story*. New York: Macmillan, 1982.

Halacy, D. S., Jr. *Return from Luna*. New York: Norton, 1969.

Haldeman, Joe. *Worlds*. New York: Viking, 1981.

———. *Worlds Apart*. New York: Viking, 1983. Rpt. New York: Ace, 1984. *Worlds* and *Worlds Apart* are linked novels.

Hamilton, Cecily. *Theodore Savage*. London: Parsons, 1922. Rev. and reissued as *Lest Ye Die: A Story from the Past of the Future*. New York: Scribner, 1928.

Hamilton, Edmond. *City at World's End*. New York: Fell, 1951. Rpt. London: Museum Press, 1952; New York: Ballantine, 1983.

Harrison, Harry. *Make Room! Make Room!* New York: Doubleday, 1966. Rpt. London: Penguin, 1967. Rpt. Boston: Gregg Press, 1979; New York: Ace, 1984. Filmed as *Soylent Green*.

Harrison, Helga. *Catacombs*. London: Chatto and Windus, 1962.

Harrison, M. John. *The Committed Men*. Garden City, N.Y.: Doubleday, 1971; London: Hutchinson, 1971.

Harrison, William. "Roller Ball Murder." *Esquire*, September 1973. Filmed as *Rollerball*, 1975.

Hartley, L. Pa. *Facial Justice*. London: Hamilton, 1960.

Hartridge, Jon. *Earthjacket*. London: Macdonald, 1970; New York: Walker, 1970.

Heinlein, Robert A. *Beyond This Horizon*. Reading, Pa.: Fantasy Press, 1948. Rpt. London: Panther, 1967; Boston: Gregg Press, 1981; New York: Signet, 1974.

———. *Farnham's Freehold*. New York: Putnam, 1964. Rpt. London: Dobson, 1965; New York: Medallion, 1984.

Herbert, Frank. *The White Plague*. New York: Putnam, 1982. Rpt. New York: Berkley, 1983.

Herzog, Arthur. *Heat*. New York: Simon & Schuster, 1977.

Hill, Douglas Arthur. "The Huntsman" Novels: *The Huntsman*. New York: Argo/Atheneum, 1982. *Warriors of the Wasteland*. New York: Argo/Atheneum, 1983. *Alien Citadel*. New York: Argo/Atheneum, 1984.

Hoban, Russell. *Riddley Walker*. New York: Simon & Schuster, 1980.

Hodgson, William Hope. *The Night Land*. London: Nash, 1912.

Holm, Sven. *Termush. [Termush, Atlanterhavskysten, 1967]*. Trans. Sylvia Clayton. London: Faber & Faber, 1969.

Hoover, H. M. *Children of Morrow*. New York: Four Winds, 1973; London and Baltimore: Penguin, 1985.

Horrakh, Livio. *Grattanuvole*. Piacenza, Italy: La Tribuna, 1977.

Houghton, Claude. *This Was Ivor Treat*. London: Heinemann, 1935.

Hoyle, Fred. *The Black Cloud*. London: Heinemann, 1957; New York: Harper, 1957.

Hoyle, Fred, and Geoffrey Hoyle. *The Inferno*. London: William Heinemann, 1973; New York: Harper, 1973.

Hoyle, Trevor. *The Last Gasp*. New York: Crown, 1983. Rpt. New York: Zebra, 1985.

Hubbard, L. Ron. *Battlefield Earth*. New York: St. Martin's Press, 1982. Rpt. New York: Bridge, 1984.

———. *Final Blackout*. Providence, R. I.: Hadley, 1948.

Hudson, W. H. *A Crystal Age*. London: 1887. Rpt. New York: Doric Books, 1950.

Hume, Fergus. *The Year of Miracle*. London: Routledge, 1891.

Hunter, Thomas O'D. *Softly Walks the Beast*. New York: Avon, 1985.

Huxley, Aldous. *Ape and Essence*. New York: Harper, 1948. Rpt. London: Chatto & Windus, 1949.

———. *Brave New World*. London: Chatto & Windus, 1932. Rpt. in *Brave New World* and *Brave New World Revisited*. New York: Harper, 1964; reissued 1979.

Ibuse, Masuji. *Black Rain*. Trans. John Bester. Tokyo and Palo Alto, Calif.: Kodansha International, 1969. London: Secker & Warburg, 1971. Rpt. New York: Bantam, 1985. First appearance in English: *Japan Quarterly* 14 (1967), nos. 2–4; 15 (1968), nos. 1–3.

Ing, Dean. *Pulling Through*. New York: Ace, 1983. Rpt. New York: Charter Books, 1987.

———. "The Systemic Shock" Trilogy. *Systemic Shock*. New York: Tor/Pinnacle, 1981. Rpt. 1986. *Single Combat*. New York: Tor/Pinnacle, 1983. *Wild Country*. [working title; not yet published]

Jane, Fred T. *The Violent Flame*. London: Ward, Lock, 1899.

Jeffries, Richard. *After London*. London and New York: Cassell, 1885. Rpt. London: Duckworth, 1911; New York: Arno, 1974.

Jeury, Michel. *Le Territoire Humain*. Paris: Laffont, 1979.

Johnson, Annabel, and Edgar Johnson. *The Danger Quotient*. New York: Harper & Row, 1984.

Johnstone, William W. "The Out of the Ashes" Series. *Out of the Ashes*. New York: Zebra, 1983. *Fire in the Ashes*. New York: Zebra, 1984. *Anarchy in the Ashes*. New York: Zebra, 1984.

Jones, D. F. "The Colossus" Series. *Colossus*. New York: Hart-Davis, 1966. Rpt. New York: Berkley, 1985. *The Fall of Colossus*. New York: Putnam, 1974. *Colossus and the Crab*. New York: Berkley, 1977.

Jones, Raymond F. *Renaissance*. New York: Gnome Press, 1951.

———. *The Year When Stardust Fell*. Philadelphia: Winston, 1958.

Kahn, James. *Time's Dark Laughter*. New York: Ballantine, 1982. Rpt. New York: Del Rey, 1985.

———. *World Enough and Time*. New York: Ballantine, 1985. Rpt. New York: Del Rey, 1985. *Time's Dark Laughter* and *World Enough and Time* are linked novels.

Kaul, Fedor. *Contagion to the World*. [*Die Welt Ohne Gedachnis*, 1930.] Trans. Winifred Ray. London: Bles, 1933.

Kavan, Anna. *Ice*. London: Peter Owen, 1967. Rpt. New York: Doubleday, 1970; Norton, 1985.

Kaye, Marvin, and Parke Godwin. *The Masters of Solitude*. New York: Doubleday, 1978.

Kelleher, Victor. *The Beast of Heaven*. St. Lucia, Queensland, Australia: University of Queensland Press, 1984.

Kennedy, Leigh. "Belling Martha." *Asimov's Science Fiction Magazine,* May 1983. Coll. in *Isaac Asimov's Space of Her Own*. Ed. Shawna McCarthy. New York: Dial/Davis, 1984.

Kilian, Crawford. *Tsunami*. New York: Bantam, 1984.

King, Stephen. *The Stand*. Garden City, N.Y.: Doubleday, 1978. Rpt. New York: Signet, 1980.

Knight, Damon. "A for Anything." *Fantasy and Science Fiction,* November 1957. Rpt. *A for Anything*. New York: Walker, 1970.

———. "Not with a Bang." *Fantasy and Science Fiction,* Winter-Spring 1950. Coll. in *The Best of Damon Knight*. Garden City, N.Y.: Doubleday, 1967. Rpt. in *The Magazine of Fantasy and Science Fiction: A 30-Year Retrospective*. Ed. Edward L. Ferman. Garden City, N.Y.: Doubleday, 1980.

———. "World without Children." *Galaxy,* December 1951. Coll. in *Five Galaxy Short Novels*. Ed. H. L. Gold. New York: Pocket Books, 1960.

Knight, Norman. *See* Blish.

Komatsu, Sakyo. *Japan Sinks*. Trans. and abrid. Michael Gallagher. New York: Harper, 1976. Vt. *The Year of the Dragon*.

———. *Fukkatsu No Hi [Resurrection Day]*. Tokyo: Kadokawa, 1964. Basis of the 1980 Kadokawa film *Virus*.

Kornbluth, C. M. *Not This August*. New York: Bantam, 1956. Rpt. as *Chrismas Eve*. London: Joseph, 1956, and as *Not This August*. New York: Tor/Pinnacle Books, 1981.

Kuttner, Henry. "Atomic." *Thrilling Wonder Stories,* August 1947.

———. *Mutant*. New York: Gnome, 1953. Rpt. New York: Garland Press, 1975. Coll. stories orig. published in *Astounding,* 1945 and 1953 under the name of Lewis Padgett.

———. "Way of the Gods." *Thrilling Wonder,* April 1947.

Lamb, William. *The World Ends*. London: Dent, 1937.

Lane, Mary E. *Mizora: The Narrative of Vera Zarovitch*. New York: G. W. Dillingham, 1889.

Lang, Herrman. *The Air Battle: A Vision of the Future*. London: William Penny, 1859.

Lange, Oliver. *Vandenberg*. New York: Stein & Day, 1971.

Lanier, Sterling E. "The Hiero" Novels: *Hiero's Journey: A Romance of the Future*. Radnor, Pa.: Chilton, 1973. Rpt. London: Sidgwick & Jackson, 1975; New York: Ballantine, 1983. *The Unforsaken Hiero*. New York: Bantam, 1983.

Lavers, Norman. *The Northwest Passage*. New York: Fiction Collective, Brooklyn College. Distributed by Flatiron Books, 1984.

Lee, Tanith. *Days of Grass*. New York: DAW, 1985.

Le Guin, Ursula. *Always Coming Home*. New York: Harper & Row, 1985.

Leiber, Fritz. "Coming Attraction." *Galaxy,* November 1950. Coll. in *A Pail of Air*. New York: Ballantine, 1964.

———. "The Creature from Cleveland Depths." *Galaxy,* December 1962. Retitled "The Lone Wolf" and coll. in *The Night of the Wolf*. New York: Ballantine, 1966.

———. "The Night of the Long Knives." *Amazing,* January 1960. Retitled "The Wolf Pair" and coll. in *The Night of the Wolf*. New York: Ballantine, 1966.

———. *A Specter is Haunting Texas*. New York: Walker, 1969.

————. *The Wanderer*. New York: Ballantine, 1964. Rpt. Boston: Gregg Press, 1980.

Leinster, Murray. *The Murder of the U.S.A.* New York: Crown, 1946.

Leourier, Christian. *The Mountains of the Sun.* [*Les Montagnes du Soleil,* 1971.] New York: Berkley, 1974.

Lessing, Doris. *The Memoirs of a Survivor.* New York: Knopf, 1975.

————. *Re: Colonised Planet 5: Shikasta.* New York: Knopf, 1979. Rpt. New York: Random House, 1981.

Levy, D. *The Gods of Foxcroft.* New York: Arbor House, 1970.

Lightner, A. M. *The Day of the Drones.* New York: Norton, 1969.

Ligny, Jean-Marc. *Succubes.* Paris: Plasma, 1983. Vol. 2 of *Le Cycle Des Chimeres,* a "collective creation" set of novels.

Llewellyn, Alun. *The Strange Invaders.* London: Bell, 1934.

Llewellyn, Edward. *Prelude to Chaos.* New York: DAW, 1983. Rpt., 1986.

London, Jack. *The Scarlet Plague.* New York: Paul R. Reynolds, 1912. Rpt. New York: Macmillan, 1915; London: Mills & Boon, 1915.

Lowndes, Robert A. W. *See* Blish.

Macauley, Robie. *A Secret History of Time to Come.* New York: Knopf, 1979.

McCann, Edison. *Preferred Risk.* New York: Simon & Schuster, 1955. [Pseudo. of Lester del Rey and Fred Pohl.]

McClary, Thomas Calvert. *Rebirth: When Everyone Forgot.* New York: Bartholomew House, 1944. A greatly rewritten version of a story of the same name that appeared originally in *Astounding,* February 1934. Rpt. as *When Everyone Forgot.* Westport, Conn: Hyperion Press, 1976.

MacDonald, John D. "Spectator Sport." *Thrilling Wonder Stories,* February 1950. Rpt. in *Science Fiction of the 50's.* Ed. Martin Harry Greenberg and Joseph D. Olander. New York: Avon, 1979.

McEnroe, Richard. *Warrior's World.* New York: Ace, 1981.

McIntosh, J. T. *The Fittest.* New York: Doubleday, 1955. Rpt. London: Corgi, 1961. Rpt. as *The Rule of the Pagbeasts.* New York: Fawcett, 1956.

————. *One in Three Hundred.* New York: Doubleday, 1954.

McIntyre, Vonda. *Dreamsnake.* Boston: Houghton Mifflin, 1978; London: Gollancz, 1978. Rpt. New York: Dell, 1986.

————. *The Exile Waiting.* New York: Doubleday, 1975. Rpt. London: Gollancz, 1976; New York: Tor, 1985.

MacLennan, Hugh. *Voices in Time.* New York: St. Martin's Press, 1980.

McLoughlin, John C. *The Helix and the Sword.* Garden City, N.Y.: Doubleday, 1983. Rpt. New York: Tor, 1984.

McQuay, Mike. *Jitterbug.* New York: Bantam, 1984.

Maine, Charles Eric. *Alph.* New York: Doubleday, 1972. First pub. as *World without Men.* New York: Ace, 1958; London: Digit, 1963.

————. *The Darkest of Nights.* London: Hodder & Stoughton, 1962. Has also appeared as *Survival Margin.* New York: Fawcett, 1968; revised as *The Big Death.* London: Sphere, 1978.

————. *The Tide Went Out.* London: Hodder & Stoughton, 1958. Rpt. New York: Ballantine, 1959. Rev. and rpt. as *Thirst.* London: Sphere, 1977; New York: Ace, 1978.

Malamud, Bernard. *God's Grace.* New York: Farrar, Straus & Giroux, 1982. Rpt. New York: Avon, 1983.

Mano, D. Keith. *The Bridge*. Garden City, N.Y.: Doubleday, 1973.

Martel, Suzanne. *The City Underground*. Trans. Norah Smaridge. New York: Viking, 1964. Orig. title. *Quatre Montréalais en l'an 3000*. Montreal: Editions de jour, 1963.

Matheson, Richard. *I Am Legend*. New York: Fawcett Gold Medal, 1954. Filmed initially as *The Last Man on Earth*, 1964; then as *The Omega Man*, 1971.

Mead, Harold. *The Bright Phoenix*. 1955. Rpt. New York: Ballantine, 1956.

Merle, Robert. *Malevil*. Trans. Derek Coltman. New York: Simon & Schuster, 1973. Orig. pub. Paris: Gallimard, 1972.

Merril, Judith. *Shadow on the Hearth*. New York: Doubleday, 1950. Rpt. London: Sidgwick & Jackson, 1953.

Messac, Regis. *Quinzinzinzili*. Paris: Fenetres Ouverte, 1935.

Mielke, Thomas R. P. *Der Pflanzen Heiland. [The Plant Savior]*. Munich: Heyne Verlag, 1981.

Miller, Walter M., Jr. *A Canticle for Leibowitz*. Philadelphia: Lippincott, 1959. Rpt. London: Weidenfeld & Nicholson, 1960; New York: Bantam, 1976; New York: Harper & Row, 1986.

————. "Dumb Waiter." *Astounding*, April 1952.

Mitchell, J. Leslie. *Gay Hunter*. London: Heinemann, 1934.

Mondolini, Jacques. *Je Suis une Herbe*. Paris: Editions J'ai Lu, 1982.

Monteleone, Thomas. "The Guardian" Novels: *Guardian*. Garden City, N.Y.: Doubleday, 1980. *Ozymandias*. Garden City, N.Y.: Doubleday, 1981.

Moorcock, Michael. "The Dancer at the End of Time" Series: *An Alien Heat*. New York: Harper & Row, 1972. *The Hollow Lands*. New York: Harper & Row, 1974. Rpt. New York: Avon, 1977. *The End of All Songs*. New York: Harper & Row, 1976. Rpt. New York: Avon, 1978. *The Transformation of Miss Mavis Ming*. London: W. H. Allen, 1977. Retit. *Messiah at the End of Time*. New York: DAW, 1978.

————. *The Ice Schooner*. 1969. Rev. ed. New York: Harper & Row, 1977.

————. "The Jerry Cornelius" Novels: *The Final Programme*. New York: Avon, 1968. Filmed first as *The Final Programme* and then as *The Last Days of Man on Earth*. *A Cure for Cancer*. London: Allison & Busby, 1971. *The English Assassin*. New York: Harper, 1974.

Moore, Ward. *Greener Than You Think*. New York: Sloan, 1947. Rpt. London: Gollancz, 1949.

————. "Lot." *Fantasy and Science Fiction*, May 1953. Rpt. in *The Best from Fantasy and Science Fiction 3*. Ed. Anthony Boucher and J. Francis McComas. New York: Doubleday, 1954.

————. "Lot's Daughter." *Fantasy and Science Fiction*, October 1954. Rpt. in *A Decade of Fantasy and Science Fiction*. Ed. Robert P. Mills. New York: Doubleday, 1960. "Lot" and "Lot's Daughter" were the basis for the film *Panic in the Year Zero*, 1962.

Morris, William. *News from Nowhere, or an Epoch of Rest*. Boston: Roberts, 1890. Rpt. Hammersmith, U.K.: Kelmscott Press, 1892; London and Boston: Routledge, 1970.

Moxley, F. Wright. *Red Snow*. New York: Simon & Schuster, 1930.

Nation, Terry. *The Survivors*. New York: Coward, McCann, 1976. After television series of the same title.

Niven, Larry, and Jerry E. Pournelle. *Lucifer's Hammer*. Chicago: Playboy Press, 1977. Rpt. New York: Fawcett, 1985.

Noel, Sterling. *We Who Survive*. New York: Avon, 1960.

Nolan, William F. "Logan" Novels: *Logan's Run*. With George Clayton Johnson. New York: Dial Press, 1967. Filmed under same title. *Logan's World*. New York: Bantam, 1977; London: Gollancz, 1978. *Logan's Search*. New York: Bantam, 1980; London: Corgi, 1981.

Norton, André. *Star Man's Son*. New York: Harcourt Brace, 1952. Rpt. and retitled, *Daybreak—2250* A.D. New York: Ace, 1954. Rpt. as *Star Man's Son*. New York: Ballantine 1985.

Nowlan, Philip Francis. *Armageddon 2419* A.D. *Amazing*, 1928. Rpt. New York: Avalon, 1962.

Noyes, Alfred. *The Last Man*. New York: Stokes, 1940. Vt. *No Other Man*.

O'Brien, Robert C. *Z For Zachariah*. New York: Atheneum, 1975.

O'Donnell, Kevin, Jr. *War of Omission*. New York: Bantam, 1982.

Offutt, Andrew. *The Castle Keep*. New York: Berkley, 1972; London: Magnum, 1978.

O'Neill, Joseph. *Day of Wrath*. London: Gollancz, 1936.

Orgill, Douglas, and John Gribben. *The Sixth Winter*. New York: Simon & Schuster, 1979. Rpt. New York: Ballantine, 1981.

Palmer, David R. *Emergence*. New York: Bantam, 1984.

Pangborn, Edgar. *The Company of Glory*. New York: Pyramid Books, 1975.

———. *Davy*. New York: St. Martin's Press, 1964. Expanded from "The Golden Horn." *Fantasy and Science Fiction*, February 1962, and "A War of No Consequence." *Fantasy and Science Fiction*, March 1962. Rpt. New York: Ballantine, 1982.

———. *The Judgment of Eve*. New York: Simon & Schuster, 1966. Rpt. New York: Avon, 1976.

———. *Still I Persist in Wondering*. New York: Dell, 1978. Coll. all of the *Davy* stories.

Parker, Richard. *The Hendon Fungus*. London: Gollancz, 1967.

Paxson, Diana L. "The Lady of Light" Novels: *Lady of Light*. New York: Timescape, 1982. *Lady of Darkness, The Second Book of Westria*. New York: Timescape/ Pocket Books, 1983.

Pedlar, Kit, and Gerry Davis. *Mutant 59: The Plastic Eaters*. New York: Viking, 1972.

Pendleton, Don. *The Day the World Died*. New York: Pinnacle, 1970.

Percy, Walker. *Love in the Ruins*. New York: Farrar, Straus & Giroux, 1971; Dell, 1971. Rpt. New York: Avon, 1978.

Phillips, A. M. "An Enemy of Knowledge." *Astounding*, April 1947.

Phillips, Rog. "So Shall Ye Reap." *Amazing*, August 1947.

Pischeria, Doris. *Earth in Twilight*. New York: DAW, 1981.

Poe, Edgar Allan. "The Colloquy of Monos and Una." *Graham's Ladies and Gentleman's Magazine*, no. CLXXXVIII (August 1841). Coll. in *The Complete Works of Edgar Allan Poe*. Ed. James A. Harrison. New York: Crowell, 1902. Rpt. New York: AMS Press, 1965. Also rpt. in *The Science Fiction of Edgar Allan Poe*. Ed. Harold Bever. New York: Penguin, 1976.

———. "The Conversation of Eiros and Charmion." Burton's *Gentleman's Magazine*, December 1839. Coll. in *The Complete Works of Edgar Allan Poe*. Ed. James A. Harrison. New York: AMS Press, 1965. Also rpt. in *The Science Fiction of Edgar Allan Poe*. Ed. Harold Bever. New York: Penguin, 1976.

———. "The Masque of the Red Death." *Graham's Magazine*, May 1842. Coll. in

The Complete Works of Edgar Allan Poe. Ed. James A. Harrison. New York: AMS Press, 1965. Rpt. in *The Fantasy Hall of Fame* Ed. Robert Silverberg and Martin H. Greenberg. New York: Arbor House, 1983.

Pollack, Frank Lillie. "Finis." *The Argosy,* June 1906. Rpt. as "The Last Dawn," in *Horror Omnibus.* Ed. Kurt Singer. London: W. H. Allen, 1965, and as "Finis," in *The Arbor House Treasury of Science Fiction Masterpieces* Ed. Robert Silverberg and Martin H. Greenberg. New York: Arbor House, 1983.

Priest, Christopher. *Fugue for a Darkening Island.* London: Faber, 1972. Amer. title: *Darkening Island.* New York: Harper, 1972.

Rand, Ayn. *Anthem.* London: Cassell, 1938. Rpt. New York: Signet, 1961.

―――. *Atlas Shrugged.* New York: Random House, 1957. Rpt. New York: Signet, 1970.

Rhinehart, Luke. *Long Voyage Back.* New York: Delacorte, 1983. Rpt. New York: Dell, 1984.

Roberts, Keith. *The Chalk Giants.* London: Hutchinson, 1974. Rpt. New York: Berkley, 1975.

―――. *The Furies.* New York: Berkley, 1966.

―――. *Pavane.* New York: Hart Davis, 1968.

Robinson, Kim Stanley. *Wild Shore.* New York: Ace, 1984.

Rose, Horace F. *The Maniac's Dream: A Novel of the Atomic Bomb.* London: Duckworth, 1946.

Roshwald, Mordecai. *Level 7.* London: Heinemann, 1959. Rpt. New York: McGraw-Hill, 1960.

Rosny Aine, J.-H. *La Mort De La Terre [The Death of the Earth]* 1912. Rpt. Paris: Denoel, 1958; 1983.

Saberhagen, Fred. "The Empire of the East" Novels: *The Empire of the East.* New York: Ace, 1979; reissued 1983. Coll. *The Black Mountains, The Broken Lands,* and *Changeling Earth* in one volume.

The Broken Lands. New York: Ace, 1968.

The Black Mountains. New York: Ace, 1971.

Changeling Earth. New York: DAW, 1973.

St. Clair, Margaret. *Sign of the Labrys.* New York: Bantam, 1963; London: Corgi, 1963.

Sargent, Pamela. "Heavenly Flowers." *Asimov's Science Fiction Magazine,* September 1983. Coll. in *Isaac Asimov's Space of Her Own.* Ed. Shawna McCarthy. New York: Dial/Davis, 1984.

Scortia, Thomas. *Earthwreck!* New York: Fawcett, 1974. Rpt. London: Coronet, 1975; New York: Fawcett, 1981.

Sellings, Arthur. *Junk Day.* London: Dobson, 1970.

Serviss, Garrett Putnam. *The Second Deluge.* New York: McBride West, 1912; London: Richards, 1912. Rpt. Westport, Conn.: Hyperion Press, 1974.

Shanks, Edward (as Richard Buxton). *Ruins: A Story of the English Revolution and After.* London: Stokes, 1920.

Shaw, Bob. *The Ground Zero Man.* New York: Avon, 1971. Rpt. London: Corgi, 1976.

Shelley, Mary Wollstonecraft. *The Last Man.* London: Henry Colburn, 1826. Rpt. Omaha: University of Nebraska Press, 1965. Rpt. Honolulu: Hogarth, 1985.

Sherriff, R. C. *The Hopkins Manuscript.* London: Gollancz, 1939; New York: Macmillan, 1939. Rev. as *The Cataclysm.* London: Pan, 1958. Rpt. as *The Hopkins Manuscript.* New York: Macmillan, 1963.

Shiel, M. P. *The Dragon*. London: Richards, 1913. Rpt. New York: Clode, 1914. Retitled *The Yellow Peril* and rpt. London: Gollancz, 1929.

———. *The Purple Cloud*. London: Chatto & Windus, 1901. Rpt. London: Gollancz, 1929; New York: Vanguard Press, 1930. Rpt. Cleveland, Ohio: World, 1946. Ranald MacDougall's script for the film *The World, the Flesh and the Devil* is loosely based on this novel.

———. *The Yellow Danger*. London: Richards, 1898. Rpt. New York: Fenno, 1899.

———. *The Yellow Wave*. London: Ward Lock, 1905.

Shute, Nevil. *On the Beach*. New York: Morrow, 1957. Rpt. Ballantine, 1978.

Sibson, Francis. *Unthinkable*. New York: Smith & Hass, 1933.

Silverberg, Robert. *Time of the Great Freeze*. New York: Holt Rinehart, 1965.

———. "When We Went to See the End of the World." In *Universe 2*. Ed. Terry Carr. New York: Ace, 1972. Coll. in *Unfamiliar Territory*. Ed. Robert Silverberg. New York: Scribner, 1973.

Simak, Clifford D. "City." *Astounding*, July 1944. Expanded as *City*. Reading, Pa. Gnome Press, 1952. Rpt. New York: Ace, 1981.

———. *A Heritage of Stars*. New York: Berkley, 1977. Rpt. London: Sidgwick & Jackson, 1978.

Sinclair, Upton. *The Millennium: A Comedy of the Year 2000*. Girard, Kans.: Haldeman Julius, 1924. Rpt. London: Laurie, 1929.

Smith, Wayland. *The Machine Stops*. London: Hale, 1936.

Soldati, Mario. *The Emerald*. Trans. William Weaver. New York: Harcourt, 1977. Orig. pub. as *Lo Smeraldo*. Milan: Mondadori, 1974.

Southwold, Stephen (pseud. Neil Bell). *The Gas War of 1940*. London: Partridge, 1931.

———. *The Lord of Life*. Boston: Little, Brown, 1933.

———. *The Seventh Bowl*. London: Partridge, 1930.

Spinrad, Norman. "The Big Flash." In *Orbit 5*. Ed. Damon Knight. New York: Putnam, 1969. Coll. in *No Direction Home*. New York: Pocket Books, 1975; London: Millington, 1976.

———. *The Iron Dream*. New York: Avon, 1972. Rpt. London: Panther, 1974; New York: Avon, 1975.

———. "The Lost Continent." In *Science against Man*. Ed. Anthony Cheetham. New York: Avalon, 1970. Coll. in *No Direction Home*. New York: Pocket Books, 1975; London: Millington, 1976.

———. *Songs from the Stars*. New York: Simon & Schuster, 1980. Rpt. New York: Bantam, 1985.

Spitz, Jacques. *La Guerre des Mouches*. Paris: Gallimard, 1938.

Stapledon, Olaf. *Last and First Men*. London: Methuen, 1930. Rpt. New York: Dover, 1968. Rpt. more recently by Dover but undated.

———. *The Star Maker*. London: Methuen, 1937. Rpt. New York: Dover, 1968. Rpt. more recently by Dover, but undated.

Start, Edward A. "The Last Sunset." *The Red Book*, March 1907.

Stevenson, Dorothy Emily. *The Empty World: A Romance of the Future*. London: Jenkins, 1936.

Stewart, George. *Earth Abides*. New York: Random House, 1949. Rpt. London: Gollancz, 1950; New York: Fawcett, 1983.

Stone, George. *Blizzard*. New York: Grosset & Dunlap, 1977.

Stoutenberg, Adrien. *Out There*. New York: Viking, 1971.

Streiber, Whitney, and James Kunetka. *War Day*. New York: Holt, Rinehart & Winston, 1984.

Sturgeon, Theodore. "Memorial." *Astounding*, April 1946. Vt. "The Atomic Memorial."

———. "Thunder and Roses." *Astounding*, November 1947. Rpt. in *The Road to Science Fiction #3: From Heinlein to Here*. Ed. James Gunn. New York: Signet, 1979.

Sullivan, Mary W. *Earthquake 2099*. New York: E. P. Dutton, 1982.

Sullivan, Sheila. *Summer Rising*. 1975. Amer. title: *The Calling of Bara*. New York: Dutton, 1976.

Sullivan, Timothy Robert. "The Comedian." *Asimov's Science Fiction Magazine*, June 1982.

Sutphen, Van Tassel. *The Doomsman*. New York: Harper, 1906. Rpt. Boston: Gregg Press, 1975.

Swigart, Rob. *The Book of Revelations*. New York: Dutton, 1981.

Szilard, Leo. "My Trial as a War Criminal." *University of Chicago Law Review*, Autumn 1949. Rpt. in *The Voice of the Dolphin and Other Stories*. New York: Simon & Schuster, 1961.

Tanaka, Koji. *Daimetsubo [Die Off]*. Tokyo: Shodensha, 1975.

Tarde, Gabriel de. *Underground Man*. Trans. C. Brereton. London: Duckworth, 1905. Rpt. Westport, Conn: Hyperion Press, 1974. Orig. titled *Fragment d'Histoire*, 1896.

Taylor, Robert Lewis. *Adrift in a Boneyard*. New York: Doubleday, 1947.

Tenn, William. "Eastward Ho!" *Fantasy and Science Fiction*, October 1958. Rpt. in *Alpha 4*. Ed. Robert Silverberg. New York: Ballantine, 1973.

Tevis, Walter. *Mockingbird*. New York: Doubleday, 1980.

Thompson, Joyce. *Conscience Place*. Garden City, N.Y.: Doubleday, 1984. Rpt. New York: Dell, 1986.

Tilley, Patrick. *Cloud Warrior*. New York: Macmillan, 1984.

Tiptree, James, Jr. "The Man Who Walked Home." *Amazing*, May 1972. Coll. in *Ten Thousand Light Years from Home*. New York: Ace, 1973.

———. "The Snows Are Melted, the Snows Are Gone." *Venture Science Fiction*, November 1969. Coll. in *Ten Thousand Light Years from Home*. New York: Ace, 1973.

Tucker, Wilson. *The Lond Loud Silence*. New York: Rinehart, 1952.

Turner, George. *Beloved Son*. London: Faber & Faber, 1978.

———. *Vaneglory*. London: Faber & Faber, 1981.

———. *Yesterday's Men*. London: Faber & Faber, 1983.

Vance, Jack. "The Dying Earth" Novels:

    The Dying Earth. New York: Curl, 1950. London: Mayflower, 1972. Rpt. New York: Timescape, 1982. Coll. of six related stories.

    The Eyes of the Overworld. New York: Ace, 1967; London: Mayflower, 1972. Rpt. New York: Timescape, 1980.

    Cugel's Saga. New York: Baen Enterprises, 1984.

———. *The Last Castle*. New York: Ace, 1966. Rpt. New York: Berkley, 1986.

Van Greenaway, Peter. *graffiti*. London: Gollancz, 1983.

———. *The Crucified City*. London: New Authors, 1962.

Van Vogt, A. E. *Empire of the Atom*. Chicago: Shasta, 1957. Coll. several related stories prev. pub. in *Astounding*.

———. "The Monster." *Astounding,* August 1948. Retit. "Resurrection," and rpt. in *The Last Man on Earth.* Ed. Isaac Asimov, Martin Harry Greenberg, and Charles G. Waugh. New York: Fawcett, 1982.

———. *The Wizard of Linn.* New York: Ace, 1962. Orig. appeared in *Astounding,* August 1948.

Varley, John. *Millennium.* New York: Berkley, 1983. Rpt. Berkley, 1985.

Venning, Hugh. *The End: A Projection, Not a Prophecy.* Buffalo, N.Y.: Desmond and Stapleton, 1947.

Verne, Jules. "L'Eternel Adam." Coll. in *Hier et Demain: Contes et Nouvelles.* Paris: Hetzel, 1910. Rpt. as "Eternal Adam," *The Best of Jules Verne.* Ed. Alan K. Russell. Secaucus, N. J.: Castle, 1978.

Vidal, Gore. *Kalki.* New York: Random House, 1978; London: Heinemann, 1978.

Vinge, Joan D. "The Crystal Ship." In *The Crystal Ship.* Ed. Robert Silverberg. Nashville, Tenn.: Nelson, 1976.

———. "Legacy." In *Binary Star #4.* New York: Dell, 1980. Expansion of "Media Man." *Analog,* October 1976.

———. "Mother and Child." In *Orbit #16.* Ed. Damon Knight. New York: Harper, 1975. Rpt. New York: Dell, 1978.

———. *The Outcasts of Heaven Belt.* New York: Signet, 1982.

———. "Phoenix in the Ashes." In *Millennial Women.* Ed. Virginia Kidd. New York: Dell, 1978.

———. *The Snow Queen.* New York: Dial Press, 1980. Rpt. New York: Dell, 1984.

Vinge, Vernor. "Conquest by Default." *Analog,* May 1968. Rpt. in *War and Peace: Possible Futures from Analog.* Ed. Stanley Schmidt. New York: Dial, 1983.

Vonnegut, Kurt, Jr. *Cat's Cradle.* New York: Holt Rinehart, 1963; London: Gollancz, 1963. Rpt. New York: Dell, 1986.

Wallace, Doreen. *Forty Years On.* London: 1958.

Waterloo, Stanley. *Armageddon.* Chicago: Rand McNally, 1898.

Watson, Ian. *Deathhunter.* London: Gollancz, 1981.

Weinbaum, Stanley. *The Black Flame.* Reading, Pa.: Fantasy Press, 1948. Coll. "The Black Flame" and "Dawn of Flame." "The Black Flame" appeared originally in *Startling Stories,* January 1939, "The Dawn of Flame," in *Thrilling Wonder Stories,* June 1939.

Wells, H. G. "The Empire of the Ants." 1905. Coll. in *The Complete Short Stories of H. G. Wells.* New York: St. Martin's Press, 1970. This story was originally in *Country of the Blind and Other Stories.* London: Thomas Nelson, 1911. Rpt. in *Amazing,* 1926.

———. *In the Days of the Comet.* New York: Macmillan, 1906. Rpt. in *Seven Science Fiction Novels of H. G. Wells.* New York: Dover, 1934. Rpt. Honolulu: Hogarth, 1985.

———. *The Shape of Things to Come: The Ultimate Resolution.* London: Hutchinson, 1933; New York: Macmillan, 1933. Rev. as film story, *Things to Come.* London: Cresset Press, 1935; New York: Macmillan, 1935.

———. *The Time Machine: An Invention.* London: Heinemann, 1985; New York: Holt, 1895. Rpt. New York: Bantam, 1982.

———*The World Set Free.* New York: Dutton, 1914.

White, E. B. "The Morning of the Day They Did It." *New Yorker,* February 1950. Coll. *A Treasury of Great Science Fiction.* Ed. Anthony Boucher. New York: Doubleday, 1959.

A Treasury of Great Science Fiction. Ed. Anthony Boucher. New York: Doubleday, 1959.

White, James. *Second Ending.* New York: Ace, 1962.

Wilhelm, Kate. *Where Late the Sweet Birds Sang.* New York: Timescape, 1981.

Williams, Jay. *The People of the Axe.* New York: Walck, 1974.

Williams, Nick Boddie. *The Atomic Curtain.* New York: Ace, 1956.

Williams, Paul. "The Pelbar" Novels:

The Breaking of the Northwall. New York: Ballantine, 1981.

The Ends of the Circle. New York: Ballantine, 1981.

The Dome in the Forest. New York: Ballantine, 1982. Rpt. New York: Ballantine, 1985.

The Fall of the Shell. New York: Ballantine, 1982.

An Ambush of Shadows. New York: Ballantine, 1983.

The Song of the Axe. New York: Ballantine, 1984.

Williamson, Jack. "Jamboree." *Galaxy,* December 1969.

Wilson, Richard. "Mother to the World." In *Orbit 3.* Ed. Damon Knight. New York: Putnam, 1968.

Wilson, Steve. *The Lost Traveler.* New York: St. Martin's Press, 1977.

Wright, S. Fowler. *Dawn.* New York: Cosmopolitan, 1929. Rpt. New York: Arno, 1975.

———. *Deluge.* London: Fowler Wright, 1927. Rpt. New York: Cosmopolitan, 1928. Rpt. New York: Arno, 1975. Filmed as *Deluge,* 1933.

Wul, Stefan. *Niourk.* Paris: Fleuve Noir, 1957.

Wylie, Philip. *The End of the Dream.* New York: Doubleday, 1972. Rpt. Morley, Yorkshire: Elmfield Press, 1975; New York: DAW, 1984.

———. *Tomorrow.* New York: Rinehart, 1954.

Wylie, Philip, and Edwin Balmer. "*When Worlds Collide*" Novels: *When Worlds Collide.* New York: Stokes, 1933; London: Paul, 1933. Filmed under same title. *After Worlds Collide.* New York: Stokes, 1934; London: Paul, 1934. Rpt. New York: Warner Books, 1963.

Wyndham, John. *The Chrysalids.* London: Joseph, 1955. Amer. title: *Re-Birth.* New York: Ballantine, 1955.

———. *The Day of the Triffids.* New York: Doubleday, 1951; London: Joseph, 1951. Rpt. as *Revolt of the Triffids.* New York: Popular Press, 1952; as *The Day of the Triffids.* New York: Ballantine, 1987.

Yano, Tetsu. *Chikyu Reinen [Earth: Year One].* Tokyo: Hawakawa Shobo, 1969.

Yarbro, Chelsea Quinn. *False Dawn.* Garden City, N.Y.: Doubleday, 1978.

Yourell, Agnes Bond. *A Manless World.* New York: G. W. Dillingham, 1891.

Zebrowski, George. *Macrolife.* New York: Harper & Row, 1979.

Zelazny, Roger. *Damnation Alley.* New York: Putnam, 1969. Rpt. London: Faber & Faber, 1971. Rpt. New York: Berkley, 1977; New York: Tor, 1984. Basis for the film entitled *Damnation Alley.*

———. *Deus Irae. See* Dick.

———. "For a Breath I Tarry." *Fantastic,* September 1966. While this story was first published in *New Worlds,* March 1966, it was badly garbled through a publishing error.

———. *This Immortal.* New York: Ace, 1966. London: Hart Davis, 1967. Rpt. New York: Ace, 1982. Orig. serialized in two parts as "*Call Me Conrad,*" *Fantasy and Science Fiction,* October and November, 1965.

FILMOGRAPHY FOR REMADE WORLD LITERATURE

Carl B. Yoke

It has not been my intention in this list to catalog all remade world films. Instead, I have attempted to provide a representative list so that those who are interested in pursuing the subject further may do so.

While other subgenres of fantastic literature have produced some brilliant films (Fritz Lang's *Metropolis,* Charlie Chaplin's *Modern Times,* and the early 1930s productions of *Dracula, Frankenstein,* and *Phantom of the Opera,* to mention a few), remade world films have been conspicuously unremarkable, until recently, despite a large body of excellent material from which to draw. Budgets were small, special effects were poor, and adaptations had little to do with original stories for most of those films that were made.

As the social climate and public consciousness have changed in recent years, however, gifted directors and writers have turned their attention to the remade world film. Whether to send a warning (as with *Threads* and *Testament)* or to serve other purposes (see Chapter 17 for an excellent overview of the development of such films), the product has been getting better and better. No longer will remade world films be limited to the ghetto of ''B'' movies.

Especially useful in compiling this list were *The Video Times Magazine*'s *Your Movie Guide to Science Fiction/Fantasy Video Tapes and Discs* and Roger Ebert's *Movie Home Companion.*

Abbreviations used in this list are:

Dir	director
Pro	producer/producers
St	star/stars
Vt	variant title
W	writer/writers

Blade Runner, 1982. Dir: Ridley Scott. W: Hampton Francher and David Peoples. St: Harrison Ford, Rutger Hauer, Joanna Cassidy. Based very loosely upon Phil Dick's novel *Do Androids Dream of Electric Sheep?*

A Boy and His Dog, 1975. Dir: L. Q. Jones. St: Don Johnson, Jason Robards, Charles McGraw, Susanne Benton. Based upon the Harlan Ellison story of the same name.

Colossus: The Forbin Project, 1970. Dir: Joseph Sargent. W: James Bridges. St: Eric Braden, Susan Clark, William Schallart. Based upon D. F. Jones' novel *Colossus.*

Crack in the World, 1965. Dir: Andrew Marton. W: Jon Manchip White and Julian Halvey. St: Dana Andrews, Jenette Scott, Alexander Knox.

Damnation Alley, 1977. Dir: Jack Smight. W: Alan Sharp and Lucas Heller. St: Jan-Michael Vincent, George Peppard, Dominique Sanda, Paul Winfield. Based very loosely on Roger Zelazny's novel of the same name.

The Day After, 1983. Dir: Nicholas Meyer. St: Jason Robards, JoBeth Williams, Steve Guttenberg.

The Day The World Ended, 1955. Dir: Roger Corman.

Deluge, 1933. Dir: S. Fowler Wright. St: Fred Kohler, Stanley Blackmur, Peggy Shannon. Based upon Wright's novel of the same name.

The End of August at the Ozone Hotel, 1965. Dir: Jan Schmidt.

Escape from New York, 1981. Dir: John Carpenter. St: Kurt Russell, Donald Pleasance, Lee Van Cleef, Adriene Barbeau, Harry Dean Stanton, Ernest Borgnine.

The Final Programme, 1973. Dir: Robert Fuerst. St: Jon Finch, Sterling Hayden, Patrick Magee, Jenny Runacre, Hugh Griffith, Harry Andrews, George Courlis.

Five, 1951. Dir: Arch Oboler. St: William Phipps, Susan Douglas.

Genesis II, 1973. W: Gene Roddenberry. St: Alex Cord, Mariette Hartley, Ted Cassidy.

In the Year 2889, 1965. Dir: Larry Buchanan. Remake of Roger Corman's *The Day the World Ended.*

The Last Chase, 1981. Dir: Martyn Burke. St: Lee Majors, Burgess Meredith.

The Last Child, 1971. Dir: John Moxey. W: Peter S. Fisher. St: Van Heflin, Michael Cole, Janet Margolin.

The Last Days of Man on Earth, 1973. Dir: Robert Fuerst. Based on Michael Moorcock's novel *The Final Programme.* This is the American version of *The Final Programme,* prepared by Roger Corman. It is less bitter than the original and the biting satire has been muted.

The Last Man on Earth, 1964. St: Vincent Price. Based upon Richard Matheson's *I Am Legend.* It follows the novel fairly closely. See also *The Omega Man.*

The Last Woman on Earth, 1960. Pro: Roger Corman. W: Robert Towne. St: Antony Carbone, Betsy Jones-Moreland, Edwin Wain.

Logan's Run, 1976. Dir: Michael Anderson. W: David Goodman. St: Michael York, Richard Jordan, Jenny Agutter, Farrah Fawcett Majors. The movie takes great liberties with the William F. Nolan and George Clayton Johnson novel of the same name.

"The *Mad Max* Films"

Mad Max, 1979. Dir: George Miller. St: Mel Gibson, Joanna Samuel.

The Road Warrior, 1981. Dir: George Miller. St: Mel Gibson.

Beyond the Thunderdome, 1985. Dir: George Miller and George Ogilvie. W: Robert Terry Hayes and George Miller. St: Mel Gibson, Tina Turner, Bruce Spence, Angelo Rossitto, Paul Larsson, and Angry Anderson.

The Martian Chronicles, 1979. Dir: Michael Anderson. W: Richard Matheson. St: Rock Hudson, Gail Hunnicutt, Darren McGavin, Bernadette Peters. PBS production based upon Ray Bradbury's collection of linked stories.

The Mutations, 1974. Dir: Jack Cardiff. W: Robert D. Weinbach and Edward Mann. St: Donald Pleasance, Tom Baker, Michael Dunn, Jill Haworth.

1990: The Bronx Warriors, 1983. Dir: Enzo G. Castellari. W: Dardano Sacchetti. St: Vic Morrow, Christopher Connelly, Fred Williamson.

No Blade of Grass, 1970. Dir: Cornell Wilde. W: Sean Forestal and Jefferson Pascal. St: Nigel Davenport, Jean Wallace.

The Omega Man, 1971. Dir: Boris Sagal. W: John William Carrington and Joyce M. Carrington. St: Charleton Heston, Rosalind Cash, Anthony Zerbe. Based upon Richard Matheson's novel *I Am Legend,* but takes great liberties with the story.

On the Beach, 1959. Dir: Stanley Kramer. W: John Paxton and James Lee Barrett. St: Gregory Peck, Fred Astaire, Ava Gardner, Anthony Perkins. Based upon Nevil Shute's novel of the same name.

Panic in the Year Zero, 1962. Dir: Ray Milland. Vt: *The End of the World.* Based upon Ward Moore's "Lot" and "Lot's Daughter."

"The *Planet of the Apes* Films"

Planet of the Apes, 1968. W/Dir: Michael Wilson and Rod Sterling. St: Charleton Heston, Maurice Evans, Kim Hunter, Roddy McDowell. Loosely based upon Pierre Boulle's novel of the same name *(Les Planete des Singes).*

Beneath the Planet of the Apes, 1970. Dir: Ted Post. St: Charleton Heston, James Franciscus, Kim Hunter, Roddy McDowell.

Escape from the Planet of the Apes, 1971. Dir: Don Taylor. W: Paul Dehn. St: Roddy McDowell, Kim Hunter.

Conquest of the Planet of the Apes, 1972. Dir: J. Lee Thompson. W: Paul Dehn. St: Roddy McDowell, Don Murray, Ricardo Montalban, Hari Rhodes, Natalie Trundy.

Battle for the Planet of the Apes, 1974. Dir: J. Lee Thompson. St: Roddy McDowell, Claude Akins.

Back to the Planet of the Apes, 1974. Dir: Don Weis and Arnold Laven. St: Roddy McDowell, Ron Harper, James Naughton. Pilot film for television.

The Quiet Earth, 1986. Dir: Geoff Murphy. St: Bruno Lawrence, Alison Routledge, Peter Smith.

Quintet, 1979. Pro: Robert Altman. St: Paul Newman, Vittorio Gassman, Fernando Rey, Bibi Anderson.

Rollerball, 1975. Dir: Norman Jewison. W: William Harrison. St: James Caan, John Houseman, Ralph Richardson, Maud Adams, John Beck. Based on W. Harrison's "Roller Ball Murder."

Soylent Green, 1973. Dir: Richard Fleisher. St: Charleton Heston, Edward G. Robinson, Leigh Taylor-Young, Chuck Connors, Brock Peters, Joseph Cotten. Based on H. Harrison's novel, *Make Room! Make Room!*

Strange New World. Dir: Robert Butler. St: John Saxon, Kathleen Miller, James Olson.

The Terminator, 1984. Dir: James Cameron. W: James Cameron and Gale Anne Hurd. St: Arnold Schwarzenegger, Michael Biehn, Linda Hamilton, Paul Winfield.

Testament, 1983. Dir: Lynne Littman. St: Jane Alexander, William Devane, Roxana Zal.

Things to Come, 1936. Dir: William Cameron Menzies. W: H. G. Wells. St: Raymond Massey, Edward Chapman, Ralph Richardson, Cedric Hardwicke, Margaretta Scott. Based on Wells' novel, *The Shape of Things to Come.*

Threads, 1984. Dir: Mick Jackson. W: Barry Hines. St: Reece Dinsdale, Karen Meagher,

Rita May, David Brierly, Harry Beety, Henry Moxon, Nicholas Lane, Victoria O'Keefe.

The Time Machine, 1960. Dir: George Pal. W: David Duncan. St: Rod Taylor, Yvette Mimieux, Alan Young, Sebastian Cabot. Based upon Wells' novel of the same name.

Virus, 1980. Dir: Kinji Fukasaku. St: Masao Kusakari, Chuck Connors, Glenn Ford, George Kennedy, Bo Svenson, Robert Vaughn, Olivia Hussey. Based upon the Sakyo Komatsu novel entitled *Resurrection Day [Fukkatsu No Hi].*

The War Game, 1967. Dir: Peter Watkins. St: Michael Aspel, Dick Graham.

Warlords of the 21st Century, 1981. Retitled and re-released as *Battletruck.* Dir: Harley Cokliss. St: Michael Beck, Annie McEnroe, James Wainwright.

When Worlds Collide, 1951. Dir: Rudolph Mate. W: Sidney Boehm. St: Richard Derr, Barbara Rush, Larry Keating, Peter Hanson, John Hoyt. Based on the Philip Wylie and Edwin Balmer novel of the same name.

Wizards, 1977. W/Dir: Ralph Bakshi. (Animated).

The World, the Flesh, and the Devil, 1959. W/Dir: Ranald MacDougall. St: Harry Belafonte, Inger Stevens, Mel Ferrer. Alleged to be loosely based upon M. P. Shiel's novel *The Purple Cloud.*

INDEX

ABOUT THE EDITOR AND CONTRIBUTORS

PAUL BRIANS, an associate professor of English at Washington State University, has translated and edited *Bawdy Tales from the Courts of Medieval France* and published numerous articles on medieval and modern literature. For the past five years, he has researched nuclear war in fiction, periodically taught a course on the subject, and published a number of articles and reviews based on his research. His book *Nuclear Holocausts: Atomic War in Fiction 1914–1984,* will appear in 1987.

EDGAR L. CHAPMAN, an associate professor of English, has taught Renaissance and modern literature at Bradley University since 1963. Educated at William Jewell College and Brown University, where he was an S. W. Marston Scholar, he has published articles on mainstream novelists Thomas Berger and Patrick White and science fiction and fantasy authors Suzette Hadin Elgin, Hope Mirrless, Philip Jose Farmer, and Talbot Mundy. He has also published *The Magic Labyrinth of Philip Jose Farmer* and is currently completing a study of Robert Silverberg.

MICHAEL R. COLLINGS, an associate professor of English and director of creative writing at Pepperdine College, has published *Piers Anthony, Brian Aldiss,* and six critical studies of Stephen King, among them *Stephen King as Richard Bachman, The Many Facets of Stephen King, The Films of Stephen King,* and *The Annotated Guide to Stephen King.* His critical articles have appeared in anthologies on fantasy and science fiction as well as major journals, and several have been translated into foreign languages. In addition to his criticism, Collings edited *Reflections of the Fantastic* for Greenwood Press and published two volumes of poetry: *A Season of Calm Weather* and *Naked Sun*.

DONNA M. DE BLASIO, currently program supervisor of the Ohio Historical Society's Youngstown Industrial Museum and part-time history instructor at Youngstown State University, served for two years as an oral history field resident for Indiana University. Her publications include several book reviews for historical journals and essays on oral history. A member of the Organization of American Historians, the Oral History Association, and the Ohio Academy of History, she is treasurer of the Oral History in Ohio Association. Her article on Leigh Brackett was delivered at the Twentieth Century Women's Writers Association at Hofstra University in 1983.

DAVID DESSER teaches a number of film courses in the Unit for Cinema Studies and the Department of Speech Communications at the University of Illinois–Urbana. He has published extensively on Japanese cinema, including *The Samurai Films of Akira Kurosawa* and recently completed a book-length treatment of Japanese New Wave cinema. He has also published a handful of articles on *Blade Runner* and recently turned his attention to the Jewish experience in American cinema.

THOMAS P. DUNN, professor of English at Miami University (of Ohio), has presented more than forty lectures and papers on science fiction and fantasy literature. With Richard D. Erlich (also of Miami University), he has presented a series of papers on human-machine interaction in science fiction and has edited two volumes of essays: *The Mechanical God: Machines in Science Fiction* (1982) and *Clockwork Worlds: Mechanized Environments in SF* (1983). A contributing editor to *The Year's Scholarship in Fantastic Literature,* he is also a member of the editorial board of *Extrapolation* and a frequent contributor to *Fantasy Review*.

JOSEPH FRANCAVILLA, instructor of English and writing at the State University of New York at Buffalo, has published fiction in *Ethos, Leighdt,* and *New Dimensions* and articles and reviews in *Cinefantastique, Extrapolation, Science Fiction Studies, The American Book Review,* and *The Transcendent Adventure*. He is presently writing a science fiction novel, a book on the historical development of science fiction, and a study of the fiction of Edgar Allan Poe and Franz Kafka.

CARL GOLDBERG is in private practice in New York City and associate clinical professor of psychiatry at Albert Einstein Medical School. He has taught at the University of Virginia, George Washington University Medical School, Antioch University, and the Virginia Institute of Group Psychotherapy. He is the author of many journal articles and among his published books are *In Defense of*

Narcissism: The Creative Self in Search of Meaning and *On Being a Psycho-therapist—The Journey of the Healer.*

JUDITH B. KERMAN, director of two-year technical programs and assistant professor of technology at Kent State University, has been a professional computer programmer and has published four books of poetry, among them *Mothering* which received Honorable Mention in the 1978 Great Lakes Association New Writers competition. Her research interests in technology and culture have led to publications and conference papers on science fiction and urban/technological folklore. She is currently editing an anthology of essays, *Blade Runner's Dilemma: More Human Than Human?* for Bowling Green University's Popular Press.

WILLIAM LOMAX, a Nebraskan now living in Los Angeles, has taught music and English in the Los Angeles Unified schools for eighteen years. Currently completing his doctoral work at UCLA in English literature, he has written a biography of the Austrian conductor Richart Lert and has published articles in a number of education journals and in the *Dictionary of Literary Biography*. He is working on a book-length study of science fiction.

HAROLD LEE PROSSER, a former sociology instructor at Southwest Missouri State University, holds degrees in English, sociology, and social science. Under the pen name of Justin Willard Pinoak, he has more than eight hundred publications in various genres since 1963. His most recent fantasy includes ''Desert Whispers'' in *Uncle,* ''Summer Wine'' in *Missouri Short Fiction,* and ''Absalom'' in *Cold Sweat.* His ''Teaching Sociology with Ray Bradbury's *The Martian Chronicles*'' appeared in *Social Education.* Forthcoming books include *Frank Herbert: The Prophet of Dune, Robert Block: The Man Who Walked through Mirrors,* and *Charles Beaumont.* Now residing in Missouri with his family while he does sociological research and writing, he is currently working on books dealing with Woody Allen and with reincarnation.

NADINE S. ST. LOUIS, professor of English at the University or Wisconsin–Eau Claire, is a specialist in science fiction and seventeenth-century English literature. She has also taught American studies and English as a second language at the Oberstufenkolleg of the University of Bielefield in West Germany. Her work on H. G. Wells' *The World Set Free* grew out of a multidisciplinary faculty colloquium, *Humanity in the Shadow of the Bomb,* at UW–Eau Claire in the spring of 1983.

JOE SANDERS, professor of English at Lakeland Community College in Mentor, Ohio, is a frequent book reviewer who has published several essays on science fiction, fantasy, and futurism. He is the compiler of *Roger Zelazny: A Primary and Secondary Bibliography* and the author of *E. E. ''Doc'' Smith.* At present he is assembling a collection of essays on science fandom for Greenwood Press.

GREGORY M. SHREVE, an associate professor of anthropology at Kent State University and former dean of its Geauga campus, spent the 1985–86 academic year as an exchange professor at Karl Marx University in Leipzig, East Germany. He has an extensive interest in information science, semiotics, and science fiction criticism. He has published a two-volume work entitled *Genesis of Structure in African Narrative,* as well as several papers and articles on science fiction and fantasy. His essay on Jack Vance appeared in Greenwood Press' *Death and the Serpent.*

THEODORE L. STEINBERG has taught in the English department at the State University of New York College at Fredonia since 1971. During 1985–86, he learned a great deal about apocalyptic thought by serving as assistant dean for general studies and special programs. His major areas of study are medieval and Renaissance literature and he has completed a book-length study of *Piers Plowman.* Other publications include works on Spenser, Lyly, Yiddish literature, medieval cosmography, and other medieval topics. He hopes that the end of the world will not precede the end of the baseball season—any baseball season.

C. W. SULLIVAN III teaches American folklore and northern European mythology at East Carolina University. He edited the science fiction textbook/anthology *As Tomorrow Becomes Today* and is currently editor of *The Children's Folklore Newsletter.* His articles on science fiction, fantasy, folklore, and mythology have appeared in a number of journals and anthologies.

MARSHALL TYMN, professor of English at Eastern Michigan University, is the author of numerous reference books and articles on science fiction and fantasy literature. He is series editor of Greenwood Press' *Contributions to the Study of Science Fiction and Fantasy* and editor of the annual bibliography *The Year's Scholarship in Fantastic Literature.* Presently the president of the International Association for the Fantastic in the Arts, he has received wide acclaim for his books on the papers of Thomas Cole, a pivotal figure in early American landscape painting.

WYN WACHHORST has taught American history and American studies at the University of California, San Jose State University, and Stanford University. His previous publications include a book on Edison as a culture hero, *Thomas Alva Edison: An American Myth,* which was a History Book Club selection. He has contributed to anthologies and to such periodicals as *Isis* and *Extrapolation.* His long-term interest lies in synthesizing various popular culture topics that illuminate the twentieth-century transformation in cultural worldview.

CAROLYN WENDELL, an associate professor of English at Monroe Community College in Rochester, New York, teaches a variety of literature and writing courses, her own favorites being science fiction and professional communication. Previous publications include a *Guide to Alfred Bester,* various book reviews of science fiction novels, and articles on teaching science fiction, women characters in science fiction, and Vonda MacIntyre.

CARL B. YOKE, associate professor of English at Kent State University and vice president of the International Association for the Fantastic in the Arts, has published *A Reader's Guide to Roger Zelazny* and *Roger Zelazny and André Norton: Proponents of Individualism* as well as coediting *Death and the Serpent* (Greenwood Press, 1985). His shorter works appear in *Dictionary of Literary Biography, Contemporary Literary Criticism, Survey of Modern Fantasy Literature, Twentieth Century Science Fiction Writers, The Mechanical God, Postmodern Fiction, and The Dune Encyclopedia* among others. Formerly associate editor of *Extrapolation,* he will edit a new critical journal to be entitled *Journal of the Fantastic in the Arts.*